April 2004

# A
# New
# Christianity
# for a New World

## Other Books by John Shelby Spong

*Honest Prayer*

*Dialogue in Search of Jewish Christian Understanding*
with Rabbi Jack Daniel Spiro

*Christpower*
Compiled and edited by Lucy Newton Boswell

*Life Approaches Death—A Dialogue in Medical Ethics*
with Dr. Daniel Gregory

*The Living Commandments*

*The Easter Moment*

*Into the Whirlwind: The Future of the Church*

*Beyond Moralism*
with the Venerable Denise Haines

*Survival and Consciousness: An Interdisciplinary Inquiry into
the Possibility of Life Beyond Biological Death* (Editor)

*Living in Sin?: A Bishop Rethinks Human Sexuality*

*Rescuing the Bible from Fundamentalism:
A Bishop Rethinks the Meaning of Scripture*

*Born of a Woman: A Bishop Rethinks the Virgin Birth and
the Role of Women in a Male Dominated Church*

*This Hebrew Lord: A Bishop's Search for the Authentic Jesus*

*Resurrection: Myth or Reality?: A Bishop Rethinks the Meaning of Easter*

*Liberating the Gospels: Reading the Bible with Jewish Eyes*

*Why Christianity Must Change or Die: A Bishop Speaks to Believers in Exile*

*The Bishop's Voice: Selected Essays 1979–1999*
Compiled and edited by Christine M. Spong (Crossroad)

*Here I Stand: My Struggle for a Christianity of
Integrity, Love, and Equality*

# A
# NEW
# CHRISTIANITY
# FOR A NEW WORLD

*Why Traditional Faith Is Dying*
*and*
*How a New Faith Is Being Born*

JOHN SHELBY SPONG

HarperSanFrancisco
*A Division of HarperCollinsPublishers*

Christianity for the Third Millennium
P.O. Box 69
Morristown, NJ 07963-0069

Readers may contact the author by e-mail
at CMSCTM@AOL.com or at the address above.

Bible quotations, unless otherwise noted, are from the New Revised Standard
Version of the Bible

A NEW CHRISTIANITY FOR A NEW WORLD: *Why Traditional Faith Is Dying and
How a New Faith Is Being Born.* Copyright © 2001 by John Shelby Spong. All
rights reserved. Printed in the United States of America. No part of this
book may be used or reproduced in any manner whatsoever without written
permission except in the case of brief quotations embodied in critical articles
and reviews. For information address HarperCollins Publishers, Inc., 10
East 53rd Street, New York, NY 10022.

HarperCollins books may be purchased for educational, business, or sales
promotional use. For information please write: Special Markets Department,
HarperCollins Publishers, Inc., 10 East 53rd Street, New York, NY 10022.

HarperCollins Web site: http://www.harpercollins.com

HarperCollins®, 📖®, and HarperSanFrancisco™ are
trademarks of HarperCollins Publishers, Inc.

FIRST EDITION

*Designed by Jessica Shatan*

Library of Congress Cataloging-in-Publication Data
Spong, John Shelby.
    A new Christianity for a new world : why traditional faith is dying and
how a new faith is being born / John Shelby Spong.—1st ed.
    p. cm.
    Includes bibliographical references and index.
    ISBN 0–06–067084–3 (cloth)
    ISBN 0–06–067063–0 (pbk.)
    1. Christianity. 2. Spong, John Shelby. I. Title.

BR124 .S665 2000
230—dc21

                                                          2001024313

01 02 03 04 05 ❖/RRD 10 9 8 7 6 5 4 3 2

# CONTENTS

# The Origins of This Book:
# From *Honest to God* to
# *Why Christianity Must Change or Die*

*Our coming of age leads us to a true recognition of our situation before God. God would have us know that we must live as those who manage our lives without God. The God who is with us is the God who forsakes us. The God who lets us live in the world without the working hypothesis of God is the God before whom we stand continuously. Before God and with God we live without God.*

*. . . God is weak and powerless in the world and that is precisely the way, the only way in which he is with us to help us.*[1]

—Dietrich Bonhoeffer

There are two tasks that I hope to accomplish with this book. The first is to move forward the work begun in the last century by a man who was my mentor and my friend. His name was John Arthur Thomas Robinson. The other is the unfinished work in my own career that did not become obvious to me until I lived both with and into the response to my book *Why Christianity Must Change or Die.*

There is probably no person in the world of Christian scholarship with whom I have felt a closer identification than I did to John A. T. Robinson. We had much in common. He was, as I am, a bishop. Only those of us who have had the privilege of living inside the expectations of that role can fully appreciate the bond that particular shared experience created for us both. He was next an author, seeking as I have done, in book after book to bridge the gap between the Christian academy and the person in the pew. Third, he was, as I am, deeply devoted to the church that he served for a lifetime, but also like me, he was uncomfortable living inside the theological straitjackets that Christianity seems so eager to force upon people in every generation.

Robinson even broke into the consciousness of his nation, just as I did, in a public controversy that grew out of the interface between religion and human sexuality. For him it was his opposition to an effort on the part of the moral purists in the United Kingdom to ban from publication D. H. Lawrence's book *Lady Chatterley's Lover.* For me it was the battle to bring gay and lesbian people fully into the life and love of the body of Christ. John Robinson and I, though separated by a generation, have followed remarkably similar life paths.

It was, however, his little book entitled *Honest to God*, published in 1963, that shaped my theological journey decisively. This book was launched with a front-page story in the *Sunday Observer* in Great Britain under the banner headline, "Our Image of God Must Go!" Robinson's life would never be the same. This book was a bold blast at the way Christianity had been traditionally understood. It was issued by one who was at that time only an assistant bishop occupying a quite secondary position in the ecclesiastical hierarchy. His title was the Bishop of Woolwich. Woolwich is one of the subdivisions within the Diocese of Southwark, which basically covers the suburbs of London south of the Thames. In this book, Robinson laid out in clear and straightforward language for the average person—whether in the pew or in the Church Alumni Association—the debates going on inside the academy. He introduced his readers to the work of Rudolf Bultmann, who was calling for the scriptures to be demythologized; Dietrich Bonhoeffer, who was calling for a Christianity apart from religion; and Paul Tillich, who was insisting that God could no longer be defined personally as a being, but must be approached nonpersonally as the Ground of All Being. The response to this book was tremendous. It was discussed in pubs, with taxicab drivers, at tea, and over dinner, and even in homes where church going had long ceased to be a habit.

But almost immediately the threatened leadership of the traditional church struck back to defend its familiar and dated theological affirmations. Led by the Archbishop of Canterbury, Michael Ramsey,[2] the hierarchy decided, in the time-honored manner of defensive people, that since they could neither embrace nor deny Robinson's message, they must attack the messenger, and attack him they did.

In an outpouring of negativity unprecedented in religious circles until the Muslims put a death price on the head of Salman Rushdie, Robinson was pilloried in the press, in letters to the editor, on radio talk shows, and from the pulpits of that land. Church careers were made by ambitious clergy attacking this young bishop in the name of something called "the faith once for all delivered to the saints" (Jude 1:3), as if such a body of fixed doctrine had ever existed.

Robinson would now suffer the fate of many a brilliant spiritual leader before him. He was quickly marginalized by his church, avoided by those who once had been his colleagues, and forced to fight to maintain his reputation and integrity. His career in the church was derailed. Normally a person of his age, education, and family background would remain an assistant or area bishop for only a few years before being made the senior bishop of a major diocese. Robinson, however, was clearly destined to be an assistant bishop forever. Finally he resigned from that position in order to return to Cambridge to teach. Even at that great university the long arm of the church was still able to bring its shunning power to bear upon his life. Robinson was never elected by the Cambridge decision makers to the position of university lecturer, despite the fact that he had enjoyed that designation in the 1950s before he was appointed to the bishop's office. So he lived out his career at Cambridge as the Dean of Chapel at Trinity College, a relatively minor position, usually filled by a recent theological graduate. He died in 1983 largely unappreciated by his church.

Because Robinson was forced after the publication of *Honest to God* to spend the balance of his life defending himself against the legions of his attackers, he never completed the task that he had begun in that book. *Honest to God* revealed quite clearly why the God-talk emanating from the church in Robinson's day was no longer credible in Robinson's world. It did little, however, except to diagnose the problem and provide a scant outline for a new direction. For this God-filled man, the issue lay not in the reality of God, which he did not question, but in the dated way in which this God had been traditionally proclaimed. Robinson had in fact made major progress in the task of deconstructing the religious patterns of our Christian past. He spelled out quite clearly the easy task of identifying what no longer works. Reconstruction, reformulating the fullness of a faith for tomorrow, however, is incredibly more difficult. Robinson clearly had this task in mind, and the hint of it was seen in his enthusiasm for Bonhoeffer's call for the church to develop a "religionless Christianity," or what Robinson came to call a "worldly holiness." But this reconstruction task was never completed. Perhaps it could not have been done at that moment, for it takes time for a new theological language and a new theological atmosphere to develop. Yet the seeds for much of the work I have done in this volume were present in that book. There is no doubt that John Robinson was my ancestor in faith. He was also my spiritual father in whose pathway I have deliberately tried to walk. That reality accounts for half of this book's origin.

The other half is rooted in the publication of *Why Christianity Must Change or Die* in 1998. This book was my attempt in a new generation to reissue Robinson's call for a radical reformation and to face the fact that the premodern biblical and creedal concepts communicate even less well at the end of the twentieth century than they did when Robinson lived. After *Why Christianity Must Change or Die* came out I drew upon the content of this book to post on the Internet, in Luther-like fashion, twelve theses that I believed needed to be debated as part of that inevitable reformation.[3] To elicit the maximum reaction of both affirmation and threat, I stated these theses in the most provocative manner I could imagine. It was a successful tactic. The response to the theses and to the book was quite revealing. In the first fifteen months of that book's life I received over six thousand letters from my readers. After that the rate slowed a bit but did not stop. The total is to this day still rising and now exceeds ten thousand, a rather remarkable number of letters for a single volume. Clearly my message had struck a chord.

But these responses were different from letters I had received after my other books had been published in more ways than just their numbers. First, they were more positive than negative by about a three-to-one margin. That was a surprise. Normally when one pushes the edges of an existing institution such as the church, as I have done throughout my career, those who feel pushed are the ones who respond by writing, and they tend to do so negatively. In my previous books the negative mail has always outnumbered the positive mail, at least in the beginning. So this was a significant shift in my experience and signaled something new.

The second noteworthy insight from this mail came when an analysis of the letters revealed that the vast majority of the positive responses, perhaps ninety percent, came from laypeople. Some were church dropouts. Some maintained their membership in the institutional church by the slenderest of threads. Some, especially in the more overtly religious parts of our nation and the world, had adopted the stance of being silent participants in the life of their churches, unconvinced but also unwilling to disturb the prevailing values of their communities. These people lived in the Bible Belt of the South, in small towns in the American Midwest, and, surprisingly, in the evangelical regions of Africa. Many of them told stories of a time when they had sought explanations from church leaders but had been informed that any stance other than acquiescence to the "revealed truth" as taught by the church or affirmed by scripture was sinful behavior.

These letter-writers resonated with my explorations. They found in my words a way to articulate their own faith-questions and to seek new answers. They also found a sense of community with me in my writing, which countered their suspicion that they were somehow peculiar—that is, the only people who felt this way. Time and again these letters expressed some version of the line, "If you as a bishop can write and say these things, then perhaps there is still room in the Christian church for someone like me." In many instances these positive letters were long and revealingly autobiographical. It was as if the writers were compelled to tell their life story to someone they felt might understand.

The negative mail, when analyzed, was equally revealing. The hostility contained in the negative letters was overt. I was called by a series of unflattering labels: heretic was one of the nicer ones; atheist, Anti-Christ, hypocrite, deceiver, the Devil incarnate, and ecclesiastical whore were among the more printable of the others. Sometimes these letters included demands that I renounce my office as a bishop and claimed that I should be expelled or deposed from the church if I were unwilling to do so.

Some even carried threats of punitive action, including my murder, that the writers either recommended or informed me of their intention of carrying out personally. God had instructed them to do this, many of them stated. However, the most surprising insight that was revealed in this negative mail was not its hostility, but the fact that the vast majority of it, perhaps as high a figure as ninety percent, came from clergy—that is, from the ranks of the ordained.

I found this contrast quite revealing. If ever I observed the deep chasm in understanding that exists in the Christian church in our day, it was here. Ordained people are seen in these responses as defending their turf with vehemence while attacking any proposed changes in their traditional formulations as evil. Laypeople are seen as living on the edges of church life and even dropping out regularly, yet they are still open to receiving new possibilities. Those among my ordained colleagues who responded seemed to be oblivious to the existence of these laypeople, who, though turned off by the small-minded defensiveness of their church leaders, were nonetheless very welcoming of my attempts to speak of God in the accents of a new day to which they could respond. If my ordained friends do not even recognize the problem they face, they can hardly address it.

Time after time when I give public lectures, the response is generally positive from those people who live on or even beyond the fringes of the church, and it is generally negative from those whose identity is somehow defined by the church. An all-clergy group is perhaps my most difficult audience.[4] I recall one series of lectures that I gave at a well-known eastern university for which a panel of three people had been officially designated to respond at the conclusion of the four-day presentation. One of the panelists was a faculty member at that university, a professor of astronomy. The second was a ranking administrative official from the theological school of a different university in the same city. The third was an Episcopal priest who had formerly been both a seminary faculty member and a missionary in Africa. Their responses amazed me.

The priest was negative, the administrator was both irrelevant and ambivalent, and the astronomer was ecstatic with gratitude. Both the priest and the administrator came with printed manuscripts, which was interesting since this meant that they had prepared their responses prior to hearing my lectures. The priest made statements that were so startlingly a response to perceived threat that I knew he lived in a world that I did not inhabit. He actually praised those who cultivated an anti-intellectual ignorance. His most gratuitous remark was that he knew of no one who "used God as a security blanket." The administrator chose this opportunity to make remarks about his understanding of homosexuality, a subject that had not been mentioned in the lectureship, taking a stance quite counter to my own well-known views on this issue. Perhaps he had waited for some time to have such an opportunity. The astronomer alone seemed to recognize the context out of which I was working, to hear the insights I sought to develop, and he expressed himself as filled with appreciation. My words, he said, had helped him move more deeply into his personal attempt to cultivate the life of the spirit.

I am constantly amazed at how threatened ecclesiastical representatives are when they confront the fact that the words they use to tell their faith-story simply no longer communicate meaningfully in the world of today's experience. Getting angry, being hostile, acting defensively, and engaging in diverting attacks on extraneous issues are responses more symptomatic of the problem than they seem to realize. I knew in that particular experience once more that the audience for whom I seek to write is represented not by the threatened priest but by the questing astronomer. It was fascinating to have the insight I had gained from the mail elicited by *Why Christianity Must Change or Die* confirmed so vividly in this academic setting.

Following publication of *Why Christianity Must Change or Die*, I lectured extensively on its content throughout the United States, in Canada, and across England, Scotland, and Wales. In that process, dealing with the questions of my listeners, I inevitably began to develop more fully some of the ideas included in that book. I found my own thought processes stretched into new arenas by this dialogue. Slowly I became aware that I was now walking beyond the traditional safety barriers of my own faith-tradition, barriers that I had heretofore observed. I discovered myself raising questions that I had previously been unwilling even to entertain, and journeying into theological arenas that I had never before entered. It was for me both an exhilarating and a fearful experience.

I began to wonder how I could stay in touch with my increasingly disparate two worlds: the world of the church and the world of my audience. I recalled such colleagues as Don Cupitt in England, Lloyd Geering in New Zealand, and Robert Funk in California, who had clearly arrived at this place before me and who had, I believed, adopted conclusions about the Christian faith that I had not been willing to adopt. Was I now moving toward their life paths and their conclusions? They had in my mind become not just exiles, but willing inhabitants of a post-Christian world with no great need to seek reconciliation with the faith that had nurtured them. I was not sure I wanted to step away from or perhaps even beyond my faith-system as radically as they had done. It was, however, clearly time for me to step beyond both Robinson's book *Honest to God* and my own book *Why Christianity Must Change or Die*. But where this journey would end, I could not guarantee. I went back to the writings of some of my mentors—people such as Paul Tillich in particular, though there were others such as Karl Barth, Don Cupitt, Norman Pittinger, and Richard Holloway—and read their works anew, concentrating this time not on their more popular books but on the writings that marked their lives when they came toward the end of their careers. They clearly had felt many of the same things that I found myself feeling. In their final writings they did not appear willing to be constrained by the traditional boundaries that mark so many representatives of the church. They seemed to have walked the paths that were now so clearly visible to me. Tillich even named one of his final books *On the Boundary*. Cupitt spoke of *After God*, and Holloway wrote of "godless morality." John Robinson's widow, Ruth, shared with me some of the unresolved theological issues in his life and in hers.

Those who had so significantly shaped or shared my theological formation did not appear to me to have been willing to stop their pilgrimage into the wonder of God because it had become fearful. They had not stepped back from the levels of honesty that had marked their careers. I knew then that I could not do so either. I too must follow where truth would lead me. Once again, the motto of my theological seminary compelled me: "Seek the truth, come whence it may, cost what it will." It is one thing for me not to be able to see the road ahead; it is quite another for me to see it and out of fear to cease my inquiry. I knew that I must continue my pilgrimage, no matter where it led.

The dialogue with my readers and my listeners made many new, unexplored pathways obvious to me. If I refused to take these pathways, it would be to close my mind to new truth, to assume that what I could see was all that could be. That was both intolerable and idolatrous. To suggest that God and one's own understanding of God are the same is not only to stop growing, it is to die to the quest for truth. If my church were ever to require that of me, it would no longer be a place in which I would want to live. For one who loves the church as deeply as I do, that thought was both a frightening conclusion and an exhilarating experience of freedom.

This was the internal process through which I traveled that caused me to recognize that the conclusions I had reached in *Why Christianity Must Change or Die* could never be the final conclusions of my life or career. Those earlier conclusions, in retrospect, appeared to be far more preliminary than I had imagined. That book and the dialogue that it created had clearly been door-opening experiences for my readers, and as time went by I was forced to see that they had also become door-opening experiences for me. My task now included an invitation—indeed a responsibility—to walk through the open doors into whatever lay beyond them, whether it proved to be comfortable for me or not.

In that former book I had analyzed effectively and competently, I still think, the profound cultural and theological problems that Christianity faces at this moment of its history. However, it was becoming more and more obvious to me that I had in those pages only begun to show hints, not well-developed ideas, about the evolving directions in which I hoped the Christianity of the future might move. It is amazing how things we think are conclusions get downgraded to hints with the passage of time! The outline of a radically reformed Christianity was present in that volume, but my accomplishment there was far more to show why the old formulas no longer worked than it was to spell out with compelling power the new vision of a reformulated Christianity. That was the incomplete, the unfinished work in my own life that I was now ready to engage. The unanswered questions that had been raised for me by my readers now flooded my mind, crying out to be addressed. What does God look like beyond a dying theism? Does such a God matter? Who is the Christ when traditional concepts such as incarnation, atonement, and the Trinity are no longer usable? Does this figure still command the respect once given to him? Could Christianity survive in a recognizable form if the reformation for which I was calling actually came to pass? Would I too, as many of my colleagues before me had done, end my career either silent before a vision I refused to enter or disillusioned by a church that could no longer either listen or move?

It was while wrestling with these profoundly disturbing issues and while entertaining the dawning awareness out of which these issues were raised that I received an invitation that would alter the course of my life. About a year before the date of my retirement as an Episcopal (Anglican) bishop, a letter arrived from officials at Harvard University inviting me to be the William Belden Noble Lecturer for the year 2000. This appointment was accompanied by an offer to live on the campus in Lowell House as a scholar in residence. Still later, an invitation arrived asking me, while in residence, to teach a class at the Harvard Divinity School. The Noble Lectureship carried with it the requirement that "every reasonable effort be made to seek the publication" of these lectures.

This was the wonderful, serendipitous opportunity I needed to encourage me to move publicly beyond the limits I had reached in *Why Christianity Must Change or Die* and to explore more fully the emergence and the shape of what might be called a postmodern Christianity. HarperCollins was eager to bring out a final Spong book that might spell out the future shape of Christianity, so Stephen Hanselman, the publisher, and John Loudon, my editor, immediately offered me a contract. It was at that moment that the two originating streams that would produce this book flowed together, and this present writing venture was born.

All of this is to say that the content of this book began its life as the William Belden Noble Lectures given at Harvard University in March of the year 2000. I have expanded that content in order to provide a proper context for my thinking and to enable me to draw fuller conclusions. I have deliberately sought to walk beyond the traditional boundaries of the Christianity in which I was raised and to develop a new vocabulary, in order to open new avenues into the holy.

I find myself today prepared to join John Robinson by laying the literalness of traditional Christianity aside in order to chart a new Christian future. I am well aware of what this means, and I am quite prepared to absorb the inevitable hostility from those traditional religious people who feel threatened by any challenge to their particular religious system. History teaches me that this response normally accompanies those who step beyond the ancient theological boundaries. I will also seek to move beyond those institutional power-claims by which Christianity has sought to present itself as an exclusive pathway to God. Christianity will always be the pathway to God on which I journey, but I am now convinced that no human system, including Christianity itself, can maintain the exclusive power-claims of its past. The world is far too small today to offer a haven for that kind of tribal religion.

In this Christianity of the future I have also sought to escape the pseudo-security that traditional Christianity has pretended to provide. The God of the everlasting arms who is ready to catch us when we fall (Deut. 33:27) and the Jesus whom we call "the Rock of Ages"[5] to whom we will forever cling, both produce, I now believe, an immature person who needs to be taken care of by the supernatural parental deity. That can never be the result of the Christianity I now envision. Rather, I see and welcome a radically new humanity emerging which must live in a religionless world. Dietrich Bonhoeffer observed, in the passage that serves as this preface's epigraph, "Before God and with God we live without God." I find a profound freedom in this newly discovered willingness to embrace the radical insecurity of the human situation. The religious promise to provide the security that enables one to cope with life's intransigence has become for me nothing more than a delusion designed to keep human beings dependent and childlike. It, like all religious delusions, must be sacrificed if Christianity is to move into the future. As Bonhoeffer described it, this is the time of our "coming of age."

In this volume I will seek to articulate a vision of Christianity so radically reformulated that it can live in this brave new world. Yet my hope is also to demonstrate that this Christianity of the future is still in touch with the experience that propelled this faith-tradition into being more than two thousand years ago. This will in all probability be the final theological book of my life and career, and I wanted it to be not an attack on the inadequacy of what is, but a vision of the power of that which might be. I offer it with no ecclesiastical imprimatur. I write only to issue an invitation to come and listen, to explore these possibilities, and to see if by traveling on a new road we can enter the reality of the God beyond theism and hear the voice of Christ speaking in the vocabulary of a post-Christian world. I will leave it to my readers to decide whether or not I have achieved this goal.

" OPEN A NEW WINDOW, OPEN A NEW DOOR "

I wish to thank Dr. Peter Gomes, the distinguished Plummer Professor of Christian Morals at Harvard University and the chair of the William Belden Noble Lectureship, for extending to me the privilege of delivering these lectures at that great center of learning. When I looked over the names of those who had in previous years filled this post and found such gigantic figures as Hans Küng, H. Richard Niebuhr, Paul Tillich, William Temple, and yes, my most admired predecessor, John A. T. Robinson, I was both deeply gratified and profoundly humbled. I also wish to thank Professor Diana Eck of the Harvard University faculty and the Reverend Dr. Dorothy Austin, associate minister at Harvard Memorial Church and associate professor of psychology and religion on leave from Drew University, for extending to my wife, Christine, and to me the joy, the companionship, and the conviviality of residing in the scholar in residence apartment in Lowell House on that campus where they serve as masters. The opportunity to live in this exciting community and to eat our meals with Harvard undergraduates, tutors, and faculty members each day was itself invigorating. Dedicating this book to the three people who made that possible is for me a special pleasure.

As this book was being formulated and written, I was also teaching a class at Harvard Divinity School entitled "Issues in Public Preaching." Inevitably, the ideas I was developing for this book came out in my lectures and comments and so had the chance to interact with the thoughts of the bright and fertile minds of these graduate students. This was for me another expanding opportunity. These candidates for the master of divinity degree, who ranged in age from the early twenties to the late fifties, forced me time after time to clarify my thoughts.

Perhaps my greatest gift to them was the tacit permission I seemed to offer that enabled them to think in new ways outside the traditional boxes. There was an exhilarating freedom present in these classes as together we engaged issues that certainly were never engaged in my own theological preparation for ministry. I found myself anticipating eagerly, as I still do today, the impact of these students on the life of institutional Christianity in the next generation. I could easily see the reformation of Christianity for which I have called being accomplished by these future clergy, who represented Episcopal, Presbyterian, Lutheran, Methodist, Baptist, United Church of Christ, Unitarian-Universalist, and Moravian traditions within Christianity, as well as Jewish and Buddhist traditions in the larger family of the world's faiths.

My readers will find these students referred to in footnotes and in the text of this book itself. But what the text cannot say is that I learned much about the meaning of prayer from a Moravian student named Christian Rice. I found a new way to approach the resurrection when I listened to a Unitarian-Universalist student named Mark Strickler. I understood atonement in a new context from a student named Sarah Sentilles. I found enormous courage being articulated by Tom Rosiello, Elizabeth Valera, and Neil O'Farrell as they processed theological truth inside personal issues. I saw science and theology wedded more effectively than I have ever seen before in a student named Eric Fossel, who had left a very successful practice of medicine to pursue theological studies. Because I am confident that these soon-to-be clergy will shape the church of tomorrow, I want to list their names both for future reference and as a way of thanking them individually for what my opportunity to teach them meant to me. They are Carrie M. Brunken, Helen Lane Dilg, Zachary P. Drennen, Kathrin M. Ford, Eric T. Fossel, Christopher E. George, Susan E. Gray, Rebecca L. Kavich,

Evan V. Keely, Melissa MacDonnell, Mark J. McInroy, Cornelius O. O'Farrell, James B. Pratt, Christian C. Rice, Veronica Garcia-Robles, Thomas A. Rosiello, Leaf Seligman, Sarah Y. Sentilles, Mark E. Strickler, Joseph R. Truesdale, Elizabeth N. Valera, Medora M. Van Denburgh, Jamie P. Washam, and David M. Zuniga.

I also wish to thank those who made the actual production of this manuscript possible: my secretary, Lyn Conrad, who has worked with me on the last four books and has continued even in her retirement to assist this process; and my editor at Harper San-Francisco, John Loudon, who has helped to sustain and expand my writing career. To Stephen Hanselman, publisher at Harper San-Francisco, and to Liza Hetherington, Kris Ashley, Calla Devlin, Margery Buchanan, Roger Freet, Terri Leonard, and Eric Brandt, who have handled production, marketing, and publicity, I express my appreciation. All of them have made my association with the house of Harper so rich over so many years. I also acknowledge Carol DeChant and Kelly Hughes of the public relations firm of DeChant and Hughes in Chicago, who have worked with me in the launch of six of my books, culminating in this one.

The final editing of this manuscript took place in St. Deiniol's Library in Wales, where the warden, Peter Francis, and his wife, Helen, were ever so gracious in their welcome and in the offer of their personal friendship. I also found the resources of that library to be wonderfully adequate and commend it to others who need a place for research and study.

Finally and above all, I want to thank my wife, Christine Mary Spong. I know that it is traditional for an author to pass accolades to his or her spouse for both support and expertise, but my readers must know that I am not engaging in that kind of hyperbole or traditional banter. Christine is not just my wife; she has been a total partner in my career, aiding me first in my role as a bishop and then in my role as an author and lecturer. In my Episcopal office she was a vital part of everything I did. I suspect that the hole created by her retirement as the bishop's wife was larger and more obvious than that created by my retirement as the bishop.

In my post-Episcopal career she has played an even more significant role. Managing my life, my writing, and my public speaking has become her full-time job. As an editor, she is the best with whom I have ever worked. She has incredibly sensitive eyes. She knows at once what communicates and what does not. She challenges assumptions that are not clear and holds her ground when her challenge is not accepted. She loves me without reservation, but that does not mean that she is not rigorously critical when my writing needs improvement. I know without doubt that I am a better writer because of her intense involvement in that process.

Besides that, there is the ultimate and undeniable truth that I love her very deeply and I find our life together to be nothing less than a rich and ever-expanding pleasure. I have been tremendously proud of her when she has filled in for me, doing my lectures on several different occasions when sickness felled me at an inopportune time, and when she edited her own book.[6] So gifted is this lady that she has herself been sought out as a lecturer in such places as California, North Carolina, Mississippi, and Oregon. She is a very talented and deeply appreciated wife, and I adore her.

Out of the solidarity of that wonderful partnership, we extend our love to our larger family. So I also want to thank our children, Ellen, Katharine, Jaquelin, Brian, and Rachel; their spouses, Gus Epps, Jack Catlett, and Julieann Hoyt; our grandchildren, Shelby and Jay Catlett and John and Lydia Hylton; our sisters and brothers, Betty Spong Marshall, Will Spong, Nancy Wentworth, Bill Bridger, and Doris Bridger; and our one surviving parent, Ina Bridger[7]—all of whom enrich our lives and add immeasurably to our happiness.

JOHN SHELBY SPONG
Cambridge, Massachusetts
September 2001

# A
# New
# Christianity
# for a New World

# ONE

# A PLACE TO BEGIN:
# THE OLD IS NO MORE;
# THE NEW IS NOT YET

*Between 1910 and 1915, in response to biblical criticism in general and to the challenge of Charles Darwin in particular, a group of conservative Christians published a series of pamphlets under the title* The Fundamentals.[1] *From those pamphlets the word* fundamentalism *as a description of the literal beliefs of conservative Christians entered the religious vocabulary.*

*The tracts defended such things as the Mosaic authorship of the Pentateuch, the Davidic authorship of the Psalms, and the accuracy of the biblical prophecy predicting specific events in the life and death of Jesus Christ. Each of these suppositions has been successfully challenged by modern scholarship. Beyond that, these tracts also defended the literal accuracy of what they called "the primary Christian themes." In time these basic fundamentals of Christianity were said to be five in number. To question or to deny the truth of any of these five doctrines was thought to be an act not just of heresy, but of actual apostasy.*

*These five fundamentals were:[2]*

*1. The inspiration of scripture as the literal, revealed word of God.*

*2. The virgin birth as the miraculous and literal means by which the divine nature of Christ has been guaranteed.*

*3. The substitutionary view of the atonement that was accomplished in the death of Jesus. The affirmation of the saving power of his blood and the gift of salvation that was accomplished by his death.*

*4. The certainty of the physical bodily resurrection of Jesus from the dead. The accuracy of both the empty-tomb and the appearance stories in the gospel tradition.*

*5. The truth of the second coming of Jesus, the reality of the Day of Judgment, which would be based on the record of one's life, and the certainty of heaven and hell as eternal places of reward and punishment.*

Today I find each of these fundamentals, as traditionally understood, to be not just naive, but eminently rejectable. Nor would any of them be supported in our generation by reputable Christian scholars.

Scripture is filled with cultural attitudes that we have long ago abandoned and with behavior that is today regarded as immoral. Concepts such as the virgin birth, the physical resurrection, and the second coming are today more often regarded as symbols to be understood theologically than as events that occurred in literal history. The substitutionary view of the atonement has become grotesque, both in its understanding of a God who requires the shed blood of a human sacrifice as a prerequisite for salvation and in its definition of humanity as fallen and depraved.

If these things still constitute the faith of Christian people, then Christianity has become for me and for countless others hopelessly *unbelievable. Surely the essence of Christianity is not found in any or all of these propositions.*

—JOHN SHELBY SPONG,
from a public speech at the Graduate Theological
Union, Berkeley, California, 2001

I am a Christian.

For forty-five years I have served the Christian church as a deacon, priest, and bishop. I continue to serve that church today in a wide variety of ways in my official retirement. I believe that God is real and that I live deeply and significantly as one related to that divine reality.

I call Jesus my Lord. I believe that he has mediated God in a powerful and unique way to human history and to me.

I believe that my particular life has been dramatically and decisively impacted not only by the life of this Jesus, but also by his death and indeed by the Easter experience that Christians know as the resurrection.

Part of my life's vocation has been spent seeking a way to articulate this impact and to invite others into what I can only call the "Christ-experience." I believe that in this Christ I discover a basis for meaning, for ethics, for prayer, for worship, and even for the hope of life beyond the boundaries of my mortality. I want my readers to know who it is who writes these words. I do not want to be guilty of violating any truth-in-packaging act. I define myself first and foremost as a Christian believer.

Yet I do not define God as a supernatural being. I do not believe in a deity who can help a nation win a war, intervene to cure a loved one's sickness, allow a particular athletic team to defeat its opponent, or affect the weather for anyone's benefit. I do not think it is appropriate for me to pretend that those things are possible when everything I know about the natural order of the world I inhabit proclaims that they are not.

Since I do not see God as a being, I cannot interpret Jesus as the earthly incarnation of this supernatural deity, nor can I with credibility assume that he possessed sufficient Godlike power to do such miraculous things as stilling the storm, banishing demons, walking on water, or expanding five loaves to provide sufficient bread to feed five thousand men, plus women and children. If I am to make a claim for the divine nature of this Jesus, it must be on some other basis than this.[3] Nature miracles, I am now convinced, say volumes about the power that people attributed to Jesus, but they say nothing about literal occurrences.

I do not believe that this Jesus could or did in any literal way raise the dead, overcome a medically diagnosed paralysis, or restore sight to a person born blind or to one in whom the ability to see had been physiologically destroyed. Nor do I believe he enabled one who was mute and profoundly deaf since birth to hear. Healing stories can be looked at in a number of ways. To view them as supernatural, miraculous events is, in my opinion, the least credible of those possibilities.

I do not believe that Jesus entered this world by the miracle of a virgin birth or that virgin births occur anywhere except in mythology. I do not believe that a literal star guided literal wise men to bring Jesus gifts or that literal angels sang to hillside shepherds to announce his birth. I do not believe that Jesus was born in Bethlehem or that he fled into Egypt to escape the wrath of King Herod. I regard these as legends that later became historicized as the tradition grew and developed and as people sought to understand the meaning and the power of the Christ-life.[4]

I do not believe that the experience Christians celebrate at Easter was the physical resuscitation of the three-days-dead body of Jesus, nor do I believe that anyone literally talked with Jesus after the resurrection moment, gave him food, touched his resurrected flesh, or walked in any physical manner with his risen body. I find it interesting that all of the narratives that tell of such encounters occur only in the later gospels. I do not believe that Jesus' resurrection was marked in a literal way by an earthquake, an angelic pronouncement, or an empty tomb. I regard these things too as the legendary traditions of a maturing religious system.[5]

I do not believe that Jesus, at the end of his earthly sojourn, returned to God by ascending in any literal sense into a heaven located somewhere above the sky. My knowledge of the size of this universe reduces that concept to nonsense.

I do not believe that this Jesus founded a church or that he established an ecclesiastical hierarchy beginning with the twelve apostles and enduring to this day. I do not believe that he created sacraments as special means of grace or that these means of grace are, or can be, somehow controlled by the church, and thus are to be presided over only by the ordained. All of these things represent to me attempts on the part of human beings to accrue power for themselves and their particular religious institution.

I do not believe that human beings are born in sin and that, unless baptized or somehow saved, they will be forever banished from God's presence. I do not regard the mythical concept of the fall of human life into some negative status as constituting an accurate view of our beginnings or of the origins of evil. To concentrate on the fall of humanity into a state of sinfulness and to suggest that this sinfulness can be overcome only by a divine initiative that will restore human life to a pre-fallen status it never had are to me strange concepts indeed, serving primarily, once again, to build institutional power.[6]

I do not believe that women are any less human or less holy than men, and therefore I cannot imagine being part of a church that would discriminate against women in any manner or even suggest that a woman is unfit for any vocation the church offers generally to its people, from the papacy to the humblest role of service. I regard the church's traditional exclusion of women from positions of leadership to be not a sacred tradition but a manifestation of the sin of patriarchy.

I do not believe that homosexual people are abnormal, mentally sick, or morally depraved. Furthermore, I regard any sacred text that suggests otherwise to be both wrong and ill-informed. My study has led me to the conclusion that sexuality itself, including all sexual orientations, is morally neutral and as such can be lived out either positively or negatively. I regard the spectrum of human sexual experience to be broad indeed. On that spectrum, some percentage of the human population is at all times oriented toward people of their own gender. That is simply the way life is. I cannot imagine being part of a church that discriminates against gay and lesbian people on the basis of their *being*. Nor do I want to continue to participate in ecclesiastical practices that I regard as based on nothing but prejudiced ignorance.[7]

I do not believe that either skin pigmentation or ethnic background constitutes a matter of superiority or inferiority, and I regard any tradition or social system, including any part of the Christian church that operates on that assumption to be unworthy of continued life. The prejudices of human beings based on race or ethnicity are to me nothing more or less than a manifestation of past tribalism; they are negative biases that human beings developed in their struggle to survive.[8]

I do not believe that all Christian ethics have been inscribed either on tablets of stone or in the pages of the Christian scriptures and are therefore set for all time. I am aware that "time makes ancient good uncouth"[9] and that prejudice based on negative cultural definitions has, through the centuries, been the basis upon which Christians have oppressed people of color, women, and those whose sexual orientation has not been heterosexual.[10]

I do not believe that the Bible is the "word of God" in any literal sense. I do not regard it as the primary source of divine revelation. I do not believe that God dictated it or even inspired its production in its entirety. I see the Bible as a human book mixing the profound wisdom of sages through the centuries with the limitations of human perceptions of reality at a particular time in human history. This combination has marked our religious convictions as a mixed witness, combining both slavery and emancipation, inquisitions and theological breakthroughs, freedom and oppression.[11]

I suppose I could expand this litany of beliefs and nonbeliefs for pages, but these few statements should be sufficient to pose the issues I wish to develop. The primary question I seek to raise in this book is this: Can a person claim with integrity to be a Christian and at the same time dismiss, as I have done, so much of what has traditionally defined the content of the Christian faith? Would I be wiser and more honest if I were to do what so many others in my generation have done—namely, resign from my membership in this faith-system of my forebears? Should I renounce my own baptism, deny that I am any longer a disciple of Jesus, take up citizenship in the secular city, and become a member of the Church Alumni Association? Am I prohibited from taking the steps necessary to abandon my faith-commitments by a lack of will, by an irrational, emotional attachment that I cannot break, or even by a spiritual dishonesty? Surely such a choice would in many ways have made my life simpler, less complicated. In the eyes of many, both in the Christian church and in the secular society, it would also have represented an act of integrity. It would not, however, have been honest, nor would it have been true to my deepest convictions. My problem has never been my faith. It has always been the literal way that human beings have chosen to articulate that faith.

I have elected, therefore, the harder, the more complicated path, even though it has on many occasions threatened to tear my very soul apart. Walking my path has subjected me to enormous religious hostility from threatened adherents of my own faith-tradition, as well as to cursory dismissal on the part of many of my secular friends, who seem to regard me as a hopelessly religious carryover from the Middle Ages. In the face of religious hostility on one side and incredulous disdain for my unwillingness to reject my faith-tradition on the other, I continue to insist that I am a Christian. I hold steadfastly to the truth of the assertion first made by Paul that "God was in Christ" (2 Cor. 5:19, KJV). I seek the God-experience which I believe lies underneath the biblical and theological explanations that through the ages have attempted to interpret Jesus. I think that it is possible to separate the experience from the explanation and to recognize the increasingly inadequate capacity of ancient words to capture the essence of any experience for all time. I therefore call the church to a radical shift from the way in which it has traditionally proclaimed its message, the way it has organized itself to broker that reservoir of spiritual power, and the way it has claimed to speak for God in human history.

I am quite certain that the reassessment of Christianity that I seek to develop must be so complete as to cause some people to fear that the God they have traditionally worshiped is, in fact, dying. The reformation needed today must, in my opinion, be so total that it will by comparison make the Reformation of the sixteenth century look like a child's tea party. In retrospect, that Reformation dealt primarily with issues of authority and order. The new reformation will be profoundly theological, of necessity challenging every aspect of our faith-story. Because I believe that Christianity cannot continue as the irrelevant religious sideshow to which it has been reduced, I seek to engage the best minds of the new millennium in this reformation. I hope that we Christians will not tremble at the audacity of the challenge. We face today, as I will seek to document, a total change in the way modern people perceive reality. This change proclaims that the way Christianity has traditionally been formulated no longer has credibility. That is why Christianity as we have known it increasingly displays signs of rigor mortis.

Christianity postulates a theistic God who does supernatural things, many of which are not by our standards considered moral. This God is described in our scriptures as hammering the Egyptians with plague after plague, for example, one of which involved the murder of the firstborn male of every Egyptian household in a divine campaign to free the chosen people from slavery (Exod. 7–10). Then this God opened the Red Sea to allow the Hebrews to escape their life of bondage and closed the Red Sea just in time to drown the pursuing army of the Egyptians (Exod. 14). Is that the handiwork of a moral deity? Do these actions reflect a God whom Egyptians could ever worship? Could any of us? Do we want to believe in such a deity?

The theistic God of scripture is also said to have stopped the sun in the sky (as if the sun actually rotated around the earth) to enable Joshua to have sufficient daylight to slaughter the Amorites in a battle (Josh. 10). Is that a justifiable cause for divine action? Putting aside any speculation about what might have happened to the force of gravity in response to such magical tampering with the universe, we are left to wonder whether the Amorites could ever have worshiped such a God. Could they have sustained the claim that human life is of infinite value when tribal prejudices were confused with God's will in that way? Can any of us make that claim today?

It was that same biblical text from the book of Joshua that enabled the leadership of the Roman Catholic Church to force the seventeenth-century scientist Galileo to recant on pain of death from his "nonscriptural" assertion that the earth was not the center of the universe and that in fact it rotated around the sun. Even though Galileo's insights have made the modern exploration of space that began in the 1950s possible, it was not until 1991 that the Christian church, in the form of the Vatican, finally admitted publicly that Galileo had been right and that the church had been wrong in condemning him. By this time neither Galileo nor most of the world's scientific community particularly cared what the official voices of the church declared about their enterprise. As Paul Davies, a Templeton Prize–winning physicist, observed, the trivial God he met in church was no longer big enough to be able to be God for his world anyway.[12] Does anyone doubt which side in that particular conflict will prevail in the march of time?

Christianity, borrowing a concept from the Jewish Day of Atonement, Yom Kippur, has traditionally interpreted the death of Jesus as a sacrifice offered to God in payment for our sinfulness. It has delighted in referring to Jesus as "the lamb of God, whose shed blood washes away the sins of the world." Is such a God—one who requires bloody human sacrifice—still worshipworthy today, when we finally raise this offensive idea to consciousness?

Borrowing from another part of the Jewish tradition, this time the festival called Passover, Christians developed the context of the eucharist, their major liturgical observance. In the original Passover ritual of the Jews, another lamb had been sacrificed and the magic power of its blood had been placed on the doorposts of Jewish homes in Egypt, to keep the angel of death from making mistakes and killing Jews instead of Egyptians (who were deemed worthy of such destruction). Then the Jews roasted and ate the slaughtered lamb before making their exodus from Egypt. Since then, members of Jewish families have gathered each year at the table to celebrate that ancient deliverance by feasting on the body and the blood of the sacrificial lamb. It is a strange ritual when its various elements are heard outside a liturgical context, yet it has shaped the Christian eucharist through the centuries. Today these concepts, still found in Christian worship, elicit images that are repugnant to the modern consciousness.

I suspect that this liturgical development began when an early Christian preacher took Paul's ecstatic exclamation that "Christ, our paschal lamb, has been sacrificed" (1 Cor. 5:7, RSV) as the text for his sermon. Then that hypothetical preacher related the Passover homiletically to the Jesus story in order to achieve a

Christian correlation with that Jewish practice. In that explanation the cross on which Jesus had been nailed became the doorpost of the world. The blood of Jesus, shed upon that cross, was seen as breaking the power of death for all people. In this way the significance of Jesus' death was explained as being like the death of the paschal lamb that had protected the Jewish people from their final enemy in a past moment of national crisis. It was but a short additional step for Christians to develop a sacramental act, as the Jews had done, which could recall that death and recreate it in the present, symbolically enabling the gathered peoples to eat the flesh and drink the blood of the new lamb of God. It was also inevitable that these symbols would in time be literalized.

But do those symbols, literalized or not, still translate in this generation? Can they still convey meaning in a postmodern world? The magic of breaking the power of death by placing blood on the doorposts or on the cross is strangely primitive. The cannibalistic ritual of eating the flesh of the deceased deity is filled with ancient psychological nuances that are disturbing to modern sensitivities. The liturgical practice of reenacting the sacrifice of the cross and claiming that our participation in that reenactment is necessary for salvation is hardly a winning modern formula. Likewise, the ecclesiastical claim that only properly authorized and ordained persons can preside over these acts is ludicrous to modern ears. Do we really expect such claims to win the loyalty of modern minds? Yet if these claims are removed from Christian worship, does anything remain?

I believe that all of the questions, issues, and difficulties noted above need to be faced openly by Christians today and then transcended with new images. For Christians who have identified God with these strange earlier understandings of divinity, the transition will not be easy. Yet the time has clearly come when all of us must move beyond the deconstruction of these inadequate and therefore rejectable symbols, which historically have been so significant in the life of the Christian church, and turn our attention to the task of charting a vision of what the church can and must be in the future.

The primary apologetic task facing the Christian church today is that of separating the extraneous from the essential, the timeless God-experience from the time-warped God-explanations of the past. Deconstruction admittedly is a far easier path to travel when seeking to describe why some ways of understanding a religious system from the past are inadequate. It is far more difficult to sketch out a vision of something new, something people have never seen, something the world has never tested. But reformers cannot just tilt against the windmills of antiquity. They must develop new visions, propose new models, chart new solutions. That is now the task I seek to accomplish.

I do not anticipate that this effort will meet with a predominantly interested or responsive ecclesiastical audience. That does not concern me, however, because the people with whom I seek to communicate constitute a very specific audience and to them I will aim my message as directly as I can.

I am not interested, for example, in confronting or challenging those conservative, fundamentalist elements of Christianity that are so prevalent today. They will, I believe, die of their own irrelevance without any help from me. They have attached their understanding of Christianity to attitudes of the past that are simply withering on the vine. Nowhere is this better seen than when one observes how the word *Christian* is used in our contemporary world. Ask yourself what image comes to your mind when you see a business that calls itself a "Christian bookstore" or hear a political commentator who refers to "the Christian vote" in a particular election.

"Christian bookstores" are known primarily for their anti-intellectual stance, their support of creation science in opposition to evolution, their volumes on childrearing which advocate tyrannical approaches that, in my mind, border on child abuse, their attempt to uphold the dying patterns of patriarchy, and their negativity toward homosexuality.

The Christian Right politically espouses similar causes, with the two issues of opposition to abortion and condemnation of homosexuality being their emotional hot buttons. Supporters of this political movement have enfolded these two issues inside a moralistic crusade that marches under such code words as "family values" and "restoring integrity to both government and America's civil life." But that crusade deals with symbols and not substance.

Both abortion and homosexual acceptance are products of a revolution in sexual thinking that has been fueled not by rampant immorality, as the proponents of yesterday's values maintain, but by dramatic breakthroughs in the way knowledge has grown and life has changed.

Those who oppose abortion on what they describe as moral grounds see it as symbolic of the removal of punishment from sexuality. When effective and safe birth control, in the form of the pill, was introduced in the middle of the twentieth century and family planning became a genuine possibility, those changes were also resisted by these same elements of society, and on the same basis. The great unstated fear was that sex and punishment were being separated. Today birth control and family planning are so universally practiced that no political candidate would seek office in opposition to either. Abortion, on the other hand, still has political cachet, especially when it is encased in moralistic slogans such as "the right to life" and is graphically described as "partial-birth abortion."

There is probably a political consensus today around the idea that abortion should be "safe, legal, and rare"—and indeed it will be so when society accepts the fact that the sexual rules have changed because life itself has changed.

Four hundred years ago, puberty commenced several years later than it does today. It has been coming down about half a year per century, the result of healthier diet and better medical practice. However, because we now believe that young women are educable in our great universities and are capable of doing graduate work and entering careers once reserved for men—those in law, medicine, business, and even the church—marriage has been pushed into the mid to late twenties. The resulting gap of some ten to fifteen years between puberty and marriage has made the revolution in sexual ethics inevitable. The abortion issue is the last vestige of that revolution, and the pending easy availability of the RU486 pill, already being used in most European countries, will effectively end this battle.

Homosexuality is the other burning issue of the Christian Right, and once more supporters of that movement maintain their prejudices by being significantly uninformed. Those in the Christian Right still define homosexuality as a choice made by people who are mentally ill or morally depraved. If mentally ill, these victims ought to seek a cure, the conservative Christians say. If morally depraved, these victims ought to seek conversion and an end to their sinful ways. This mentality is countered by the overwhelming medical, scientific, and psychological data, all of which suggest that homosexuality is more like left-handedness. It is a part of the very *being* of a minority of the human family, and therefore it is something to which one awakens, not something one chooses to be. Those organizations, most of which are identified with Christian fundamentalism or evangelicalism advertising that they can cure homosexuality are, in my opinion, not just ignorant, but actually fraudulent.

So let me be clear. I do not seek to address these conservative and, I believe, out-of-touch-with-reality believers. I do not want to convert them, argue with them, or even seek to counter them, unless they threaten to become majority voices seeking to impose their agenda on our world. I believe that the expansion of knowledge will ultimately render their attitudes irrelevant to the debate on the future of Christianity.

At the same time, I do not expect that these efforts at reformation or the stating of a new Christian vision will be greeted with

A Place to Begin

anything more than a yawning indifference from those members of our society who have already decided that almost any religion is a superstition employed by the weak. These people who have opted for life in the secular city rather than to remain members of their religious institutions are not typically interested in my efforts, which they regard as an attempt to do a face-lift on a corpse.

This attitude of the secularists was illustrated beautifully for me in London recently on a television program in which I participated. One of my fellow panel members was an iconoclastic journalist who identified himself as an atheist. This man became quite disturbed when I would not parrot the traditional religious line that he was so used to ridiculing. It was the first time that I had ever been attacked by an atheist for not believing properly! My critic knew from long experience how to deal with the traditional religious point of view and had made his peace with that by abandoning it totally. He did not wish to go through that exercise on another occasion with someone who had rejected the very things about religion that he rejected. So he became amusingly angry.

If these ideas of mine come to the attention of the secular world, it will be because of conservative attacks mounted in the public arena against my point of view. Yet even if those attacks become newsworthy, the secular city will still, in all probability, not opt to engage my viewpoint, though that will be the only chance I have to gain the attention of its citizens. In all probability, conservative attacks will sound to secular thinkers like one more religious squabble from which they are pleased to be delivered and in which they have no real interest.

Even in the mainline religious traditions, it will not be easy for me to gain a listening ear or to establish a significant foothold. Mainline churches are far more dedicated to preserving institutional power than they are to confronting these "life and death" issues. The fear felt by members of these churches will cause them to say such things as, "He has gone too far this time."[13]

I listened on one occasion to a former professor of divinity at Oxford University, known at that time as one of the Anglican Communion's most distinguished scholars, as he talked publicly about the resurrection of Jesus. It was an amazing performance, neither offending anyone nor offering any new possibilities. That performance, I suspect, will stand in all of its hearers' (and readers') memories as an eminently forgettable occasion. No growth, no excitement, no gospel. Yet somehow this theologian succeeded on that occasion in achieving his goal of diffusing questions and maintaining an aura of learnedness without drawing a single disturbing conclusion or facing a single problem.

Sometimes the failure to offend is less deliberate than coincidental. Karl Rahner, a very creative scholar, wrote in a deeply obtuse, heavily annotated way, and because of that was hardly ever read by anyone who sat in the pews of the churches of his Roman Catholic tradition. He died respected and honored by the highest officials of the Vatican. But his disciple, Hans Küng, a Catholic professor of theology at the University of Tübingen, had a tremendous gift of communication and became the most widely read Roman Catholic theologian of the twentieth century. When Küng wrote, people understood what the issues were and responded with both threat and freedom. But in the eyes of Küng's ecclesiastical superiors, he had committed the unforgivable sin: he had allowed questions to be raised in the human hearts of "the faithful"—hearts in which, in the mind of the church, only proper *answers*, not *questions*, should ever be allowed to reside—and had thereby "disturbed the people." For his "sin" he was removed from his position as a "Catholic" theologian and remains today largely unappreciated in his own tradition, a martyr to his church's neurotic need to control truth—a need that in our information age is about as possible to maintain as standing before the incoming tide at the shore and hoping to stop it.

History informs me that reformation normally rises from the ranks of the people. Reformers lift the vision, but if that vision does not ignite the people, it quickly fades. My experience teaches me not to expect reformation to come from the mainline churches or from their academic defenders until someone who is in touch with where people are in our world raises the issues in such a cogent way that both mainline leaders and academicians will be forced to respond and to join the effort.

The audience I seek to address is smaller, more distinct, and more specific. I seek to speak to those ordinary people whose name is legion. They are people who feel spiritually thirsty but know that they can no longer drink from the traditional wells of the past. At its core, this group will be a small minority of the population, but they are augmented by a much larger group of fellow travelers who will respond if given the opportunity to listen. These people will applaud, reflecting their deep and genuine appreciation. Some of them will say, "At last someone has given me permission"—as if some type of permission were actually needed—"to look at things from a new perspective beyond the traditional formulations into which my religious yearnings have heretofore been forced." This group will resonate with the idea that their own doubts and questions about God or religion do not define them as either crazy or evil. Their doubts and questions mean only that they are breathing the air of the twenty-first century. They will rejoice that they at last have found a way to put their heads and their hearts together.

This group has been my primary audience throughout my whole career. They still possess a profound God-consciousness, but that God-consciousness never quite fits the molds that religious institutions say are the only ways that one can think about God. If the new reformation of Christianity is to be achieved, then it will begin and find its roots in this group—a group generally not just unseen but also unheard by the religious leadership of our world.

As these various audiences react to and interact with my suggestions and proposals, it might be worthwhile to keep before us the ultimate question I hope to address in this book, posed earlier in the text. Will the radically reformed Christianity for which I am calling be sufficiently connected to and identified with the Christianity of the past that it will be recognized not only as its heir, but also as part and parcel of the same faith-tradition? If the answer to this question is no, as many of my critics will certainly maintain, then their charge, that what I am seeking to do is to create a new religion, will be accurate. Yet I suspect that the answer to that charge may be in doubt for many years, perhaps a generation or two. I am deeply aware that I seek to walk the razor's edge of both faith and practice by searching for a solution to Christianity's sickness that may be itself a fatal cure. My deepest hope is that the church, in its myriad institutional forms, will not rush to judgment, but will allow the process of time to determine whether I am friend or foe, prophetic in vision or deluded by hubris. ( JOEL GOLDSMITH )

Let me, however, state at the onset both my conscious desire and my conviction. I am seeking to reform and rethink something I love. I have no intention of trying to create a new religion. I am a Christian and will go to my grave as a member of this household of faith. I think that all efforts to build new religions are doomed, and inevitably so, from the very beginning. No religion, including Christianity, has ever come into existence as a *new* thing. Religious systems always represent an evolving process. Christianity, for example, emerged out of Judaism, which in fact had been shaped in part by the worship of Egypt, Canaan, Babylon, and Persia. Christianity's march into dominance in the Western world was marked by its incorporation into itself of elements from the gods of Olympus, Mithraism, and other mystery cults of the Mediterranean.

As Christianity moves today into the modern world, it is beginning to reflect insights garnered from the other great human religions. Evolution is the mode of the religious journey through history. What I will seek to do is simply to chart the evolving future of this faith-tradition. I will leave it to tomorrow's believers or critics to determine whether or not the Christianity that will survive this present twenty-first century is still in touch with the Christianity that broke upon the scene in Judea in the first century and then moved on to conquer the Roman Empire in the fourth century, dominate Western civilization in the thirteenth century, endure the face-lifting reformation of the sixteenth century, follow the flag of European colonial expansion in the nineteenth century, and shrink dramatically in the twentieth century.

I will remain rooted in my conviction that the word *God* stands for and points to something that is real. In some way, I will continue to assert that the Christ-figure was and is a manifestation of the reality that I call God, and that the life of Jesus opened for us all a way to enter that reality. That is, I will seek to maintain that Jesus was a defining moment in the human journey into the meaning of God. I will stake out a vision of how I believe this power can transcend the ages to enable people today to be touched by it and even to enter it, necessitating the creation of communities of worship and living liturgies.

Finally, to accomplish this task, I am required to strip away from this Christianity of the future every attempt to literalize the interpretive myths and explanatory legends of the past. I will attempt to free Christianity of its exclusive claims and its power-needs, which have totally distorted its message. I will seek to go behind the institutionally developed religious system that has come to mark Christianity and there explore the power which that system sought to explain and organize. Although eager to escape those limits, I have no desire to escape the experience that has compelled people through the ages, down to and including me, to say, "Jesus is Lord!"

Those are my goals. Can they be achieved? Or is this the fantasy of one who can see the dying embers of a faith-tradition and even of a life's work, but is unable to admit that they cannot be revived? I leave that for my readers to decide. As for me, I believe that this is the only way I can continue to be faithful to the baptismal vows I took so long ago: "To follow Christ as my Lord and Savior, to seek Christ in all people, and to respect the dignity of every human being."[14]

# TWO

# The Signs of
# the Death of Theism

*God. Where are you? I wish you would talk to me. God. It isn't just me. There's a general feeling. This is what the people are say-ing in the parish. They want to know where you are. The joke wears thin. You never say anything. All right. People expect that. It's understood—but people also think . . . You see, I tell you, it's this perpetual absence. Yes? This not being here—it's that. I mean, let's be honest, it's just beginning to get some of us down. You know? Is that unreasonable? There are an awful lot of people in a very bad way. And they need something besides silence. God. Do you understand?*[1]

— David Hare, playwright

The evidence that God, understood theistically, is dying or is perhaps already dead is overwhelming. I define the theistic God as "a being, supernatural in power, dwelling outside this world and invading the world periodically to accomplish the divine will." There are both rational data and emotional data to support this contention.

The rational data are seen in the way the arena in which the theistic God was believed to operate has been shrunk so dramatically by the advance of knowledge. When people say today, for example, that "the age of miracles is over," what they mean is not that miracles no longer occur, but that they never did—the age when we perceived events as miraculous is gone. The things that our ancestors called miracles and even magic are explained today without appeal to the supernatural because we understand so much more completely the way the universe operates. The scientific world no longer sees God in terms of a chain of cause and effect. We once saw God as the prime mover in the issues of sickness and health. Sickness was a reflection of God's punishment, we used to think, while health was a reflection of God's favor. But then we discovered germs and viruses, and we developed antibiotics, surgical procedures, and such things as chemotherapy. With this new knowledge it began to dawn on us that antibiotics, surgery, and chemotherapy are just as effective on sinners as they are on saints. So the realm of sickness as an area in which God operated began to shrink, and medicine joined the modern push toward secularization.

We once saw God as the source of the weather, and we interpreted drought, floods, storms, hurricanes, and tornadoes as expressions of the divine will. But then we discovered weather patterns and fronts, low- and high-pressure systems, El Niño and La Niña winds, tidal effects on climate, and so many other realities that the idea of a supernatural being directing the weather for some moral purpose has become impossible to sustain.

We once thought that God led our nation into battle, defeating our enemies or, if our faithfulness to this God had been badly compromised allowing us to taste the divine wrath in defeat. But with the advent of modern warfare, God seems always to be on the side of the nations with the greatest arsenal.

These are but a few of the numerous illustrations that could be cited to show rationally that God, understood theistically, is no longer operative in our belief systems, no matter how hard we try to hold on to this premodern deity.

Even if we wanted to return to the familiar and comforting God of our youth, we could not do so. That is true of most people in the developed nations of the world, whether they admit it or not. The God of theism is so visibly dying that only by playing a game of denial and illusion—a game that many play—can we continue to maintain that this God is still real. That is the nature of the religious dilemma of our generation.

Those who do not agree that the dismissal of the theistic understanding of the deity is the inevitable fate awaiting the God of the past must surely admit that the belief in this deity is rarely taken with any existential seriousness.

It seems not to matter whether the person is a member of the theological academy, in which the modern God-debate occurs daily, or a thoroughly secular member of the world for whom the word *God* is never spoken with seriousness; almost all people live today outside the God-consciousness of antiquity. The people who still occupy the pews of our churches seem blissfully unaware of the debate in the academies, and so they continue to use the language of the past in their hymns and liturgies. This is accomplished primarily by a willingness not to think much about its meaning. When they do engage this thought process, they find these concepts non-sensible at best and non-believable at worst. The anger that they so often express when they are made to think about it is revelatory of its fragility. But the fact remains that the dismissal of classical theism is simply the presupposition of our corporate society, even if it is not yet fully present in the stated assumptions of our conscious minds.

Carl Jung, writing to a Protestant pastor in Switzerland, declared quite matter-of-factly as early as 1959 that an "antimythological trend" is abroad today due to "the difficulties we

have in clinging to our previous mythological tenets of belief."
That had not been so in earlier centuries, Jung continued, when
people operated out of their very limited knowledge of the world
of nature. In that world, he said, one needed no sacrifice of the
intellect to believe in miracles; and the report of the birth, life,
death, and resurrection of the redeemer could all still pass as literal biography. All of this, he concluded, had radically changed
under the compelling influence of scientific rationalism. "We are
tired of the excessive effort to believe because the object of the
belief is no longer inherently convincing," was Jung's final sum-
mation of the matter.[2]

Since theism as a definition, and God as a concept, have been so
totally identified with each other in our Western Christian world,
a nontheistic position is widely assumed, at least in religious
circles, to be an atheistic position. To say it positively, a rejection
of theism is perceived as an affirmation of godlessness. People no
longer believe in God in a real and operative sense, even if they do
continue to believe in believing in God. There is a powerful difference. The signs of this functional godlessness are seen in the
statistical decline of every mainline Christian and Jewish tradition
in the developed world. It is also apparent in the hysterical revival
of fundamentalist religions throughout the world. In the West
that revival takes the form of the rise of evangelical Christianity.
In Israel it assumes the shape of a controlling militant orthodoxy.
In those parts of the Middle East that have experimented with
Western ways, it manifests itself as an Islamic Shiite fundamentalism that has achieved political power in Iran and remains a strong
aggressive minority all over the Muslim world. The counterpoint
of this fundamentalism—indeed, almost its exact opposite—is
present in the rampant secularism that in the West constitutes an
ascending majority point of view.

There are also abundant emotional data suggesting that the
security-producing role once attributed to the theistic God is no
longer working. These data manifest themselves in various ob-

servable forms of human behavior—some apparently mundane, others challengingly abhorrent—that mark our Western world in this emerging century. It is these emotional data on which I will focus here.

In this chapter on the death of theism, I ground my discussion not in terms of the rational data, which can be read almost anywhere in the world of science, or in terms of observations of the motivating values by which we increasingly live in the secular city. Rather, I seek to raise to consciousness some revealing, almost universal patterns of human behavior, which proclaim that the anxiety we once controlled by our conviction that the theistic God was alive, well, and in control is no longer holding. These data suggest, I contend, that the emotional component of human life is increasingly unable to keep its sense of trauma and hysteria under control, and thus the data provide commentary on what is really happening in our increasingly godless modern world. I urge my readers to follow this argument closely, even if it seems to start in a strange place.

How many of those who constitute my reading audience begin the day with either coffee or tea? In the United States coffee is the more popular of the two beverages—so popular, in fact, that multi-million-dollar corporations have placed coffee bars and coffee houses in almost every community of the land. A strange, compelling affinity has developed between Western life and this treasured beverage. One hears people say such things as, "It's hard to get going in the morning without my coffee." Most human beings in the Western world do seem to need some help to get started each day. Even in the United Kingdom, where tea is the drink of choice with which to start the day, a ritual of mid-morning coffee has achieved an almost universal status, serving as a kind of pick-me-up to guard against the first flagging of one's energy as the day wears on.

Since caffeine is the operative drug in both coffee and tea, and since caffeine is an *addictive* drug—indeed, far more addictive than most people imagine—we need to face the fact that addiction, at least to this mild drug, is widespread in our society and in our experience. Have you ever wondered why?

When one adds to this bit of data the fact that caffeine is also found in cola drinks, such as Coca-Cola and Pepsi, a pattern begins to emerge. Caffeine is also added artificially to many other carbonated soft drinks, including youth-oriented beverages such as Mountain Dew and Surge, in which caffeine has its heaviest concentration. Some of these drinks are marketed with wide pour-spouts to enable quicker consumption, thus accentuating the immediacy of the "fix." Furthermore, the chocolate that laces many of the desserts we eat is also laden with caffeine.

Clearly, then, caffeine plays an omnipresent role in our society; it is difficult for anyone to avoid this drug for even a single day. What does it say about the life of our postmodern Western world that we have organized it so thoroughly around the stimulant caffeine?

To pose this issue from a second perspective, look at the presence in our contemporary society of a second drug, alcohol. Think for a moment about the extensive presence and use of alcohol in our modern world. Examine your own use of this drug over, say, the past twenty-four hours. Did a cocktail precede your last dinner? A glass of wine accompany it? A beer relax you after work? Though not as universally used as caffeine, alcohol runs a close second.

Alcohol is an assumed and accepted part of the very air our culture breathes. It is offered in most restaurants. For a majority of Westerners, it is an anticipated part of every meal at which guests are welcomed into the home. Indeed, we face the negativity of the waiter if we decline what we euphemistically call "a drink" in a restaurant, and we may be thought rude or cheap if we do not serve alcohol to those invited to our homes for dinner.

How many of us have ever looked at life from the point of view of a person who has a problem with alcohol dependency? Bars are everywhere. Alcohol is an inescapable reality in our developed world. Cocktail lounges are present in almost every urban block and in the terminals of every major airport. In our peripatetic world, one cannot travel on an airplane without being offered alcohol to ease the journey.

Recent studies reveal that thirteen percent of the people in the United States are admitted alcoholics—a number that, if true, staggers the imagination since, undoubtedly many more people have alcohol problems than admit to them. I have no reason to think that the problem of alcoholism is any more or less present in the United States than it is in any other developed nation in the world. Have you ever wondered why the drug alcohol has become so powerful a part of our lives? Why does contemporary life seem to be so alcohol-dependent?

To press this inquiry to still another level, examine the popularity of the habit of smoking. Statistics suggest that the use of tobacco is actually declining in the United States, in response to the concentrated governmental efforts to curtail smoking in this country, but the fact remains that this habit continues to grow worldwide. Furthermore, recent studies suggest that even in the United States there has been a new increase in teenage smoking, suggesting that this habit is once again rising in popularity, even in the face of a massive campaign to suppress it.

The operative drug in tobacco is nicotine, known to be addictive. But beyond the appeal of this addictive drug, there is an even deeper attraction found in the act of smoking: smoking is a socially acceptable adult form of nursing. Adults can hardly go through life clinging to their mother's breast or using a pacifier in public! Yet smoking carries us, subconsciously if not consciously, back to those infantile sensations. The size of the cigarette and the size of the nipple on our mother's breast are identical. Is that accidental? The sucking motions used in smoking and in nursing are the same. The warmth of the inhaled smoke and the warmth of the ingested milk from our mothers are quite similar. Why, we must wonder, have we developed a cultural addiction to the drug nicotine that keeps us subconsciously attached to our nursing past?

We look next at the presence of clinical depression in our population. How many of those who are now reading these words have experienced the reality of depression, if not in person, then at least in someone near and dear to you? Are we not conscious of the multi-billion-dollar pharmaceutical industry that our society has spawned, a major part of the wealth of which has come from the development of drugs designed to combat depression? Who does not recognize the names Librium, Prozac, Equinil? So widely used are these drugs that their brand names have become household words. I once heard the story of a pastor, attempting to communicate in a language his culture would understand, who proposed that the benediction prayer be changed from "The peace of God that passeth all understanding" to "The peace of God that passeth Prozac be with you all evermore!" Could that substitute be suggested, even in jest, if these drugs were not universally known? What is going on in human life, we must ask, when a significant number of people—so large a group that the rest of us accept their practice almost as a norm—must be drugged or artificially medicated in order to cope with their daily life?

To press this inquiry to yet another level, I raise the difficult specter of suicide in our society. While the percentage of people who actually commit suicide is relatively small, many people have either contemplated it for themselves on some level or have known someone close to them who has. In Darwin, Australia, the phenomenon of suicide has become so normal that the months from January through March are widely known as "the suicide season." That season is discussed so publicly that one gets the impression the people of Darwin would be upset if they failed to achieve their suicide quota for any given year.

Suicide—the final act of self-destruction—is both recognized and feared in our society, even as it seems to have some appeal. Why, we must ask, does this ultimate release from life seem commonplace in our world? Does it not proclaim that a significant number of our citizens find coping with life quite difficult?

When we put this list of observable behavior patterns together, we are forced to recognize that many people are today manifesting in their actions the presence of something we might call "the pain of human existence." Not only that, but these actions have become so universally practiced that they now receive varying levels of approval. At the very least they are considered to be within the norms of human experience.

As troubling as these culturally accepted patterns of behavior have become, however, there are still other human actions that are so intensely horrifying that they shock us when we hear or read of them, though their occurrence is so frequent that they have ceased to be unexpected. I refer to the random, chilling acts of shooting, terrorism, and mass murder that have marred our life in recent years. Children from twelve years old on up have, in many schools in the United States, planned and carried out violent gun attacks upon their classmates. This pattern has become so widespread that almost every school district in our country has been forced to upgrade its security system. These acts of violence have not occurred primarily in the urban schools of the inner city to which our prejudices tend to assign such patterns of behavior; rather, they have tended to be staged in small towns, rural communities, and affluent suburbs. The perpetrators of these crimes have not been outsiders, but the sons and daughters of families who have been known and trusted in their local communities for generations and who in many cases have been churchgoers. In at least one instance in Colorado, the perpetrators, who ultimately killed themselves, were revealed, through subsequent investigation, to be devotees not only of guns and firearms but of rightwing neo-Nazi political activities.

These patterns of behavior coming from minors have given birth to national debates about the causes of antisocial pathology that are, generally speaking, as shallow as they seem to be popular. Television violence, frequently named as a culprit, has been blamed by those who do not seem to understand that television *reflects* the tastes and values in our society far more than it *creates* them. Others have suggested that these antisocial patterns could be countered if only parents and school officials would return to the practice of corporal punishment as a way to recreate a law-abiding society. Perhaps they have not heard that abused children become abusive adults. Still others, including some of those who are running for high political office, have proposed the reestablishment of mandatory school prayer accompanied by a posting on school bulletin boards of the Ten Commandments as a means of addressing this problem. They seem not to be aware that religion has spawned as much violence and killing throughout Western history as anything else.

The frightening reality is that, despite our attempts to deny it, this kind of destructive behavior is not at all limited to impressionable children. It was adults who planned and carried out the bombing of a government building in Oklahoma City and the twin towers of the World Trade Center in New York City. Both of those acts of violence had religious overtones. It was an adult day-trader in Atlanta who murdered a series of people working in a brokerage office when he could not cover his losses. It was an adult who invaded and shot members of a Jewish community center in California because he hated Jews. It was members of the adult population who in highly publicized cases brutally and personally murdered younger homosexual males in Wyoming and Alabama. It was adults who dragged a black man behind a pickup truck until he was not just dead but dismembered in Jasper, Texas. It has been adults who have carried out a series of murders related to abortion clinics and abortion practitioners. It has been adults who have succumbed to murderous road rage. It has been adults who have hijacked airplanes and placed explosive devices in luggage, resulting not only in death and mayhem but in strict airport security for all passengers.

Each of these acts of violence comes out of something that is going on in the corporate psyche of those adult human beings who dwell in the modern world. Though it might be argued that each of these deeds is individually motivated, the fact that similar violence happens with such frequency demands that we seek answers beyond the suggestion that only mentally sick individuals are responsible. When mental illness reaches epidemic proportions, it becomes a commentary on something far deeper and far more complex that is abroad in the life of the whole society. To kill those with whom one disagrees on some volatile issue, to strike out against those whom one perceives as threatening, is irrational behavior that cries out for some deeper explanation. On one level we human beings appear to have a need to drug ourselves to get through life. On another level we exhibit the desire to remove perceived threats to our well-being with violent action. What, we must ask, do all of these patterns of behavior mean?

To raise these issues from the micro to the macro level, we observe that the twentieth century gave to the Western world the terms "holocaust" and "ethnic cleansing." During the holocaust, which was carried out in Germany in the 1930s and 1940s, six million Jewish people (and many others deemed undesirable by the Third Reich) perished in mass cremations organized by the government of a highly developed, *ostensibly Christian* nation—a nation whose citizens had more doctorates per capita than any other country in the Western world. Obviously the presence of education cannot be said to be a deterrent to attempted genocide and murder! An intense revulsion was felt in the Western world in the years immediately following World War II, when pictures of Jewish bodies in mass graves at Buchenwald and Auschwitz appeared and when the full horror of what had happened to the Jews of Germany and in lands under German control entered our conscious minds.

Many people mistakenly assumed that this revulsion would be sufficient to put an end forever to any other human attempt to accomplish a program of systematic ethnic murder. Yet the civil wars occurring at the end of the twentieth century in Bosnia, Serbia, and Kosovo, and some of the conflicts in Africa, especially in Rwanda and Burundi, followed by the massive cultic murders in Uganda, have proved that such assumptions were ill-founded. There is something profoundly wrong in the human psyche out of which such behavior continues to flow. The fact that the undeclared war between Ireland's Protestant and Catholic populations continues to resist solution after centuries of conflict, or that the tensions in the Middle East seem to endure over countless generations, illustrates the depth of the problem. The fact that racism is a lingering cancerous sore in the developed nations of the world announces over and over that there is something about human life—even developed, educated human life—that is motivated by irrational forces we do not understand and by realities we apparently cannot master. Furthermore, it seems frighteningly obvious that the power of whatever this demonic force represents is growing.

I suggest that these observable behaviors, from the mundane addiction to caffeine to the terrifying reality of ethnic cleansing, are significantly related. More specifically, I suggest that they are nothing less than emotional manifestations of the death of the theistic God. I intend to buttress this assertion with the additional suggestion, which I shall document in the next chapter, that theism was itself originally born as a way of dealing with the trauma of self-consciousness; it was devised as a tool that enabled human beings to keep their hysteria, a by-product of self-consciousness, at bay.

Today, with theism dying, that bulwark against hysteria is disappearing and the signs of the reemergence of that hysteria are visibly mounting. This is the reality to which the widespread use of the drugs and tranquilizers discussed above seems to point. This is what lies behind the meaningless killings and the reemergence of our primitive survival instincts. This is what drives human life back into tribal identities that justify in frightened minds the elimination of those who threaten their tribal power, those who seem to undermine the fragile security that tribal identity seeks to resuscitate. Theism, a definition of God that was born in the dawning of self-consciousness as a way of coping with the awareness of human vulnerability and human meaningless-ness, is today dying, and human life is once again experiencing the trauma of aloneness and loss of meaning. The death of the theistic God was first announced by Friedrich Nietzsche in the nineteenth century.[3] It was then proclaimed by radical theolo-gians in the 1960s.[4] Today it has finally permeated the conscious-ness of the mass mind of the Western world.[5]

These are some of the data that I believe lie behind both the decline of traditional mainline churches and the rise of funda-mentalist churches that traffic in a security they cannot possibly deliver. This is the reality that is being proclaimed in our time by the birth of religious substitutes for theism, from the New Age movement, to Western gurus, to the religion of diet and exercise. Theism's death accounts for the fact that the great cathedrals of our generation have ceased to be churches and have instead be-come athletic arenas and sports stadiums. To these secular cathe-drals crowds of worshipers are attracted each Sunday. The objects of their devotion are dressed in colorful vestments called uniforms and are the recipients of rituals, chants, and liturgical dances. Choirs sing their praises to the objects of their devotion and create moments of ecstasy. They are even gripped, as we say, "by the Spirit."

The death of theism is also manifested in that growing gap that is today drawn between what people say they believe (faith) and the values by which they live (practice). That gap can be illus-trated in thousands of different ways.

Churches universally oppose divorce, while the divorce rate skyrockets in the Western world, even among church people. The pope speaks about the evil of "artificial" birth control, and yet polls indicate that Roman Catholics practice birth control as freely as any other segment of the population. The church in many of its manifestations condemns homosexuality as deviant and evil, and yet it is becoming increasingly apparent that the churches that most heartily condemn homosexuality have the highest percentage of homosexual persons in their ordained life. Indeed, some of the most overt hostility to homosexual people has been spoken by homosexuals hiding inside the vestments of leadership in those churches that are doing the condemning.

This same pattern is seen in the deep and unresolved racism, anti-Semitism, and even anti-Catholic prejudices that mark the lives of many evangelical and fundamentalist Protestant adherents, who reflect, far more than they seem to recognize, not the demands of their faith but the values of the security-seeking religious mentality in which they were raised.[6] It is seen in the significant number of scandals that appear to mark overtly religious people who fall prey to the very sins of the flesh, especially sex and greed, against which they so frequently rail.

In the secularizing societies of the developed nations of the West, where supernatural and superstitious explanations of life no longer suffice and are, in fact, no longer holding, we see a rise of the same emotions that engulfed the human enterprise at the dawn of self-consciousness. There is an awesome fear that comes to those whose education allows them to understand the vastness of the universe but whose emotional capacity to respond to that knowledge is marked by feelings of powerlessness, fragility, and aloneness. Only the creature who possesses self-consciousness has to confront these personal traumas.

It is these traumas that human life—whether yesterday or today—is required to manage, and they demand that some effective coping devices be developed. I contend that a theistic God, who was thought to be sufficiently powerful first to tame and then to control these fears by being our human ally, has been the major coping device through much of human history. I also argue that this theistic coping device worked for centuries. It enabled the world to advance, to build civilization, to develop art, music, and drama. It enabled human beings to perceive life as lived under the watchful eye of an all-powerful and caring deity and to suggest that they themselves were made in this God's image and therefore could curry this God's favor by learning and practicing Godlike behavior.

But as this theistic God dies visibly in the very midst of our present civilization, the hysteria, the fear, and the meaninglessness that are part of our human self-consciousness are seen to be rising once again to frightening levels. The old myth of theism has lost its power and its appeal. A new myth to which we can once again be committed is not yet in place. Before the new myth can be developed, we need to understand how the old one was born, how its power was kept intact for so long, and how it has died. Perhaps then we will have a clue where to begin in our struggle to kindle once more a faith, a way of life, even a God who is not subject to the death of theism. At least that is our next step.

THREE

# SELF-CONSCIOUSNESS AND THEISM: SIAMESE TWINS AT BIRTH

*Framing [God] jealous, fierce, at first*
*We gave him justice, as the ages rolled,*
*Will to bless those by circumstances accurst,*
*And long suffering, and mercies manifold.*
*And, tricked by our own early dream*
*And need of solace, we grew self-deceived*
*Our making soon our maker did we deem,*
*And what we had imagined, we believed.*
*Till in Time's stayless stealthy swing*
*Uncompromising rude reality*
*Mangled the Monarch of our fashioning*
*Who quavered, sank; and now has ceased to be.*[1]

— THOMAS HARDY, Nineteenth-century British poet

The theologian Paul Tillich called it "the shock of nonbeing." The father of psychology, Sigmund Freud, called it "the trauma of self-consciousness." Both were referring to that time in the churning drama of evolution when self-awareness and self-transcendence became a part of the consciousness of the first human creatures—that moment when, in Freudian vocabulary, the ego was added to the id and began the process that was to produce the superego.

It is that human capacity to be fully self-conscious that marks Homo sapiens as different from any other form of life in the natural world. That separating difference is what fills human beings with a sense of dread. Anxiety, says Paul Tillich, is born in the human recognition of finitude. It is therefore as omnipresent as humanity itself. To be human is to experience self-consciousness, to know separation, to be made aware of limits, and to contemplate ends. One cannot be human, therefore, without being filled with chronic anxiety. It sounds depressing, but surely it is true.

We note first that animals do not appear to need caffeine in order to start their day or alcohol in order to secure release from their tensions. Animals have never been known to develop nursing substitutes once they have been weaned. Animals do not appear to require tranquilizers in order to cope with life's chronic stress, nor are they prone to suicide. Animals do not seem to have to deal with their dark or shadow side. They apparently have no need to turn a murderous barrage on their own species or to seek to purge their ranks of those who are not thought to be of the same genetic purity.[2]

All of these behaviors are identified primarily with Homo sapiens because they arise out of that uniquely human capacity to achieve self-consciousness and to face the questions of meaning that emerge with "the shock of nonbeing." So we begin this discussion by making note of the fact that the thing that makes human beings anxious is identical to that which makes these same creatures human. Once that reality is embraced, then we need to examine the moment in which self-consciousness was first born, to probe its origin, and to understand how human beings have learned to cope with this reality. How do we self-conscious creatures organize our lives to deal with this threat of nonbeing, this trauma of self-consciousness?

It is important to begin this inquiry by moving as close as we can to that which was the literal beginning of life. This tiny planet we call earth has been in existence, according to the best estimates of contemporary scientists, for some four to five billion years.[3] The earliest form of life appeared on this planet as a single cell within the first billion years of this planet's history.[4] What actually caused that emergence of life is still being debated, but living things, once born, simply divided and subdivided with no further development for about three billion years. At that point, about a billion years ago, the dramatic move from monocellular to multicellular life was accomplished. The ocean appears to have been the primary home for this early life. At some point even further along, a mysterious boundary between plant life and animal life was drawn, and the forms began to proliferate on both sides of that great divide.[5]

About five hundred million years ago, fish with internal skeletons first appeared in the oceans. About that same time, plant life began to edge into the rivers and estuaries, and then finally onto the land itself. About fifty million years later, animate life in the form of insects and spiderlike creatures first invaded the barren land of the earth's largely inhospitable surface. They were followed in the next fifty million years by amphibian creatures—crossopterygian giants whose muscular fins enabled them to push across the land and who possessed primitive lungs as well as gills that were instrumental in making survival in the new environment possible. Over time these invading forms of life became increasingly complex, as cell specialization grew and countless numbers of new species developed.

Another hundred and fifty million years or so passed before these evolving creatures reached the complexity of the reptiles who dominated the land life of this planet around 250 million years ago in forms that have now become highly romanticized in tales of "the age of the dinosaurs."[6] When the reptiles began to reach the limits of their potentiality, about sixty-five million years ago, warm-blooded creatures that came to be called mammals started their pilgrimage into dominance. The earliest mammalian ancestor appears to have been a furry, mouselike creature that inhabited the forest floor, probably near the grasslands of eastern Africa.

Human life was still a long way from arriving. Homo sapiens were, in fact, a very late development in mammalian history. Depending on how one defines human life, this creature could be as old as two million years, if Homo erectus is considered human, or as young as fifty to one hundred thousand years, if full self-consciousness and language form our definition of humanity.

But regardless of how or when one dates the arrival of human beings on this planet, one is forced to recognize that for literally hundreds of millions of years, most of the living creatures who inhabited this planet were born, lived, and died with no conscious awareness of themselves. They simply passed through billions of life-cycles, guided by biological instinct and environmental necessity in an apparently endless wheel of fortune, without any need, desire, or ability to raise questions of either mortality or purpose. These living creatures were apparently content simply to follow the natural path of being born, growing to maturity, meeting basic needs for food and water, mating, or at least reproducing themselves, and dying. They had no conscious awareness of who they were or what they were doing. They defended their turf instinctively when it was invaded, or they fled, if necessary, from whatever apparent danger they perceived.

These nonsapient creatures worked out a manner of being related to the rest of nature, and when the time came to die, they did so without anticipatory fear or grief. Having no conscious sense that they actually existed or *were*, and thus lacking a conscious memory of the past or anticipation of the future, they had no sense that they were destined *not to be*. That was true no matter how death came. Sometimes it arrived suddenly and violently. Other times it came upon them as silently and as placidly as a sunset. These creatures were ushered into death by enemies both visible and invisible. The visible ones were those we think of now as natural enemies, but they were in fact only fellow participants in the endless biological struggle for survival. The invisible enemies, on the other hand, were silent—microscopic germs and viruses, or the degenerative processes of age. We now know that even germs and viruses are living creatures, but no one was aware of their existence until a century or so ago.[7]

Whether we are talking about the earliest primitive creatures or human beings today, each individual specimen of life lives for a time until it becomes the sustainer of life for yet another creature. This is true whether we are killed to be eaten or our deceased bodies become a feasting ground for worms and maggots. But in the historical phase of prehuman life, no one contemplated this routine meaninglessness or raised questions about the very purpose of life itself. No creature had the capacity to imagine, and hence no creature anticipated future needs or future dangers, and no one planned life in such a way as to prepare for any eventuality that tomorrow might bring. Rather, each subhuman creature responded only to the stimulus of the moment, raising none of the great questions of life and facing none of the anxieties that an awareness of finitude inevitably creates. So it was that for the vast majority of the years of this planet's history, the violent, churning, competitive struggle for survival that we call life went on without the possibility that some creature might understand it, be aware of its emptiness, or contemplate its lack of ultimate meaning.

Then it happened: somewhere in that almost infinite span of time, incipient self-consciousness entered the life of this planet. It emerged inside a solitary subgroup of those same creatures that had been content heretofore simply to repeat the naturally mandated life-cycle of the species. It was something radically new, and life on this planet—at least for humans, the creatures in whom this revolution was dawning—would never be the same. Self-awareness had come into being. Finitude had been experienced. Mortality had become one's anticipated and inescapable date with destiny.

As the realization of mortality grew in humans, a dreadful sense of anxiety gripped them. Tillich's shock of nonbeing and Freud's trauma of self-consciousness had come into existence, and these awakenings brought to humans the knowledge that they were distinct, in some sense separate from the rest of the world. Because of their new knowledge, humans would never again identify themselves completely with the natural world. They now experienced their selfhood as that which stood over against their world. Both the shortness and the uncertainty of human life became operative existential realities that could be contemplated abstractly and anticipated consciously. Simultaneously in these newly self-conscious creatures a tremendous need was born to find meaning, permanence, and stability in a world that suddenly seemed meaningless, transitory, and destabilized.

As the early humans confronted these realities with a new self-conscious awareness, their emotional resources were overloaded. Try to imagine the shock, the trauma, the sense of aloneness, the radical insecurity that seized these newly self-conscious creatures. They suddenly were aware of danger as a chronic state of being, of mortality as inevitable, and of a world so vast that they were reduced to a sense of themselves as almost totally insignificant. They were gripped by an overwhelming sense of *angst*—a word that our English rendition, "anxiety," only barely begins to translate.

Had these creatures, our ancient human ancestors, not learned to cope with the angst accompanying self-consciousness, that consciousness would have proved to be an ineffective evolutionary step, for no creature can live with chronic, unrelieved angst and survive. Indeed, I suspect that in those early years of human history the issue of survival for those humans who had achieved this evolutionary breakthrough was very much in doubt.

But learn to cope they did. Coping took a variety of forms. The communal life that emerged from the experience of the pack, organized under the leadership of a dominant creature who came to be designated "the chief," was one such form. Sometimes the mythology of survival required that this chief be understood to be of divine origin, or be able at least to participate in a power beyond the perceived limits of humanity. The ability to preserve and store food, a skill that had been instinctively present in some animal species, was raised to a new level of competence in humans and became a significant coping device. Finding security in a protective cave during the fearful darkness of night was still another. In time, fire was captured, heightening the safety of these self-conscious creatures and allowing them to venture into both darkness and nontropical climates. But the most powerful coping device of all, and the one that I suspect did more to secure this evolutionary breakthrough than any other at the dawn of self-consciousness, was the birth of a theistic concept of God, and thus the beginning of what we now call religion.

Sigmund Freud tried to recreate this dawning of a God-consciousness in a little monograph published in 1927 entitled *The Future of an Illusion*.[8] The fact that God was, for Freud, nothing more than an illusion should not blind us to the accuracy of his insights. Freud suggested that the primary response of human beings to the trauma of self-consciousness was the experience of hysteria. An emotional thermostat designed to control that hysteria had to be created; survival *required* it. The creation of the various theistic religious forms was a major component—indeed, *the* major component—of that thermostat.

It was inevitable that self-awareness made the early human beings conscious that they were defined against something that was other than themselves. If I am a self, separate and contained, I relate immediately to that over against which I am defined, that which is other than who or what I am. Perhaps that other is nothing but the natural world, as many philosophers have argued, but it is nonetheless different from me. But this kind of impersonal, natural assumption was not one that our primitive forebears made. Historical artifacts suggest that they related to that natural world as if it too were self-conscious and as if it too had a sense of being. Perhaps, they suggested, that which was over against them belonged to another self-aware creature.

It was the observation, and later the conclusion, of these forebears that this external world certainly had vitality. Rivers flowed. The sun rose and set each day. The moon turned on a regular axis. The stars twinkled in the vast sky. Thunder and lightning were heard and observed, and rain fell or failed to fall upon the earth from that same sky. The forests were filled with living creatures. So were the rivers and the oceans. Birds flew in the sky. Plants grew and bore fruit out of the soil of the earth. Indeed, the entire world in its totality appeared to teem with life, the same life that these now self-conscious creatures knew themselves to possess.

Since "I am a self" was the first definition of self-consciousness, it was an easy step to assume that there were many other selves that governed the vital forces apparent in all of life. If that was so, then the human creature needed to work out a modus operandi that took these other personal beings into account, a manner of living with and relating to them. He or she needed to curry their favor, gain their approval, and live in harmony with their purposes.

"Perhaps I am not alone" was the conclusion reached by that incipient self-consciousness when it viewed the world as an objective other for the first time. That conclusion then led to another: "Perhaps these powerful forces can be made to work *for* me or at least not *against* me." The ruminations continued within the breast of the first self-conscious creature: "Perhaps these other vital powers are benevolent. Perhaps they desire to help, watch over, aid, and protect me. I seem to have no power over wind and wave, sun and moon, and yet these aspects of the life of my world appear to affect me and my survival dramatically." So it was that a human definition of the selfhood of these natural forces began to emerge.

Theism in some form, I submit, was the earliest definition of the meaning of the power that was behind all that was now defined as "other" by those first self-conscious creatures—a definition that in some manifestation would last for vast ages and countless generations. But we need to note that theism was born not as the name of an external God, who had somehow revealed a divine presence from outside this world to human beings. It was born, rather, as a definition of the powers present in the world of nature that stood over against newly self-conscious human beings. God understood theistically was thus a human definition, not a divine revelation. Theism was created by frightened self-aware humans to assist them in the task of banking the fires of hysteria brought on by the trauma of self-consciousness, the shock of nonbeing. God, understood theistically, is thus quite clearly a human construct. Please let that fact register. The theistic definition of God is a *human* creation. Thus theism is not the same as God. Neither is it any more eternal than any other human definition.

Theism was the means whereby that which was experienced as other by newly self-conscious human beings was personalized. At its beginning, theism was perceived not in a single, unified way, but in a wide variety of individualistic ways. The first form of theism was the primitive assumption that every vitalizing force experienced in life was animated by a spirit. Those animating spirits might be benevolent or demonic, but in either case they were assumed to be personal, to have selfhood, to be in charge of their particular area of life, to be capable of responding to human need, and to be in possession of supernatural power. Because of this responsiveness and power, people in the early moments of human history assumed that their survival depended on their ability not only to discern a multiplicity of these spirits, but also to know their desires so that they might both honor them and please them.

The earliest form of theism, then, was the postulation, by self-conscious creatures, of the existence of self-conscious spirits as an explanation for the vitality found in life outside themselves. *Animism*, the label given to this form of theism, captures the human assumption that life was animated and that this vital aliveness in creation grew out of the aliveness of those personal spirits which inhabited all things.

Theism would take many forms over many centuries before it began to die in our generation. The animistic understanding described above was only its first and aboriginal form. It would evolve as the human experience was transformed and as human knowledge grew. When human beings moved from the stage of being nomadic hunters and gatherers into various primitive, settled, agricultural styles of life, theism adapted itself to the fertility cycle on which both agriculture and animal husbandry depended. The symbol of reproductive fertility was quite clearly feminine, and so the theistic definition of the divine power began to be expressed in terms of a matriarchal, goddess deity. The fact that both the earth and even nature itself are referred to maternally— Mother Earth and Mother Nature—in every gender-specific language of the world is but a vestigial remain of this phase of theistic development.[9] Our modern Western burial practices, which involve the opening up of Mother Earth so that she might receive her children at the end of their days, back into the fertile womb from whence they came, is yet another echo of this matriarchal form of theism, though this echo is rarely perceived by modern minds.

But the mother-goddess form of theism did not survive forever either; or, to say it more positively, it gradually evolved into ever-new forms. Perhaps the evolution came about because the role of the male in reproduction finally began to be understood. With cause separated from effect by a period of nine months in human beings, and varying amounts of time in other species, the causality of reproduction was more than our ancient ancestors could put together intellectually or even imagine intuitively. Perhaps the causal connections began to be embraced when ancient people noticed the seeds of plants falling to the ground and the subsequent emergence of the new growth of those same plants in the same places at some point a bit later. Perhaps they observed the way the rain from the sky beat upon the surface of a rather passive Mother Earth, a process apparently essential to the growth of new things. Perhaps they noted the warming rays of the sun, which also came from the sky and seemed to help growth to occur.

Whatever the catalyst, it finally dawned on human beings to postulate a male deity who ruled the sky and related to the female deity identified with the earth. In time the rain came to be thought of as divine semen sent from Father Sky to impregnate and thus to fertilize Mother Earth, to make her bear new life and bring forth new food. As the evolutionary process continued, a premium began to be placed on male skills in times of war or in the season of the hunt. This male emphasis began to replace the exclusive sense that the feminine principle was the divine source of life. But however we now explain the shift over a period of centuries, a male consort to the mother goddess was developed, and theism moved into yet another form.

In some cultures this male/female form of theism developed into a hierarchy of deities, with a Zeus and Hera or a Jupiter and Juno ruling the divine family and a variety of other deities overseeing life's various activities and mysteries. This was the primitive animism of antiquity reexpressed as polytheism.

Among nomadic, nonagricultural people such as the ancient Hebrews, theism evolved into a form of tribal monotheism. All theistic power was vested in a single tribal deity, who tended to be exclusively male. He was seen as a mighty warrior who led wandering people into battle and a great protector watching over the lands they inhabited. This deity was assumed to be the source of everything both good and evil that affected the tribe. Such tribal activities as the corporate efforts to please this deity, to obey this deity, and to worship this deity were considered necessary to the survival of the tribe itself. Tribal monotheistic gods were depicted as jealous of their prerogatives, angry when offended, punitive when disobeyed, and beneficent when pleased.

But limits were clearly placed on the power of these deities, for their authority and their dictates appeared to stop at the edges of the tribe's boundaries. The Egyptian god ruled Egypt, for example; the Assyrian god ruled Assyria; the Philistine god ruled the land of the Philistines; and so on it went. This was not a time in history when a theistic divinity would pour out the divine spirit on all the nations of the world—"Parthians, Medes, Elamites, and dwellers in Mesopotamia," as the New Testament book of Acts (2:9) would later suggest. Such a universalism could not yet be imagined.

In time this development in human thought would occur, however, and theism would come to speak of a nontribal deity who stretched beyond tribal barriers. Perhaps this step toward universalism was the product of war and trade. Perhaps it grew out of a minority idea that appeared in the mind of a religious genius—one such as Moses of the Jews or Amenhotep IV of the Egyptians, each of whom seemed to have an advanced consciousness—but remained submerged in the popular mind until its time was right. Perhaps it was even the experience of an exile, when a whole nation had been both defeated and violently removed by its enemies into a foreign captivity, where its citizens discovered that somehow they could still "sing the Lord's song in a strange land" (Ps. 137:4).

Whatever the factors were that produced the change, the time did arrive when somehow tribal boundaries were not conceived to be limits placed on the emerging understanding of the theistic divine being. It was at that moment that an embryonic form of universal monotheism, an idea that was destined to grow, made its first appearance in human experience. Even this budding universal monotheism took different cultural and liturgical forms in the various regions of the world. Christianity became its Western form; Islam its Middle Eastern form; Hinduism, Buddhism, and Confucianism its Far Eastern manifestations; with Judaism scattered like leaven in the lump of the West and minority movements like the Jains, the Sikhs, and the various mystery cults dotting the religious landscape of the rest of the world. Yet each theistic religious system talked of a single divine being who was the only God, no matter how differently these various traditions defined the Holy One. Theism had at long last reached its contemporary definition.

The theistic God in these various traditions was always other, always external to the self who was defining the God-figure, always supernatural, and, at least in the West, usually personal in the sense that individuals could know and communicate with this deity. The theistic God was also presumed to be the explanation for that which was beyond rational understanding, a being capable of miraculous power who therefore needed to be supplicated, praised, obeyed, and pleased.

Theism is thus a definition of God which has journeyed with self-conscious human beings from primitive animism to complex modern monotheism. Yet in every one of its evolving forms, theism has functioned as it was originally created to do. Theism was born as a human coping device, created by traumatized self-conscious creatures to enable them to deal with the anxiety of self-awareness. It was designed to discover or to postulate the existence of a powerful divine ally in the quest for human survival and in the process to assert both a purpose to existence and a meaning to human life. Assuming, then, that theism developed as a human response to Tillich's shock of nonbeing and Freud's trauma of self-consciousness, we should expect to see shock, trauma, and hysteria return in countless numbers of ways when theism dies as I contend it is doing today.

Let me go back now for just a moment to that original theistic stage of animism in order to lift to consciousness the elements that make up the theistic definition of God.

Once our ancient forebears had postulated the personal character of the rocks, caves, streams, animals, thunder, sun, rain, lightning, water, trees, stars, oceans, and almost everything else that they met in their self-conscious life in this world, they proceeded to design a religious system to enable themselves, as the hysterical and frightened creatures they were, to curry the favor of these supernatural powers on which they felt their survival depended. If the animating spirits were thought to be benevolent, the self-conscious creatures wanted to receive their blessing. If the animating spirits were perceived to be hostile or demonic, our ancient ancestors wanted to neutralize their destructive power. In this way, these original frightened human beings could bank their fears by pretending to gain a modicum of control over the powers in the universe that they believed existed outside themselves.

So through a variety of religious practices, the newly self-conscious creatures hoped to tame, or at least manipulate, the presumed supernatural powers in the universe to serve human needs. Having personalized these supernatural powers, people knew how to cope with them: they simply adapted human expectations and human practices to the realm of the supernatural. They continued to search for a clear knowledge of the will of this or that deity so that they could win divine favor by acting in a way pleasing to the theistic power. This served to bring together into an indivisible union the human God-consciousness and the human survival need for behavior control. That is what enabled both taboos and group survival strategies to be, in time, elevated to the status of the revealed will of God. It also created enormous arenas of power that were to be filled by the priest, the witch doctor, or the shaman—whoever claimed to be able to discern the will of the personalized deity and to be able to interpret that will accurately.

Since powerful human beings reveled in and relished the flattery of their dependent subjects, it came to be assumed that the supernatural deity or deities also delighted in the praises of those protected by theistic power. So acts of praise, hymns, and psalms were created to make the theistic deity aware of the fact that human beings recognized and stood in proper awe of the divine power. That has not ceased. Listen to the language of our own liturgies today: "Blessed art thou, O God of Hosts, praised and exalted above all forever"; "We praise you, O God; we acknowledge you to be the Lord"; "The heavens declare the glory of God"; "How great thou art"; "The firmament shows God's handiwork." Likewise, prayers were composed which, seeking the same divine approval, called God by every grandiose title that fragile human beings could imagine. Titles such as "almighty and everlasting God," "most merciful Father," and "all-loving God" are still in common use today. Human beings also used prayers to remind God of what they hoped God was: in language still heard in churches today, they said, "You are always more ready to hear than we are to pray. You are long-suffering, slow to anger, of great kindness, and ready to forgive."

We human beings even accentuated our concept of God's power by developing a language of worship in which we groveled, as slaves might be expected to do before a master. We are, we said to this deity, "miserable offenders" in whom "there is no health." We acknowledged ourselves as deserving only condemnation, for we are those "who stand condemned before the throne of grace," clearly unable to please our deity without divine aid. Somehow we humans seemed to believe that the power of our deity was enhanced by the contrasting recognition of our weakness or that our deity would be flattered and empowered by our awareness of our own lack of worth or by a human nature that was depicted as humble, dependent, and servile. It was as if this powerful theistic deity required a certain masochistic or self-derogatory theme as an essential component of our acts of worship.

Because hysteria is not well served by uncertainty, this theistic religion also developed extraordinary claims about both the rhetoric we used to describe the deity we worshiped and our human ability to grasp and to define the power of this deity. Almost every religious system asserted that its particular deity was the only true and real divine being. To keep this claim from being eroded, even more powerful claims were made, suggesting that those religious leaders or designated holy people who had defined this one true deity also possessed an absolutely certain pipeline to ultimate truth.

It was a circular argument, as all irrational arguments are: our deity is the only true deity; the truth of this deity has been given only to us, and it was given by direct revelation, so its truth cannot be questioned; since we are the sole designated recipients of this revelation, we alone can interpret it properly, and our interpretation cannot be challenged. The claims variously heard in Christian history that there is no salvation outside a particular church, that a designated church leader possesses infallibility, or that a sacred book called "the word of God" is inerrant are but latter-day expressions of this desire to remove uncertainty—a desire that arose early in the human attempt to address the angst of our self-consciousness.

So theism served to keep hysteria under control. It put a pious face on human fear and made the threat of nonbeing and the trauma of self-consciousness manageable. That has been the major agenda addressed by theistic religious systems throughout human history.

But in this postmodern world, theism is finally dying. God, as the explanation for the heretofore inexplicable, is fading from

*THE AND MAP PINS*

our view. Every new discovery about how the natural world operates cuts into the arena once reserved for God alone. The theistic
God first became the gap-filler, explaining those things that
human knowledge could not. The gaps, however, grew fewer
with each century, and more are being closed every day by the
advances of knowledge. The theistic God is becoming irrelevant,
with no real purpose. Theistic power has become impotent. As
British scholar Michael D. Goulder has observed, "God no
longer has any work to do."[10] An unemployed deity does not remain God for long.

That is where we are today. Theism is dying. The hysteria that
became apparent with the birth of self-consciousness and was
held in check by the coping mechanisms of theistic religion is
now breaking out all over. The real question facing the human
enterprise in our day is: Can the evolutionary step which led us to
self-consciousness survive without the coping mechanism of theistic religion? These two elements—self-consciousness and theism—appear to be Siamese twins, joined at birth.

The renewed trauma of self-consciousness stares at us unre-
lentingly when we embrace the death of theism and see as one
manifestation of that death the rise of hysterical, irrational fundamentalism. That trauma also lies behind our increasing dependence on chemical stimulants such as caffeine, relaxing drugs
such as alcohol, and forms of adult nursing such as smoking.
These things have become our allies in the struggle to cope with
the hysteria of self-consciousness. The renewed trauma of self-
consciousness also explains why antidepressants are household
words in our society and why suicide is a growing reality. It explains why mindless violence against those who are irrationally
defined as our enemies regularly makes news.

If theism dies, does God die? That is the question postmodern
men and women are struggling to answer. Are we really alone in a
vast and hostile universe, meaningless specks who somehow know
that we are destined for oblivion? Can we tolerate that vision

without self-destruction? Can human beings continue to evolve into higher levels of consciousness if we are not emotionally able to bear the trauma that such consciousness inevitably creates?

If theism dies, is atheism the only alternative? Is it not a possibility worth pursuing that our very self-consciousness might be the means by which our lives could be opened to nontheistic dimensions of our existence, even nontheistic definitions of God? Could not our growing self-consciousness also enable us to relate to that in which our being is grounded, that which is more than who we are and yet part of who we are? Could we not begin to envision a transcendence that enters our life but also calls us beyond the limits of our humanity, not toward an external being but toward the Ground of All Being including our own, a transcendence that calls us to a new humanity? Is there not a new maturity that can be claimed by human life when we cease the search for a supernatural being who will parent us, take care of us, watch over and protect us? Is there not a new human dignity that can be found in the rejection of those groveling patterns of our past through which we attempted to please the theistic deity in the early years of evolutionary history? In place of that groveling, are we not now able to open ourselves in new ways to discover the Ground of Being that is met and known in the self that is emerging as expanded consciousness? These, it seems to me, are the profoundly religious questions of the new millennium.

It is no longer either desirable or possible to expend our energy trying to resuscitate the dying theisms of yesterday. No revival of these dying systems is possible. To deny this reality is to perpetuate an enduring religious delusion. Hysterical fundamentalism is not the way into the future; it is the last gasp of the past. It will not work. The time has come to create a new thing. Not a new religious coping device that will enable us to bank the fires of hysteria for another generation, but a new way to affirm self-consciousness as an asset and to seek within it that which is timeless, eternal, real, and true.

That is, I believe, what the world in a variety of ways is now seeking. Can the religious systems of the past change sufficiently to provide the basis for an expanded consciousness tomorrow, a heightened humanity, a more noble creature than either we or our primitive ancestors could imagine? Or will self-consciousness demand too high an emotional price—a price that creatures like us will not be able to pay?

These are the questions before religious systems today. How we answer them will determine, I believe, the future of the human race. No more existential concern has ever faced those who have walked our evolutionary path. It strikes me as curious indeed that these issues are seldom if ever addressed inside those institutional structures that have been built to enable people to seek the presence of the holy. Perhaps that is why these structures are so increasingly lifeless. They may not be capable of changing; but if they do not, they will die. The time has surely come when human beings must begin a new exploration into the divine, must sketch out a vision of the holy that is beyond theism but not beyond the reality for which the word *God* was created to point.

# FOUR

# BEYOND THEISM BUT
# NOT BEYOND GOD

*If we perform the radical surgery [on Christianity] that is required, not only will certain traditional formulations of faith fall by the wayside, but also much of the presumed content of Christianity, and rightly so. Our only consolation is that if we do not intervene radically and soon the patient will die.*[1]

— THOMAS SHEEHAN, professor of
religious studies, Stanford University

G od.
 If theism must be abandoned, is God also at risk? If our historical understanding of God must be dismissed, is God also dismissed? How does one speak of that which, by definition, lies outside the capacity of the human mind? What language does one use? There is no God-language available for human use, only our own limited and limiting words. Can God be contained in the categories and concepts of a vocabulary that has been culturally

created and historically shaped? If "otherness" is a part of who or what God is, then God must be a presence that, while it can be experienced, can never be defined. If that judgment is correct, we have to wonder why the human drive to explore the experience of God rationally is so intense. What do we hope to accomplish? Is our human propensity to think theologically anything more than perpetual illusion?

If our understanding of God has been couched in the language of "a being, supernatural in power, dwelling outside this world and invading the world periodically to accomplish the divine will"—the definition of the theistic God that I suggested in Chapter 2—then perhaps God is, as Freud suggested, nothing more than a human creation, designed to assist us in banking the fires of hysteria, controlling the trauma of rampant anxiety created by self-consciousness. To make that assertion is to elicit frightening concerns and questions that religious people would rather ignore. Church leaders seem to prefer to continue the game of "let's pretend," shouting ever more loudly their ancient formulations and attacking anyone who dares to wander into this inviting, but dangerous territory. When they level the accusation that these challenges threaten their religious security, it is clear that truth is not their primary goal. But I am convinced that we Christians of the twenty-first century must face these issues openly and honestly. There is no alternative if we wish to continue to be believers in this postmodern world.

As we enter this discussion, it is worth noting that in some form these concerns have always marked the human experience. They have typically traveled in some subterranean part of the human consciousness as a kind of minority report. They bubble to the surface in a peculiar way in this generation, however, because whether we like it or not, today's knowledge revolution and an emerging human maturity have conspired to make the theistic patterns of the past unbelievable. Theism, with its supernatural God ready to take care of us, is revealed as a delusion that encourages worshipers to remain in a state of passive dependency.

When we view theism in this way, we see that its death may represent not something fearful and bad, but rather a step toward maturity, toward a human coming of age, toward a growing unwillingness on the part of spiritually discerning people to continue defining human life as if we were children relating to the heavenly parent. If the death of theism does in fact represent these things, it ought to be widely and gratefully celebrated by our religious institutions. Instead, I sense that it is being ignored or castigated by the increasingly conservative churches around the world today.

Yet there is no doubt in my mind that the Christianity and even the spirituality of the future will require the opening of every life to the exhilarating new humanity that is being born as the theistic God is gradually dying. So part of the task of envisioning the God of tomorrow will be to explore both the weight and the fear of maturity—something religious people never seem to enjoy. Paul Tillich has suggested that this is the primary doorway through which we must walk if we are to arrive at what he called "the new being."[2]

I am deeply aware that this journey I am proposing is not easy—not for anyone. There is something frightening and lonely about recognizing that we can no longer be children dependent on the theistic parent-God. It is rather like the desolation I felt when I buried my last parent and realized that there was no one left on whom I could depend as I had once depended on my father and mother. But if we are able to move beyond this anxiety to face the new reality, there is, as I hope to demonstrate, something deeply invigorating about discovering a new maturity and realizing that God can be approached, experienced, and entered in a radically different way. I refer here not to a deity who is "a being," not even if we claim for God the status of the *highest* being. I speak rather of the God I experience as the Ground and Source of

All Being and therefore the presence that calls me to step beyond every boundary, inside which I vainly seek dependent security, into the fullness of life with all of its exhilarating insecurities.

I intend to demonstrate that probing this new God-possibility begins with a search for clues in our religious past—indeed, in such places as our sacred scriptures, which indicate that even our ancestors in faith could not fully ignore what seems to us to be a modern problem. The limits on the theistic definition of God have been present for centuries. More than three thousand years ago the Jews listed among the first of their commandments a prohibition against all human attempts to create an image of God out of anything (Exod. 20:4–6). These Jews, our spiritual ancestors, understood that every human image of God, including the prevailing theistic one, would finally be inadequate.

The Jews also refused to allow the faithful ever to speak the holy name of God. It was their assumption that to be able to name an entity was to know it, to have power over it, and even to define it. One could never do those things to the Jewish God. Adam and Eve, in the Jewish myth of human origins found in the book of Genesis (2:4-3:end), were empowered to name the animals in the Garden of Eden, reflecting the human claim to have dominion over all that God had made. God, however, could never be named in that sacred Jewish text. How could any being name the Source and Ground of All Being? Even the ancients, you see, were forced to wonder about that, recognizing that their theistic images were in fact limited human fantasies pointing toward a reality but incapable of embracing it.

In the Christian West today, we are far too sophisticated to erect idols of wood or stone and call them our gods. We know that such an activity no longer has credibility. In our intellectual arrogance, however, we Westerners—especially the Christian theologians among us—have time after time erected idols out of our words and then claimed for those words the ability to define the holy God. We have also burned at the stake people who refused to acknowledge the claim that God and our definitions of God were one and the same. Truth now demands that we surrender these distorting identifications forever.

Christians, for example, assert that God is a Holy Trinity, as if human beings could figure out who or what God is. The Holy Trinity is not now and never has been a description of the being of God. It is rather the attempt to define our human experience of God. There is a vast difference between the two. All of our theological disputes and our religious wars throughout history that have been fought over differing versions of the way God is defined, represent nothing less than the folly of human thinking. The Jews understood that God does not dwell in temples or altars made with human hands. Twenty-first-century Christians must now come to understand that God does not inhabit creeds or theological doctrines shaped with human words.

To say these things is not to launch an attack on God; it is rather to state the obvious: that no human words, no human explanations, will ever capture the essence of God. We surely ought to be suspicious of the fact that the theistic God we have defined so precisely is said to have the primary vocation to care for, watch over, and meet the needs of the very creatures who defined this God. When the ultimate result of the worship of the God that we have defined is to make us—the definers—feel good about our human situation, we must suspect ourselves of self-serving motives. Are human beings really made in God's image, as the ancient wisdom has attested, or have we deluded ourselves into thinking such a thing to justify the obvious—namely, that the theistic God of the past was created by us and in our own image? As I have suggested in a previous book, "If horses had gods would they not look like horses?"[3] We humans, even we religious humans, cannot escape the subjectivity of our own being. We now need to stop pretending that we can.

Another clue from our sacred texts can be discovered in a charming narrative that I chanced upon in one of my journeys through scripture. It is a biblical story that reveals, in a primitive way, that even our ancestors in faith had to face the limitations present in all of their "God-talk." In the book of Exodus, Moses is portrayed as demanding the opportunity to see God face-to-face (Exod. 33:17–23). Up to the moment of this request, God had been manifested to Moses, the text suggests, only in a cloud, or in the thunder, or perhaps by a connecting light from heaven. This, however, was now not good enough for the one who was called the father of the Jewish nation. So the request for a face-to-face meeting with the Holy One was uttered by Moses in this interesting tale.

But the text tells us that God declined Moses' presumptuous attempt at intimacy. This should not surprise us, because there was a perception, even a *conviction*, among the Hebrews that the holiness of God was so intense that no human being could see God and continue to live. Moses, however, was undaunted by that conviction; he continued to press for a face-to-face meeting. Once again the request was denied. As great as Moses was, he, like every other mortal, was not to be allowed to look upon the divine countenance.

At this state in the deliberations between God and Moses, perhaps in deference to Moses' great stature, God is said to have offered Moses a compromise: if Moses would cover his eyes, God would pass before him; and then, as God went around the bend in the mountain, Moses could open his eyes and stare momentarily on God's "back parts" or "hindquarters," as one translation puts it. Later versions of the Bible would render this word with the less salacious concept of God's "backside" or "back."[4]

I do not think I have ever heard a sermon preached on that particular text in my entire life. I suspect it might be too difficult for a preacher not to titillate the congregation with references to the divine derriere. But beneath this amusing level of literalness, the ancient writer was pointing to something far more profound than our literal minds could ever imagine: he was asserting the common human experience that mortal men and women can never see who God is but only where God has been. We see God's tracks. We visualize and experience God's effects, not God's being. We never see God as a disincarnate or separate Self.

To embrace that simple truth is to watch the whole theistic theological enterprise totter under the weight of its own irrelevance. It is also to recognize that those endless rows of weighty theological tomes that fill library shelves in great centers of learning—every page of which attempts to explain God—must now be recognized as little more than monuments to human egos. I do not argue for a moment that God is not real. Indeed, the reality of the God-experience overwhelms me every day of my life. I assert only that no human words, no human formulas, and no human religious systems will ever capture that reality. To claim that any one at any time has ever done so is idolatrous.

Human beings can approach God only by human analogy, nothing more. We can speak of God only in human words. We have no other. Yet the anthropomorphic language that we do possess, we now must recognize, is always distorting.

Those religious folk who cannot get their minds beyond the limits that language imposes, and they are numerous, will always hear these words as an attempt at deicide. The death of theism will be understood by them only as the death of God or as the affirmation of atheism. At the same time, the more secularized members of our society will hear in my words echoes of what came to be called "deism" in the aftermath of the Enlightenment. Deism was an affirmation of God, but one that located God so far beyond the life of this world that there was no possibility of a divine relationship. It was for most people nothing more than the first step to which human beings were driven by the advances of knowledge on our inevitable pilgrimage from the theism of the past through the deism of the present into the atheism of the future.

Both groups will be wrong. To deny theism is not to be an atheist. To propose that we step beyond theism is not to join the secular sojourn in a meaningless deism. I believe passionately in God. Yet I now find the theistic definition of God far too limiting. I want to move to a place where I can propose something new. I am no longer interested in clinging to the theistic answer because the questions that theism is supposed to address are no longer being asked.

I seek rather to walk beyond what I regard as a meaningless debate between three inadequate definitions of God—theism, deism, and atheism—in order to suggest some new possibilities, because I am convinced that the death of the first two does not make atheism the only remaining alternative, nor does it bring to an end the possibility of confronting in a new way the reality of God.

Given the limits on our humanity that the biblical writer faced in relating the story of Moses' request to look upon the selfhood of God and that we face as a postmodern people, I propose to begin this inquiry by accepting the countering divine invitation that was offered to Moses in that story. Though like Moses we cannot visualize who God is, we can gaze with him upon where God has been. So I want to examine what our anthropomorphic language might call "God's footprints." I want to go where I perceive that God has been, to concentrate, if you will, on God's "hind parts."

My questions are these: Can I experience God without being able to define God? Is there anything to the sense of transcendence; is there an experience of otherness that is not a delusion born out of fear? Is there a spiritual realm that calls me beyond my boundaries into the expansiveness of Being itself or into that sense of a new being? Is there a reality that we agree to call by the word *God* whose face may be hidden but whose effects I can see? Are there places I can go where this reality has been encountered? The God I seek must be beyond the theistic definitions of the past. I neither need nor desire that protective parental God any longer. So I inaugurate a new quest for God understood in a new way.

I shall never forget the first time I invited a group of people into this quest. It occurred in an adult class one Sunday morning in an urban congregation in Hoboken, New Jersey, a town best known as the birthplace of Frank Sinatra, just across the Hudson River from Manhattan. This congregation was made up of young, attractive, urbane, upwardly mobile, artistic, and overtly nonpious people who were nonetheless regular churchgoers, an unusual combination in this secular generation in urban America. This congregation had bent the mold of what *church* means in its struggle to break out of the traditional patterns of the religious past. It had edited out of its liturgy, creeds, and hymns some of the more primitive elements of our theological heritage. I posed for their discussion that Sunday morning a carefully worded question, deliberately designed not to close people's imaginations: "What content comes to your mind when you hear the word *God?*" Their responses amazed me.

The first word mentioned was *energy*. Then, in quick succession, followed *wind, nature,* and *love.* None of the first four words was what we would normally think of as personal or theistic. Other words then poured forth, a jumble of nouns and adjectives: *center, connection, living, present, enveloping, creative, strength.* I was startled to realize just how far removed the members of this congregation were from the theistic definitions of yesterday. Far more than I had imagined, the revolution in theological thought had taken hold at the grassroots level.

Only when this list of impersonal concepts had filled the chart at the front of the room did echoes of the personal deity of yesterday begin to emerge. That was when I began to hear the words *powerful, demanding, angry, busy, forgiving, tender, having a sense of humor, listening.* When I raised to their awareness the impersonal quality of their first responses and then compared those with their second tier of definitions—the latter implying a rather personal being—they made an additional fascinating distinction.

"I don't think of these latter words as personal," one woman responded. "I think of them as communal." I pressed her to clarify her meaning, so she continued: "When we speak of God as a person, what we're really doing is personalizing the values by which we live as a community. To live together as a family demands a combination of love, structure, and discipline. The values that make community possible are invested with Godlike dimensions. That is when we speak of God as angry, demanding, busy, forgiving, tender, and possessing a sense of humor."[5]

I listened in astonishment, for at least in this congregation the traditional theistic God "up there"—the divine Mr. Fix-It, the invasive miracle-working deity of our religious past—had clearly faded from view. Yet these parishioners were not atheists. They were not nonbelievers. They still gathered on Sunday mornings to probe the mysteries of their God-experience, to listen to the details of their Christian faith-story, in which they, by a specific decision-making act, continued to live and to celebrate their relationships with one another as members of a community dedicated to the reality of God. I thought on that particular Sunday morning that perhaps I had glimpsed a vision of the direction in which the church of the future must and inevitably will move. The kingdom of God was breaking into the world in Hoboken, New Jersey. Frank Sinatra would have loved it.

I next led this group of adults in an exploration of the sacred story as it is portrayed in the Torah, the first five books of the Hebrew Bible, known as The Law or The Books of Moses—they are of course also the first five books of the Christian Bible. I noted that the stories contained in these texts are filled with the traditional personal-God concepts. The biblical focus is clearly on a supernatural being who watches over human life from some vantage point outside this world.

This God is said in the First Testament to have "walked with Adam and Eve in the cool of the evening," to have warned Noah to prepare for the coming flood by building an ark. God is said to have chosen Abraham to be the father of a new people, to have enabled Sarah to conceive in her old age. She was ninety: no wonder, the text suggest, that she laughed when she heard the news! God is portrayed as acting like a good Jewish matchmaker by picking out a wife for Isaac. God is said to have called and empowered Moses to be the agent of freedom from slavery, to have rained bread from heaven to feed the hungry Israelites while they journeyed through the wilderness, to have chosen David to be the founder of a new royal line, to have fought the wars of this people, and even to have given them victory when they were deserving and defeat when their behavior warranted it. This God is said to have raised up prophets and through these prophets to have predicted the actual events that would occur in the future. All of these activities are portrayed in our sacred texts as performed by a supernatural being to whom the word *God* has been attached.

I wanted these listeners of mine to see how they would respond to the insight that the God who dominated the sacred tradition of which they now claimed to be a part was vastly different from the God they had been describing. I wanted them to be aware that when they jettisoned theism, they were jettisoning the primary image of the biblical God, which meant that they were also jettisoning all aspects of bibliolatry, including that perception of the Bible as our source of theistic revelation. I think we need to feel the full weight of that before we will ever move beyond it.

But if, as I have suggested, all any human being can ever really do is see where God has been, not who God is or what God does, then we can read these biblical stories quite differently—nonliterally, nonsuperstitiously—moving beyond their primitive quality so that we can make nontheistic sense out of the experiences that the Bible sought to depict theistically, for that was the only way in which ancient people could think.

The Jews in this story, we are told in the book of Exodus, had journeyed from the slavery of Egypt—an extreme experience in human dependency—to the freedom of the wilderness. Could it be that these Jewish ancestors in faith were so incapable of embracing the maturity of freedom found in the wilderness that they were emotionally forced to substitute a dependency on a theistic God named Yahweh for their prior dependency on the Egyptians? Might they have achieved survival—simply by trading masters? Is it possible that all they did was opt for a more benevolent despot over their earlier cruel one? Perhaps there is some progress in that shift, but is it not slight indeed? The Bible hints at this possibility by informing us that these freed slaves actually yearned on several occasions to return to the security of Egypt (Exod. 14:10–12).

Security is so seductive, and insecurity is so frightening. But security is always false, and insecurity is always real. No religion can make anyone secure, though it, like the drugs on which our society is so dependent, can give the illusion of security. True religion enables one to grasp life with its radical insecurity and to live it with courage. It does not aid us in the pretense that our insecurities have been taken away.

But once these Jewish folk had survived their time in the wilderness, they credited their survival to that theistic deity who continued to reward them and punish them as a parent might deal with a child. These narratives attempted to convince the Jews that those things which human beings, since the dawn of self-consciousness, had assigned to the theistic God had in fact been done for them. As I argued in the previous chapter, the purpose of the God of theism is and always has been to keep human anxiety and human hysteria in check.

We are told in this sacred text that the very laws of God—what we now call the Ten Commandments, spelled out in Exod. 20:1–17 and in Deut. 5:7–21, were delivered to the Jewish people amid the cloud and smoke of Sinai, complete with thunder and earthquake. The compelling need for security that we analyzed at the birth of theism among our primitive forebears can be seen in this biblical story: the reason a people must have God's laws is so that they can please their deity with their behavior and thus gain divine protection for themselves despite their anxious self-consciousness.

Some of the laws handed down at Sinai defined the Jewish people's duty to their God. This God could have no other gods as rivals, for example. That is an interesting thing for a deity who claims to be the only God to say. This God could not be imaged. This God's name was to be held in honor, and the day of this God was to be observed.

Once those duties to the deity were stated, laws governing the community and enabling its survival were also articulated. Parents were to be honored. Social Security and pensions had not yet been created, so survival depended on the younger generation caring for the older one. Life was too sacred to kill. Relationships were to be held in respect as something holy. Possessions were not to be stolen. One's word was to be trustworthy. Finally, these commandments concluded, greed could not be allowed to disrupt the social patterns.

The theistic God, it was said, would punish the offender, but the fact is that the *community* punished the offender and justified its actions on the basis of its God-claim. The personal qualities attributed to God were indeed communal values that had been elevated to the realm of the divine.

Beneath the literal words of the Torah there was a sense that God and life were not separate. God was seen as the source of life—the depth, the meaning, the experience of life. If one has the eyes to see beneath the text, the external God of theism was, even for the Jews, but a vehicle to invite the people beyond their personal limitations into a recognition of their unity with each other, their responsibility for each other, and the mutuality of their dependence on each other. Theism was part of the tribal call for members to step beyond their individuality into the experience of life itself, with its ever-widening, ever-expanding consciousness. The theistic God was a human symbol for the divine depth of life, that vast consciousness which we encounter in the center of life and to which we can contribute, when our lives expand or when we are able to expand the lives of others. That is a new God-thought creating new God possibilities that invite us to journey more deeply in this direction. So my first definition of a nontheistic God is this: God is the ultimate source of life. One worships this God by living fully, by sharing deeply.

The Torah also tells us that the theistic God requires us to love our deity with all that we have: our minds, our hearts, our strength—indeed, our whole humanity (Deut. 6:5). It says that experiencing this theistic God is a call to journey beyond the narcissistic limits of our own love. Human love begins as a love for the image of ourselves that we project onto others and then receive back onto ourselves. That projection is what happens when we love those who are, initially, only extensions of ourselves. We love our primary caregivers first, and then in ever-widening circles we move to our immediate family, our extended family, our friends, our neighbors, our tribe, our nation, and finally humanity itself. We pause in a kind of fearful anxiety at every boundary that marks a transition into a larger orbit. The further out we venture, the more difficult we discover it is to love; for increasingly, as the circles widen, we begin to see that we have to love for *love's* sake, not for *our* sake. The theistic God is thus a symbol of that human drive to escape narcissism and be lovers of God in all others—even in those who frighten us because they are different.

These different ones we have both categorized and rejected time and time again in our attempts to capture our security inside our religious systems. We have called the different ones by a wide variety of titles. They are the unwashed, the uncircumcised, the unbaptized, the unfit. We have called them Samaritans and Gentiles. We have called them lepers, the ritualistically unclean, the heretics, and the religiously incorrect. We have called them mentally ill, racially diverse, and sexually different. We have said of them that they speak in strange accents, have unusual customs, and worship in unfamiliar ways. Since we cannot comprehend the God of these different ones, we assume that the unknown deity is demonic and evil. As a result, we spit on that which these different ones call holy. We even justify our warfare against them as a religious act. Yet once we identify the God we ourselves claim to worship with love, all of these concepts of discrimination are challenged, and we are forced to grow beyond the limiting barriers that have made our ability to love so puny, so compromised.

In that process of coming to know that which we name as divine, the God who is love is slowly transformed into the love that is God. Let me repeat that. In that process, the God who is love is slowly transformed into the love that is God—boundless, eternal, passing beyond every limit and calling us to follow this love into every crevice of creation. We journey into this God by being absorbed into wasteful, expansive, freely given love. The more we enter and share this love, the more our lives are opened to new possibilities, to the sacredness of otherness, to a limitless transcendence.

Ultimately we discover that our God-experience is like swimming in an eternal ocean of love. It is also like interacting with the unperceived presence of the air. We breathe love in, and we breathe love out. It is omnipresent, omniscient, omnipotent. It is never exhausted, always expanding. When I try to describe this reality, words fail me; so I simply utter the name *God*. That name, however, is no longer for me the name of a *being*—not even a supernatural being or the supreme being. It is not the title for a miracle-worker, a magician, or a rescuer. It is rather something as nebulous and yet as real as a holy presence. It is a symbol of that which is immortal, invisible, timeless.

This love is something like the footprints of God in which I seek to walk, even as I discover that to walk in these footprints is to go places that I fear to go. But when I look up, I can see ahead of me, ducking around the edges of the unknown, what one might call the hindquarters of the divine. Then I discover that the reason I cannot see God but only where God has been is that

God is clearly *in* me, just as God is *before* me. God is part of who I am and part of who you are. God is love, and so love is God. Thus my second definition of a nontheistic God is this: God is the ultimate source of love. One worships this God by loving wastefully, by spreading love frivolously, by giving love away without stopping to count the cost.

The God we once saw theistically as a being can also now be seen as a symbol of Being itself. It is a characteristic of our human life that we cling to our being with an intensity that befits the profound struggle that all creatures have endured through the billions of years of history. The evolutionary pathway has been a journey from single-celled life to the complexity of self-conscious humanity, with its ability to know transcendence. Yet look at what our self-aware but fragile humanity, so desperately seeking the bondage of security, does with the gift of being. We take that precious but fragile gift and surround it with all of our defenses. We clutch it tightly. We try to protect it from all encroachments. We need to recognize that being is not a gift that can be embraced and preserved or even held in perpetuity. Protected being is dying being. Unrisked being can never become expanded being. The only thing one can do with being is to give it away.

Holding that insight firmly, we now return to another biblical story. In the narrative of the burning bush, God is said to have confronted Moses in a dramatic scene (Exod. 3:1–14). This vision challenged Moses, the story tells us, to be a liberator, to set the slave people free—free to live, free to love, and free to be. Once again the theistic image found in this story points beyond itself to new possibilities. Moses inquired of God, "What is your name?" The divine voice responded, "I am who I am is my name." "I am," says the Bible, is the name of God. Was that enigmatic answer the ancient biblical writer's way of suggesting that God is not a being, but Being itself? Thus my third definition of a nontheistic God is this: God is Being—the reality underlying everything that is. To worship this God you must be willing to risk all, abandoning your defenses and your self-imposed or culturally constructed security systems. THE PRIVILEGE OF THE

The theistic God-image in the story of the burning bush is a IN-human creation, designed to enable us to do what it is not easy to STANT" do. If we interpret its God-message nontheistically, we hear the instruction, "You must shout your 'I am' to the world!" In other words, you must stretch beyond all of your limits. If God is the Ground of Being, you worship this divine reality by having the courage to be all that you can be—your deepest, fullest self. You worship the God who is the Ground of Being by walking into the unknown, by giving your being away, by valuing the being of others as equal to and even more precious than your own. To have the courage to be is to move beyond the self-absorbed survival mode to which human life is so deeply attached. It is to live for another. It is to worship the God who is not a being but Being itself.

This God is not a supernatural entity who rides into time and space to rescue the distressed. This God is the source of life, the source of love, the Ground of Being. The theistic God of yesterday is a symbol for the essence, the being of life in which we share. God is life, we say, and we worship this God by living fully. God is love, we say, and we worship this God by loving wastefully. God is Being, we say, and we worship this God by having the courage to be all that we can be. Ultimately, it is in the act of living, loving, and being that we go beyond the boundaries of our existence and know transcendence, otherness, and eternity. It is in that moment, I am convinced, that the God beyond theism— the God Tillich described as the God beyond the gods of men and women—begins to come into focus.

So as one who worships this God, I now must learn to climb over my protective fences and walk past the barriers of my fears—barriers that always confront me at the edges of my humanity. But when I walk beyond these fears, I discover that I touch a transcendent presence that I cannot help but call God. This presence is far beyond the image of the theistic external deity that once I served. This realization causes me not to mourn, but to rejoice that the blinding idolatry of traditional theism has finally departed from my life. God is so much more than the supernatural being, the divine Santa Claus, or the heavenly Mr. Fix-It.

The death of theism calls us into responsibility. It provides us with the opportunity to step boldly into the fullness of life. It is an invitation to give up the pitiful human quest for security, which we all at some level know does not exist except in our pretense, and to experience the power found in the acceptance of the fact that radical insecurity is the very mark of our humanity. It enables us to grasp this humanity without denial and to enter the fullness of life with a mature new confidence. This enhanced humanity in turn opens us to a new awareness that we are not alone. It is not that our loneliness is overcome by a parental God in the sky waiting to come to our aid. Rather, it is that we experience ourselves as part of that which is eternal. There is a reality we call God that is the source of the life we live, the power of the love we share, the Ground of Being that calls us to be all that we can be. I live today in the conviction that I am not separate from this God. I participate in that which is eternal, infinite, and beyond all boundaries. My being is expanded by this experience. Otherness confronts me. Transcendence calls me. God embraces me.

Do not confuse this God with the God we served in the childhood of our humanity. This God is not identified with doctrines, creeds, and traditions. The reality of this God is beyond all of that. This God can never be captured in words or made to serve our power-needs. The God beyond theism is beyond *everything*. This God is unavoidable, inescapable, omnipresent. Perhaps that is what the psalmist had in mind when he said, "Whither shall I flee from thy presence? If I ascend to heaven, thou art there! If I make my bed in Sheol, thou art there! If I take the wings of the morning and dwell in the uttermost parts of the sea, even there thy hand shall lead me, and thy right hand shall hold me"

(Ps. 139:7b–10, RSV). If God is the Ground of Being, then my being is a part of this inescapable divine reality. When I separate the theistic explanations from the God-experience, I discover that even the ancient formulas were open-ended, pointing beyond themselves to that which they could not begin to articulate.

I venture into this new terrain with a deep sense not of fear but of relief. I no longer have to expend enormous energy defending that theistic God who appeared to act so capriciously and to violate the standards of justice so consistently; I no longer have to produce the tongue-twisting and elaborate theological explanations that have sustained this image through the centuries. I am free of the God who was deemed to be incomplete unless constantly receiving our endless praises; the God who required that we acknowledge ourselves as born in sin and therefore as helpless; the God who seemed to delight in punishing sinners; the God who, we were told, gloried in our childlike, groveling dependency. Worshiping that theistic God did not allow us to grow into the new humanity that we now claim. Rather, it kept us as the clay passively seeking to be molded by the divine potter.

Yes, of course growth is painful. In this quest beyond theism, we have sacrificed the one who was presented to us as our eternal and omnipotent protector. That loss, however, is balanced by our gaining what Paul called the "glorious liberty of the children of God" (Rom. 8:21). We have gained the freedom to live and to love and to be. We are not alone, as our critics clinging to their dying theistic images and anchored to the definitions of the past like to claim. God is not dead. We have indeed entered God. We are God-bearers, co-creators, incarnations of what God is.

In these new roles, we claim no magic or miracle. We make no attempt to suggest that life is fair or to defend the theistic deity when life is harsh. We do not cultivate a false security; we are aware that danger lurks in many corners, and we know that the external protection we once sought was but an illusion. That illusion we have now set aside, since we understand that illusions do not become reality simply because we *need* them to be so. Immaturity does not disappear if we do not take hold of our lives and live them responsibly. God is not made real because we think it would be nice if it were so. God is real only if God *is* real.

That is the God-reality which is now my experience. I grasp it boldly and without apology. I believe that it is an experience of that which is timeless and true. The God-experience about which I now seek to be articulate is all that I could ever desire God to be. My life reveals the divine life. I love with the divine love. I understand what St. Catherine of Genoa meant when she said, "My Me is God," as well as her assertion that selfhood cannot be found except in God. This theme was also echoed time and again in the writings of great medieval mystics such as Meister Eckhart and Julian of Norwich.[6] I know what the author of the Epistle of John meant when he wrote, "God is love" (1 John 4:16). I understand the God at the burning bush who was named the great "I am." I know what Paul of Tarsus meant when he wrote, "By the grace of God I am what I am" (1 Cor. 15:10). I know what Paul Tillich meant when he urged us to live out "the courage to be."[7] As one who is no longer a dependent child asking to be protected, but a mature human being, I now accept my share of the responsibility for shaping my world. I claim this new spiritual awareness. The death of the parent-God of theism is similarly a call to religious maturity—a call to be a God-bearer, a source of life, love, and being to the world. It is a call to be what Christians have called the "body of Christ," the community of people through whom God is experienced.

Many will ask whether this God-concept that I grope to find words to convey is of sufficient continuity to connect me with what they tend to describe as the more emotionally satisfying parent-figure, that deity that we once thought inhabited the sky. I answer that question with a resounding yes. My affirmation reflects my conviction that the experience of God is always the same. It is only our description of this God that changes, and our description is *ever*-changing. Theism is a human description of God that has died. I seek to walk beyond the carnage of that description into a new sense of God—a God met not outside of life but at the very heart of life.

My mind, my integrity, my intellectual questioning, and my God-experience all come together in this new image. My religious schizophrenia is at an end. Theism is dead, I joyfully proclaim, but God is real. When I stand in the presence of this God who inhabits the heart of life, I know just why I define myself as a joyful, passionate, convinced believer in the reality of God.

# FIVE

# THE ORIGINAL CHRIST:
# BEFORE THE THEISTIC DISTORTION

*We have been betrayed by the Bible. In the half-century just end-
ing, there is belated recognition that biblically based Christianity
has espoused causes that no thinking person or caring person is any
longer willing to endorse. We have had enough of the persecution
of the Jews and witches; of the justification of black slavery; of the
suppression of women, sex and sexuality; and of the stubborn defense of a male dominated, self-serving clergy. . . . We cannot, we
must not shrink from engagement with the ignorance and misun-
derstanding that fuels such egregious misuse of scripture.*[1]

— ROBERT W. FUNK, director of the Jesus Seminar

By now we have embraced the possibility, perhaps even made
the decision, that the theistic God is dead. When we arrive at
that conclusion, we discover that it requires us to relinquish that
deity forever. But suddenly it dawns on us with terrifying force
that once theism is relinquished, much of what we hold sacred—

concepts and beliefs deeply tied to that theistic definition—will also disappear. We are up against a profound theological domino effect. Recognizing these ramifications, we are tempted to draw back in fear. But that temptation must be resisted. There is only one life-affirming alternative when a reformation dawns, and that is to step boldly into the new spiritual arena—an arena in which all the definitions of the past are up for debate and reformulation—and to breathe deeply of this new air. That is now our situation: We must choose between the stultification of the past and the fresh, invigorating air of the future. Too MUCH—

I hope that in the previous chapters I have established a major marker: to move beyond the theistic definition of God is not to move beyond God. Indeed it is, rather, to open our God-experience to an array of vast new explanatory possibilities. It is to invite the people of our world who are spiritually hungry, though not for a dying theism, to enter a new source of meaning. It is to move beyond the narrow base of Western approaches to God as part of a worldwide spiritual awakening, envisioning the possibility and working toward the reality of a dialogue that leads to an interfaith union never before thought possible. It is to embrace the radical reformation that will be required if Christianity is to live into the years of this third millennium as anything more than a marginalized irrelevance dwelling at the edges of a secular society. But as gigantic as the step away from the theistic definition of God is, it is nonetheless just the *first* step. As exhilarating as it might be, we are only at the very beginning of our journey.

Because we are children of the West, we must look first at the primary symbol in our faith-story: Jesus, who is called Christ. Is it conceivable that we might be able to tell the Christ-story apart from the concept of a theistic God? The future of Christianity and the possibilities for a new reformation will be determined, I am convinced, by how we answer this question. My own immediate response is that we can and we must. It is, however, the *must* part of that statement that I need to address first, for that is where we face the deconstruction of yesterday's now-inadequate religious conceptions. These conceptions must be laid aside. The *can* part of my answer involves a reconstruction that, I am now convinced, will be built only upon a different foundation. This reconstruction, which will follow logically at the appropriate time, constitutes the very essence of this book.

Why must we tell the Christ-story apart from the theistic concept of God? Quite simply, we must do so because the residual theism of the past is today strangling the very life out of Christianity. The theistic God-content, that has been so tightly wound around Jesus of Nazareth from a very early date, makes it all but impossible today to see Jesus as having any meaning at all. So unless we loosen the hold that theism has on Christ, the death of theism will surely mean the death of Christianity.

If the supernatural being who lives above the sky, invading life periodically to accomplish a divine purpose, has fallen into disrepute and is no longer a possibility for the belief systems of modern men and women, then surely we must acknowledge that Jesus *understood as the incarnation of this theistic deity* is equally without a future. The Jesus of the supernatural entry into life through the miracle of the virgin birth; the Jesus of the supernatural exit from this world through the miracle of the cosmic ascension; the Jesus who in his earthly existence did such Godlike things as walking on water, stilling the storm, healing the sick, raising the dead, and feeding the multitude with but five loaves—this Jesus is little more than an earthly portrait of the theistic God in human form. If theism is dying today, a casualty of advancing knowledge, then the understanding of Jesus as the incarnation of this theistic deity is also mortally wounded.

But is that all there is to Jesus? Does he disappear when his theistic clothing is removed? Is there anything to Jesus that remains once the theistic interpretation of his life has been lifted from his shoulders? Whenever this subject has been broached in traditionally liberal circles—and it has been discussed often through the intervening centuries—the resulting portrait of Jesus has been that of a great teacher. One of my most esteemed mentors, Professor Walter Russell Bowie, constantly referred to Jesus as "the Master."[2] That title portrays Jesus as good and even noble, but it does not suggest external origin or eternal value.

Furthermore, the content of Jesus' teaching was not terribly original. Much of what Jesus said can be located in the Hebrew scriptures that informed his life. The summary of the law—to love God first and to love one's neighbor as oneself—can be found in the Torah (Deut. 6:5; Lev. 19:18). The so-called golden rule is sometimes stated negatively, but it is present in many other sacred texts. The long teaching sections of Mark (10–12), Matthew (19–20), and Luke (9:51–19:40), which cover the time of Jesus' journey from Galilee to his rendezvous with destiny in Jerusalem, is patterned, I would argue, deliberately after the story of Moses giving his final instructions on many issues to his people prior to his departure from them as chronicled in the book of Deuteronomy.[3] Many of the parables attributed to Jesus can also be related to Old Testament or Talmudic sources.[4]

Joachim Jeremias, a noted New Testament scholar, has argued that the only really unique thing about the teaching of Jesus is his use of the intimate Aramaic word *Abba*—"Beloved Parent"—to refer to God.[5] All of this suggests that the human Jesus understood primarily as a teacher or sage would hardly be worthy of the significance that his life has been accorded; it argues that to remove the theistic interpretation from him is to destroy him as an ultimate or unique religious thinker.

Robert Funk, the founder of the Jesus Seminar, has suggested that Jesus needs a demotion.[6] This attention-capturing phrase is for some people a call into a new freedom, but for those who are more traditional it is threatening and even insulting. An unusual and gifted scholar, Funk gives voice in this suggestion to the fact that the theistic framework in which Jesus has been captured is no longer either compelling or believable in our generation. For

Christians not to face that fact is to be out of touch with reality. However, like so many critics of supernaturalism and theistic thinking, Funk also seems to assume that the only alternative to supernaturalism is naturalism and the removal from Jesus of any divine claim. If removing the theistic interpretive material from around Jesus constitutes the demotion that Funk feels to be necessary, then I am all for it. But the Jesus who remains when Funk has completed his task looks to me not like a demoted Jesus but a court-martialed Jesus, a destroyed Jesus. This approach never addresses the question of what there was about Jesus' life that caused the theistic interpretations to be thought appropriate in the first place.

I suggest that we begin this discussion by recognizing that theism is only one definition of God and that *no* definition of God is to be equated with God. The God-claim for Jesus must not be dependent on an outdated God-definition. So I am quite willing to follow Robert Funk's suggestion and join in the task of stripping the theistic claims from around Jesus' life, but in the process I will begin to point to a new God-definition that resonates with the humanity of Jesus.

Perhaps the secret lies in the way critics of non-theistic thinking try to make their case against Jesus' deconstruction. If Jesus is not the incarnation of the theistic deity, they say, then he is "just" a human being. I find their use of this word *just* to be intriguing. I believe we can expand our limited conception of what it means to be human until it is broken open and a new vision of human grandeur or transcendence can be embraced. The result will be a humanity so deeply and powerfully drawn that the artificially imposed barrier between the human and the divine will fade and we can recognize that these two words—*human* and *divine*—do not point to separate entities; rather, they are like two poles of a continuum that appear to be separate and distinct, yet when one travels from one to the other, the discovery is made that their shadows blend into and invade each other. I seek a Christology that preserves divinity but not supernatural theism, which is a distinction not often made. I seek in Jesus a human being who nonetheless makes known, visible, and compelling the Ground of All Being. I remind my readers once again that I enter this field of inquiry specifically as a Christian, as one who believes that I have met the holy God in Jesus of Nazareth.

The first thing that must be recognized is that the theistic concepts which have been used to capture and interpret Jesus of Nazareth are what is at stake in this analysis, not the God-presence that these concepts were designed to communicate. The primary insight that I seek to establish is that the theistic interpretation of Jesus does not appear to be original. Indeed, if we look properly at the texts, we can actually watch theism being introduced into the Jesus story. We can see it grow until finally it excludes all other possibilities.

The best way to engage this insight is to read the New Testament not in the order that is preserved in our present Bibles, but in the chronological order in which the various books that now constitute the New Testament were written. According to a majority of biblical scholars today, that means that we must start with the two earliest written records we have in the New Testament: Paul and what is called "the Q document." Some would add the recently discovered *Gospel of Thomas* to that list. I shall examine all of these briefly.

I take the Q document first, because it is least well understood and is still subject to vigorous debate. The name *Q* is shorthand for the German word *Quelle*, which means "source." Since German scholars made the discovery of this material in the nineteenth century, the name they gave it has stuck. The Q theory was derived from a comparison of the gospels of Matthew and Luke. It is self-evident that both of these gospel writers used Mark in the construction of their texts. Matthew used about ninety percent of Mark, basically following Mark's text after loading the front of it with a genealogy (Matt. 1:1–17), a birth narrative (1:18–2:23), an expanded baptism story (3:1–17), an expanded temptation story (4:1–11), a long section that we call the Sermon on the Mount (chapters 5–7), and other material. From Matthew 13 on, this author tracks Mark both closely and rather faithfully.

The author of Luke's gospel is less dedicated to his Marcan source than Matthew, but he does follow Mark's basic outline, again with a significant front-end load. In the process Luke incorporates a bit more than fifty percent of Mark into his text. Thus Matthew and Luke clearly have a Marcan source in common. One can therefore place Matthew and Luke side by side and remove from each of these gospels all of their dependency on Marcan material. When that is done, a fresh insight becomes obvious: Luke and Matthew still have a significant amount of shared common material, none of which is Marcan.

When this second body of shared material is lifted out of these two gospels and studied, the possibility emerges that in these similar verses we are in contact with an earlier document, now lost, that was once available to both Matthew and Luke. This fascinating theory has inspired scholars such as Burton Mack to write books about "the lost gospel."[7] Others have made the study of the Q material their life's work.[8] Volumes on the theology of the Q document have been written.[9]

The date assigned to the Q material, according to some scholars, ranges back as far as the middle of the first century C.E.[10] If that dating is correct, Q becomes an early and primary witness to the Jesus-inquiry. Serious Jesus scholars, such as those found in the Jesus Seminar, regard the Q material as a key to their endeavors, since it gets them back to a point in time closer to the historical Jesus than any other document.

The elevation of the *Gospel of Thomas* into the canon of scripture by the Jesus Seminar[11] and the attempt to date that work early in Christian history are driven by the need of historical-Jesus scholars to demonstrate that they are basing their conclusions on very early documents. Indeed, the discovery of the almost complete text of a Coptic translation of the *Gospel of Thomas* in Nag Hammadi, Egypt, in 1945 was thought to confirm both the reality of the Q document and the probability of its early origins. That discovery demonstrated, this argument contends, that collections of Jesus' sayings, such as the Q document and the *Gospel of Thomas*, did occur quite early in Christian history.

If we accept the validity of the Q hypothesis and the early dating of both the Q material and the *Gospel of Thomas* for a moment, it is noteworthy for my purpose to recognize that there are no miracle stories in either Q or *Thomas*. There is also no story in either of a supernatural birth or supernatural ascension. There is not even an account of the crucifixion and resurrection. There are no parables. There is nothing that presents Jesus in the supernatural theological language that later was to surround him. He appears to be a wise teacher, a sage, and sometimes even a comic.

So if the case can be made both for the independent origin and the early dating of Q and *Thomas*, these sources do seem to present a Jesus of Nazareth who was not a visiting deity, not an incarnation of a supernatural God, and not a miracle-worker. At the very least, this suggests that the supernatural suit of armor that was later attached to Jesus was not original. It does not, however, give us much more than the picture of a wise man and a teacher well enough respected that his sayings were deemed worthy of preservation.

If the Q hypothesis is not accepted and the early dating of *Thomas* is not confirmed, then we are back to the canonical texts of the Bible as the earliest sources on which to base our analysis.[12] The first of the writers of the canonical texts of the New Testament was Paul. Although it is commonplace in the world of scholarship to acknowledge the primacy in time of Paul, that insight has not widely permeated the minds of the people who sit in the pews of our churches. This probably is because the New Testament begins with the gospels, then moves to Acts before coming to the writings of Paul. Paul describes life *after* the time of

Jesus, while the gospels purport to record the things that Jesus actually said and did. As a result, people tend, often unconsciously, to read Paul through the eyes of the gospels.

Yet the facts are that Paul was converted and baptized, became a missionary, engaged in the controversial task of defining the Christian faith against powerful opponents such as Peter and James whom he called "the Lord's brother", completed all of his journeys, wrote all of his epistles, and was imprisoned and executed in Rome before any of the four canonical gospels was written. There is no evidence that Paul ever had access to a gospel, even a sayings gospel, if any had in fact been written. Paul's epistles are dated generally between 50 and 64 C.E. The earliest gospel, Mark, is generally dated in the 65–75 C.E. range. I tend to date Mark on the high side of that scale, around 72 C.E., as I shall explain later.[13] The point is that in Paul we have the earliest extant undisputed witness to the Jesus-story.

Isolating Paul and deliberately attempting not to read him through the eyes and stories of the later gospels produces some fascinating insights.[14] There is, for example, in Paul no reference to a miraculous birth. He says that Jesus was "born of a woman, born under the law" (Gal. 4:4). There is no hint of the concept of virginity in Paul's use of the word *woman*. He seems to be referring to a normal birth, one no different from that which happens to any other person. He later says that Jesus was "descended from David according to the flesh" (Rom. 1:3). That hardly sounds miraculous. Furthermore, there are no miracle stories anywhere in the writings of Paul.

There is also no sense in Paul's writing that the apostle understands the resurrection of Jesus to be a physical resuscitation. Yet resurrection is certainly real for Paul. He argues that apart from the resurrection of Jesus, one's faith is in vain (1 Cor. 15:14)—but it has nothing to do with flesh and blood: Paul has a profound sense of Jesus as alive, as a continuing divine presence. In Philippians (2:5–11) he portrays Jesus as the life in whom the divine one has emptied the divine nature. In 2 Corinthians (5:19) he indicates his conviction that one engages God when one meets the Christ, who is for Paul the human portrait of God's reconciling act. In Romans (1:1–4) he says that God designated Jesus to be the Son of God at the time of the resurrection, which can be read as the moment in which God adopted Jesus into God's eternal presence and perhaps even into God's divinity.

Paul's understanding of resurrection also appears to suggest that what the church later separated into distinct events— namely, the resurrection and the ascension—were for Paul two sides of the same coin. God had, for Paul, raised Jesus from death into the presence and meaning of God. It was from the heavenly place into which Jesus had been elevated that the risen Christ was revealed to chosen witnesses, in Paul's understanding.

In support of this understanding is the fact that Paul lists his own conversion experience as a resurrection appearance not unlike all the other resurrection appearances that he describes, except that his was last (1 Cor. 15:1–10). There is in Paul no mention of an empty tomb, suggesting that the empty-tomb story is not known to him.[15] He does use the symbol "three days" when referring to resurrection (1 Cor. 15:4), which seems to link him into the tradition in which the first day of the week is set aside for celebrating the resurrection; but that is as far as we can press Paul into the later developing traditions.

On two occasions Paul says that he is passing on an understanding that was handed down to him, wording that suggests an even earlier tradition. Analyzing these occasions, we can postulate some interesting conclusions. One of the references in question is his relating of the events that we now associate with Maundy Thursday and the inauguration of the church's eucharistic meal (1 Cor. 11:23–26). There Paul uses the Greek word that literally means "handed over," but it can also mean, and has been traditionally translated in the biblical text, "betrayed." Interestingly enough, however, Paul reveals no sense that this handing over was done by one of the twelve disciples, which might indicate that the Judas betrayal story is also a later-developing tradition.

This idea is reinforced when we read the second Pauline passage that refers to passing on an earlier understanding, a received tradition—which refers to the final events of Jesus' life (1 Cor. 15:1–10). There Paul says that Jesus was put to death, that he was buried, that on the third day he was raised, and that he was thereafter seen by various witnesses. After the primary appearance to Cephas (i.e., Peter), Paul says, the risen Christ manifested himself "to the Twelve," a group that certainly included the one called Judas Iscariot. It appears once again that Paul had never heard the account which was later to suggest that one of the Twelve, Judas, had been the one who "handed him over"—that is, betrayed him. After the Judas story enters the tradition, Christian writers such as Matthew have Jesus appear only to *eleven* disciples.

These passages from Paul begin to open our minds to the possibility that much of the passion narrative, including the story of the traitor and the elaborate burial tradition, is developed legend.[16]

So in Paul we find little of the theistic framework and little of the imposed supernaturalism that was to develop later. Yet we cannot read Paul without coming away with a powerful sense that for this Jewish learned man, this pupil of Gamaliel, God was somehow powerfully present in Christ. There was in Paul a real sense that the story of the resurrection meant that Jesus had been lifted by God into the realm of the divine, that Jesus was now somehow one with God, and that no one could ever understand this Jesus apart from the God who had been revealed in him.

Even God now seemed to Paul to be incomplete apart from Jesus (Phil. 2:9–11; Rom. 1:4). That was quite a witness. It must not be minimized, though it was a witness not yet understood in the theistic language of the invading supernatural deity. Perhaps Paul was too deeply a Jew to allow the God he worshiped, even the God he met in Jesus, to be imaged, defined, or even embraced intellectually. Paul had that Jewish sense that one lived in

God. Indeed, when Paul talked about being "in Christ," he clearly understood that state to be the same as being in God (Phil. 1:21, 23). So the argument that the theistic definition that came to surround Jesus was original, and that apart from it Jesus' divine nature is in debate, comes up against the early witness of Paul; and the argument's claims are punctured and deflated.

I do not mean to suggest that Paul did not see God theistically, as did all Jews of his day. He certainly did. God for Paul was a being who lived above the sky. "If you then be risen with Christ," he wrote, "seek those things which are above where Christ is sitting at the right hand of God" (Col. 3:1). He also told of one who in a kind of mystical experience had been lifted up to the "third heaven" (2 Cor. 12:2–5). What I am suggesting is that the incarnational and trinitarian language of a developed theism had not yet been wrapped around Jesus, though a God-experience had nonetheless been claimed for him. My argument is that since this theistic language was not original with Jesus, it is time-related and therefore not eternal. So Paul is the first canonical witness to support this insight, joining Q and *Thomas*, for those who are convinced of their early dating, in forming a different witness.

By the time of the writing of Mark (65–75 C.E.), the theistic interpretation of Jesus was on the rise, but it had not yet won the day even in this first gospel. Mark opens his story with the assertion that this will be "the beginning of the gospel of Jesus the Christ, the Son of God" (1:1), and Mark has God make this point and affirm that definition with a heavenly voice at the time of Jesus' baptism (1:11). But in Mark's story it is God's spirit being poured out on Jesus that designates Jesus as a God-presence, a human being infused with God's spirit not a theistic deity masquerading as a human being.

Miracle stories, however, do appear in Mark's text. Jesus is capable of healing the sick, including the crippled (1:40–2:12), giving sight to the blind (8:22–26), and casting out demons (1:21–28). Mark gives no account of Jesus giving hearing to the deaf, but he does record that it has happened (7:32, 37), and such healing is also affirmed in the later gospels (Matt. 11:5; Luke 7:22). In Mark Jesus is portrayed also as having power over the forces of nature (6:45–53). He can feed the multitudes from the meager supply of five loaves and two fish (6:30–44), for example.

Yet there is in Mark no miraculous-birth story, and the mother of Jesus is portrayed in a rather negative light. She goes with Jesus' brothers and sisters to take Jesus away. The suggestion in this account is that she and the other members of Jesus' family see him as mentally disturbed; he has become an embarrassment to their clan (3:20–35, 6:1–6). That is hardly the way a virgin mother visited by an angel, and told by that angel that she would be the bearer of God's son (Luke 1:26–35), would act. Mark has clearly never heard of the miraculous-birth tradition. It is for him not a necessary ingredient in relating the experience of the God-presence that Mark clearly perceives to be the meaning found in Jesus of Nazareth. Mark has Peter confess that Jesus is the Christ, the Messiah, a God-presence (8:27–30).

Mark also incorporates some symbols of Jewish apocalyptic thought into his story of Jesus' crucifixion. The darkness that covered the earth, the symbol of three days, and the location of Easter on the first day of the week are familiar symbols to writers of apocalyptic literature.[17]

Strangely enough, however, there is a minimum of supernaturalism in Mark's account of the resurrection, which is the first biblical narrative of that experience. The raised Jesus, for example, never appears in Mark's text. There is instead the story of the women's visit to the tomb at dawn on the first day of the week. It is followed by the picture of the tomb as empty and the word of the messenger, not yet described as an angel, who tells the women that Jesus has been raised and that they are to tell the disciples and Peter that he will go before them to Galilee, where they will see him (16:1–8). Instead of passing this message on,

Mark says, the women flee in fear and say "nothing to anyone" (16:8). On that note Mark's gospel ends.

Later Christians found that ending so disconcerting, in the light of a rising tide of supernatural and theistic images, that they composed new endings to what was thought to be an *incomplete* gospel. Those endings—a longer one and a shorter one—have been incorporated into the King James Bible and into the footnotes of other texts.[18] New Testament scholars, however, are quite certain that the authentic gospel of Mark that we possess ended at what is verse 8 of chapter 16, though they are not unanimous that this is where Mark *intended* to end his gospel, and some even speculate that Mark's real ending has somehow been lost. I suspect that Mark concluded his gospel where he did, at verse 8 of chapter 16, because he had not yet been fully captured by the theistic definitions of God that were beginning to wrap themselves around the story of Jesus.

Indeed, I believe that we can still detect in Mark the influence of Jewish synagogue worship. This means that many of the stories that we think of as reflecting a supernatural theistic understanding of Jesus are in fact Mark's attempts to interpret Jesus in terms of the symbols of the Jewish faith-story.

Paul referred to Jesus as "our paschal lamb" (1 Cor. 5:7), likening him to the animal slaughtered in Jewish worship at the time of the Passover. Mark makes that reference explicit by telling the story of Jesus' death in terms of the Passover celebration (14:1–15:42). When one connects on a calendar the story of Jesus' death with the killing of the paschal lamb and then rolls Mark's gospel back across the rest of the liturgical year of the Jews, one discovers an amazing confluence of similarities. It appears that Mark has established a correlation between his telling of the story of Jesus' life and the liturgical celebrations of first-century Judaism.

The story of Jesus' transfiguration (Mark 9:2–8), for example, is placed by Mark at that point in the liturgical year of the Jews when they were observing the Festival of Dedication. In that festival Jews celebrated the time when the light of God was restored to the Temple. Now, says Mark, with the Temple destroyed (as it was in 70 C.E.),[19] we have in Jesus the new temple, the new meeting place between God and human life. So in the story of the transfiguration as Mark tells it, the light of God is said to have been poured out not upon the Temple, but upon Jesus, while Moses, the father of the law, and Elijah, the father of the prophets, the pillars of temple worship, are both made to bear witness to the primacy of Jesus (9:2–8).

Next, still working backward in the liturgical year of the Jews, we come to the eight-day Feast of Tabernacles, the Jewish harvest festival, and at exactly that point in the gospel Mark portrays Jesus as telling harvest parables and demonstrating divine power over nature (4:1–41), with sufficient material to cover eight days.

Continuing from that correlation to roll the text backward across the Jewish liturgical year, we come to Yom Kippur, the Day of Atonement. At exactly that place Jesus is portrayed in Mark as healing the sick, curing the paralytic by forgiving his sins, calling the unclean tax-collector Levi into discipleship, and talking about fasting (1:21, 2:22). In that era sickness was thought to be caused by sin, so a purging on the Day of Atonement could bring wholeness and health to sin's victims. Casting out demons was also Jesus' divine task, since the kingdom of God was breaking into history through him and the demonic forces were the enemies of the kingdom. Demons were the supernatural interpretation in the first century for such abnormalities as mental illness, epilepsy, and deaf-muteness. This series of episodes clearly had a Yom Kippur flavor.

Finally, still rolling backward the scroll of Mark, we discover that Mark appears to begin his Jesus-story at the time of the Jewish New Year, Rosh Hashanah. That would certainly have been an appropriate starting place if Mark's gospel was written to provide Christian lections to augment the synagogue's celebrations of the major feasts and fasts of the Jewish liturgical year from

New Year to Passover. Rosh Hashanah called the people to an expectation that the kingdom of God was at hand and urged them to prepare for it with repentance. Mark places this Rosh Hashanah message on the lips of John the Baptist, associating him with the familiar liturgical words of the synagogue employed in the New Year celebration, "Prepare ye the ways of the Lord, make his paths straight" (Mark 1:1–11). This theme is enhanced in Matthew, where John proclaims the essential message of Rosh Hashanah, "Repent, for the Kingdom of heaven is at hand" (Matt. 3:2).

If we can establish that the liturgical year of the Jews at least from Rosh Hashanah (New Year) to Passover (the story of deliverance) was the organizing principle and therefore the basic outline of Mark's gospel, then the conclusion would be drawn appropriately that the first written gospel was designed to tell the Jesus-story in such a way that it could be read at Sabbath services of corporate worship in the synagogue, with the Easter narrative as the climax of that story, to be read on the Sabbath after the Passover. Mark's gospel would thus be demonstrated to be not a biography at all, as many have supposed, but a liturgical text that later got misinterpreted as a story of history and biography.

At Rosh Hashanah, as the Jews prayed for the kingdom of God to come, they also rehearsed the signs that would accompany the kingdom's arrival. These signs were taken primarily from Isaiah 35, a popular reading in the synagogue during this festival. In that passage the prophet writes that when the kingdom of God comes, the blind will see (35:5), the deaf hear (35:5), the lame walk (35:6), the mute speak (35:6). It could certainly be argued that John the Baptist, under the influence of Mark's quill, had become the human *shofar*, the trumpet of God, blown at Rosh Hashanah to gather the people to announce the in-breaking of the kingdom of God. Jesus was both the instrument to bring in the kingdom and the first fruits of that kingdom, so it was said of him that his life was marked by the signs of the kingdom's presence. That is what later readers of Mark's gospel, who did not understand his use of Jewish symbols, literalized. Instead of seeing these miraculous episodes as signs of the kingdom of God being attributed to Jesus, they read them as the invasion into human history of the theistic God, and thus they interpreted Jesus as the incarnation of a supernatural theistic power. He was a miracle-worker, this interpretation said. He demonstrated his supernatural power by healing the sick, giving sight to the blind, and giving hearing to the deaf.

It is my belief that these healing stories, as Mark used them, were not miracle narratives, as Western people have traditionally interpreted them to be, but only Mark's theological way of claiming for Jesus' life the signs of the presence of the kingdom of God. The transformation from theological interpretation to literal miracles was not quite a theistic takeover, though it lent itself to that later.

So the earliest witnesses to Jesus—Paul, perhaps Q and *Thomas*, and even Mark—portray a Jesus whose life has not yet been squeezed into the theistic mold. Yet it is a Jesus who is seen as a God-presence, a life through which the kingdom of God is breaking into human history. He is one, in whom and through whom God is seen. That is the experience we need to embrace. Jesus was a human life through which people experienced the presence of God, and this experience is documentable prior to the time when the later theistic explanations were laid upon him. The theistic explanations can be set aside, as indeed they have been in our generation, but the experience can remain intact. It is a delicate interpretive line one has to walk to separate experience from explanation. But a living Christ, seen as the originator of a new Christianity for a new world, requires it.

Remember that Mark closes his story of the crucifixion with the words of the centurion: "Surely this man was the Son of God" (15:39). By extricating Jesus from the dying concepts of theism, we might be able to make that same claim in our day with renewed and authentic power. It is at least worth noting that in the earliest records of our faith-story, Jesus is not the victim of a total theistic distortion. That distortion comes soon enough, as we shall see, but it is not original; it was added to an earlier portrait of Jesus. Because it was added to Jesus, it can also be taken off: the theistic interpretation of Jesus does not have to be eternal; theism can die.

Still, something about this Jesus made it essential that in his time theistic language would be used in order to explain him. It is that "something," that God-presence, that we seek to find. That "something" antedates the theistic takeover, and because it does, it may not have to die when theism collapses. We file this insight for now, planning to return to it in Chapter 8, when this biblical analysis is complete.

# SIX

# WATCHING THEISM
# CAPTURE CHRISTIANITY

*The living faith seems to be transformed into a creed to be believed;
devotion to Christ into Christology; the ardent hope for the coming
of the Kingdom into a doctrine of immortality and deification;
prophecy into technical exegesis and theological learning; the min-
istries of the spirit into clergy; the brothers [and sisters] into lay
[people] in a state of tutelage; miracles and miraculous cures disappear altogether or are priestly devices; fervent prayers become
solemn hymns and litanies; the spirit becomes law and compulsion.*[1]

—ADOLF HARNACK, church historian

When we come to the ninth decade of the Christian era,
more than fifty years after the earthly life of Jesus had
come to an end, Matthew's gospel and possibly Luke's enter the
Christian arena. Matthew is generally dated in the early eighties
and Luke in the late eighties or early nineties. Both texts add
enormously to the theistic interpretation of Jesus of Nazareth.

Matthew is the first Christian writer to relate the story of Jesus' miraculous birth. He highlights that narrative with a spectacular sign in the universe: a luminous star that travels through the sky at a pace so slow that it can lead its followers to their specific destination (2:1–12). Matthew uses quotations from Jewish scripture to indicate that the things he is describing are not accidental but came about in accordance with the divine plan, as revealed in the sacred story of the Hebrew people (2:6, 15, 17, 23). He portrays God as revealing divine truths and even quoting proof texts to Joseph in a dream (1:23).

The Jesus depicted in Matthew's narrative is no longer quite human. His father is the Holy Spirit and his mother is a virgin (1:18), though Matthew doesn't divulge just how the Holy Spirit is supposed to have impregnated her. The proof offered for this divine act is a verse in Isaiah (7:14), which Matthew interprets to mean that a virgin named Mary would conceive and bear a son named Jesus, who would be Emmanuel, which means "God with us" (1:23).[2] This narrative was a giant step into that portrayal of Jesus which indicated that he was at his birth not really human but the incarnation of a theistic deity. Matthew presses that point home with the previously mentioned miraculous traveling star that enabled non-Jewish magi to find the babe in Bethlehem and present their gifts—gifts that helped Matthew's audience to interpret Jesus as Matthew intended: gold, the gift for a king; frankincense, the gift for a deity; and myrrh, to symbolize a life of suffering and death (2:11).

Moving beyond the events of Jesus' birth, Matthew, in his baptism story, follows Mark's lead by having God declare Jesus to be God's son, though that declaration is not as necessary for Matthew as it had been for Mark, since Matthew places it after the virginal conception (Matt. 3:17).

In the expansion of Mark's brief temptation story, Matthew portrays Jesus as one in combat with the Devil, who is a specific tempter. Both Jesus and the satanic one quote scripture to justify their claims (Matt. 4:1–11).

If the lectionary theory of gospel formation is correct, as the previous chapter suggested, then Mark had provided readings only for that part of the Jewish liturgical year from Rosh Hashanah to Passover. Matthew then decided to expand Mark's story so that he could cover the entire Jewish calendar with Christian readings. The crucifixion was clearly meant to correspond to the Passover sacrifice. Then, Matthew, like Mark, closed his narrative with a resurrection story that comes on the Sabbath Sunday after Passover. This meant that Matthew had to start his gospel account on the second Sabbath or Sunday after Passover, which would place that beginning in mid April or five and a half months before Rosh Hashanah. Given that timing, Matthew needed to provide a Christian reading for every Sabbath or Sunday for that long gap in Mark from mid April to the end of September, either expanding the brief Marcan narratives or loading up his gospel with original stories. He also had to cover the one great Jewish festival, Pentecost/Shavuot, which fell in that omitted part of Mark's year. This theory is supported by the text, making it appear that this is exactly what Matthew did.

Pentecost, which literally means "fifty days after Passover," was originally a Canaanite holy day marking the early wheat harvest. The Jews had taken it over and given it new and specifically Jewish content. Pentecost celebrated the gift that the Jews considered the greatest that God had ever given them—namely, the Torah, or the law. So on Pentecost they recalled Moses at Mount Sinai. Pentecost was for the Jews a twenty-four-hour liturgical celebration. Psalm 119, a hymn of praise to the wonder of the law, was written to be used during this long vigil service, and that is why this particular psalm is the length that it is. It begins with an introduction, followed by eight segments, one of which could be read in each of the three-hour watches of the twenty-four-hour celebration.

Matthew's task was to create a proper scene from Jesus' life that would serve as a Christian reading appropriate for the Jewish Pentecost. It is fascinating to see just how he accomplished that.

In Matthew's Pentecost narrative, Jesus, like Moses, goes up to a high mountain. There he begins to deliver a new interpretation of the Torah. The Torah begins with pithy, easy-to-remember sayings that we have come to call the Ten Commandments. Matthew has Jesus parallel that in his reinterpretation, opening with short, pithy, easy-to-remember sayings that we call today the Beatitudes (5:1–10). Psalm 119 opens with two verses beginning with the word *blessed*. Clearly the eight Beatitudes, which also begin with the word *blessed*, were inspired by that source.

An analysis of this part of Matthew, which has come to be called "the Sermon on the Mount," reveals that it is structured to be an eight-part commentary on the Beatitudes, working backward from eight to one,[3] which makes it even more obvious that Matthew is following the outline of Psalm 119. Since that psalm provided a segment for each of the three-hour units of the Jewish vigil, so Matthew is providing a Christian lection to be used in each of the eight segments of what was evolving into a twenty-four-hour Christian vigil. Throughout the Sermon on the Mount, Jesus, as portrayed by Matthew, reinterprets Moses: "You have heard it said of old"—that is the voice of Moses; "But I say unto you"—that is the voice of Jesus (5:21, 27).

Clearly, then, there is considerable textual support for the theory that Matthew is continuing and amplifying Mark's pattern of placing the story of Jesus against the background of the calendar of feasts and fasts in the Jewish liturgical year. It is quite obvious, however, that Matthew also heightens the sense of the miraculous power of Jesus as he develops his story.

Since Jesus' entry into the world is, for Matthew, seen as miraculous, so the final events of Jesus' life also have to be seen as miraculous. When we recognize that Matthew has Mark in front of him as he writes, it is easy to show exactly where this heightening of the original story occurs. For example, Matthew writes an earthquake into the story of Jesus' crucifixion, accompanying that with a rather bizarre episode in which the graves of the saints are opened and the long-deceased bodies of the dead rise from their tombs and enter the city of Jerusalem to be seen by many (27:51–53). That peculiar narrative is repeated nowhere else in the Bible.

Matthew also writes an earthquake into the story of the resurrection (28:2). On the wings of that latter earthquake, a supernatural angelic being in lustrous apparel evolves from Mark's nonsupernatural messenger, who was simply dressed in a white robe (compare Matt. 28:3 with Mark 16:5). In Mark the women wondered how they would roll the stone away from the tomb but arrived to discover that it had already been removed (Mark 16:3, 4). How that wonder was accomplished is not disclosed. But Matthew leaves no mystery unsolved. The angel did it, he says. After rolling the stone away, this supernatural being sits on top of the stone to make the resurrection announcement (28:2–6). The women in Matthew's account do not recoil in fear and flee, saying nothing to anyone, as they had done in Mark (Mark 16:8). Matthew's women are more faithful: they do as they are told and go quickly to tell the disciples, who are not yet present at the tomb (Matt. 28:7ff.). Mark had hinted that they were already in Galilee (Mark 16:7, 14:28). Matthew leaves that detail ambivalent.

As if to reward them for their faithfulness, Matthew allows the women to see the risen Christ in the garden (Matt. 28:9ff), even though Mark had said that the women did not see him (Mark 16:8). Luke, writing later and, like Matthew, having Mark in front of him, will also say that the women do not see the risen Lord (Luke 24:5–11). So if it is *history* that we are seeking, the witness of Matthew as to whether the women saw the risen Christ at the tomb is a minority report even in the New Testament.

Nevertheless, in Matthew the women recognize Jesus and grasp him by his feet (28:9). Since feet cannot be grasped unless they are physical, I submit that this is the first place in the New Testament to assume that Jesus' resurrection was that of a physically resuscitated, formerly dead body. Though the evidence against the authenticity of this Matthean story about the women touching Jesus is significant, it is nonetheless in this questionable passage that the physicality of the resurrected body of Jesus enters the Christian tradition—a physicality destined to grow and become more and more miraculous as the years went by.

But even this disputed story of the physical resurrection did not enter the tradition until the ninth decade, by which time Christianity's initial birth was more than a half-century old. Easter clearly propelled the Christian church into existence, but it took more than fifty years to tie that incredible burst of energy to the account of the physical, bodily resurrection of Jesus. That is the insight we need to hear and to embrace.

It is that insight that drives us to ask, "To what was that original source of life and power connected?" The fundamentalist assertion that it was tied to the physical resurrection of Jesus is simply not so. Supernatural power incarnate, as the way to interpret the presence of God in the person of Jesus, was clearly not an original part of the Jesus-story.

Let me repeat what is almost a mantra in this book: if we can demonstrate that this theistic overlay of supernaturalism on Jesus is not original, then clearly it also cannot be eternal; and if it was added to the Jesus-story well into Christian history, it can certainly be removed from that same story later in Christian history without destroying the core of the story. The theistic interpretation is not the essence of the resurrection experience; it is a later explanation of the essence of that experience. It is therefore not eternal, nor does it capture or exhaust the meaning of Jesus. There is a hopeful burst of freedom in the interpretive process when that realization is grasped.

When Matthew tells his second story of a sighting of the risen Christ (28:16–20), it is Jesus' chosen disciples who see him—the first and only time in Matthew that they do so. But resurrection is portrayed quite differently in the second narrative than in the first. Now Jesus is not a resuscitated body walking out of a tomb but is rather the glorified Lord of heaven and earth who is clothed with the authority of the Son of Man and comes riding on the clouds of heaven. He exclaims that all power in heaven and on earth has been given to him. He commissions the disciples, who have climbed up to the top of a high mountain so that they can be near him in the heavenly place out of which he has appeared: they are to go into all the world to preach the gospel and to baptize. He even gives the trinitarian formula of Father, Son, and Holy Spirit, and he makes the Emmanuel claim, affirming that the God who is now part of Jesus' identity will be with them always, even to the end of the world. That is as close as Matthew comes to elucidating a concept of the Holy Spirit. The God-presence met in this Christ will be with them forever.

It is interesting to note that this Matthean portrait of the resurrected Jesus appearing to his disciples shows him to be dwelling in God's heavenly presence. Yet the story of the ascension of Jesus has still not been told. So there is a hint in Matthew, compromised certainly by his account of Jesus appearing to the women, but a hint nonetheless, that Matthew also views resurrection the way Paul did: an act of lifting Jesus from death into the meaning of the living God, not an act of resuscitating Jesus back into the physical life of human history. God raised Jesus into the divine presence, thereby making Jesus part of who God is and thus eternally available just as God is. The theistic identity that would portray him as the incarnation of an external supernatural deity was growing, but it was not yet complete. Matthew had nonetheless pushed that process along mightily.

When the Lucan corpus, which involves both the gospel of Luke and the book of Acts, appeared somewhere between the years 88 and 95, several new dimensions were added to the developing tradition.[4]

Luke incorporates Matthew's virgin-birth story into his narrative, though he changes it dramatically. In Luke's narrative the angel appears to Mary in person to announce the birth of the holy child (1:26–38). In Matthew this annunciation took place to Joseph, but in a dream, which is just a bit less supernatural (1:18–25). There is no guiding star, and there are no magi in Luke. These symbols are replaced by an angel, a heavenly host, and a group of poor shepherds (2:8–14). A humble manger and swaddling clothes become in the Lucan story the symbolic interpreters, replacing the more grandiose gifts brought by Matthew's wise men (2:7, 12, 16).

Though Luke narrates an account of the virginal conception, he does not attach it to Matthew's proof text from the book of Isaiah (7:14). Perhaps Luke recognizes that the context for this verse—God was promising a sign to the king of the land of Judah, pledging that his nation would not fall to the armies of Syria and Israel, which surrounded Jerusalem in this eighth-century moment of confrontation—is hardly relevant to the birth of a baby eight hundred years later. So Luke soft-pedals the virgin birth a bit and even has Mary say to Jesus in the episode detailing the childhood visit to the Temple, "Your father [Joseph] and I have been looking for you anxiously" (2:48). Nevertheless, Luke—who is writing for an audience less rigidly Jewish and more open to Gentile involvement in the synagogue—thinks nothing of making Jesus appear as a divine figure in human clothing.

In Luke Jesus raises the dead in the person of the widow's son at Nain (7:11–18). Unlike Mark's story of Talitha, who is also raised—but from what Jesus calls simply her "sleeping" (Mark 5:35–43)—there is no doubt in Luke that the widow's son is dead. He is being carried out on the funeral bier when Jesus raises him from death back into life.

Luke's story of the resurrection heightens the physicality of the risen body of Jesus very dramatically. Luke also unties the resurrection from the ascension, so that they are now two actions separated from each other by a passage of time. For Luke Jesus is raised from the tomb back into the life of this world (24:1–43). Then, in a later action, he ascends into the presence of God in heaven. As the resurrection narrative unfolds, Luke next tells the story of Cleopas and his companion journeying in their grief toward the village of Emmaus after Jesus' crucifixion. These two travelers are overtaken by Jesus, who becomes their companion as they walk. The text hints that Jesus materializes out of thin air (24:13–35). The Lucan risen Christ can not only walk with these travelers, but he can also talk; so he opens to them the scriptures that point to the necessity of his suffering and the expectation of his resurrection. When they recognize him "in the breaking of the bread," Luke says, he dematerializes or vanishes from their sight.

Next, says Luke, Jesus appears in Jerusalem to Peter (24:34) and then to the disciples (24:36). There he asks for food to eat, demonstrating that he has a functioning gastrointestinal system and simultaneously proving that he is not a ghost (24:41). He invites the disciples to touch his very physical flesh, and he instructs them once more in the meaning of scripture (24:39, 44–49). Only then does he rise into the sky, to be parted from them by the clouds (24:51).

When Luke retells this same ascension story in Acts 1, it is quite clear that Jesus is departing to return to his heavenly home, which in Luke's mind is located just beyond the sky. With this heightening of the identity of Jesus as a visiting deity in human form, it is no surprise that this Jesus is himself now equipped with miraculous supernatural power. In Luke miracles are almost second nature to Jesus. The theistic understanding of God—God as external, supernatural, and invasive—is clearly the God-definition through which Luke interprets Jesus.

Luke, like Matthew, uses as the organizing principle of his gospel the liturgical outline of the synagogue, which he borrows from Mark. However, as Luke's Christian community moves further into the diaspora and has increasing Gentile contact, such things as a twenty-four-hour vigil marking the Jewish observance of Pentecost and the eight-day observance marking the Jewish celebration of Tabernacles shrink into the focus of a single Sabbath/Sunday.[5] Since Luke does not need a long Sermon on the Mount–type story to mark a twenty-four-hour vigil at Pentecost in his particular church's liturgical life, he scatters Matthew's Sermon on the Mount collection of teaching materials throughout his gospel, with the bulk of it being delivered not on a mountain but on a plain (6:17–49, 12:33–36).

Luke also changes the nature of Pentecost dramatically. When he tells his Pentecost story in the book of Acts, he is clearly under the influence of Paul, who said, "We are discharged from the law, dead to what held us captive so that we serve not under the old written law, but in the new life of the spirit" (Rom. 7:6). As discussed earlier, the Jews saw Pentecost as celebrating God's greatest gift to them: the gift of the Torah. Paul, on the other hand, saw God's greatest gift not as the Torah but as the Holy Spirit. For Luke, then—influenced in this by Paul—Pentecost became a time for the Christians to celebrate the gift of the Spirit. So Luke writes in Acts, "When the day of Pentecost had come they were all gathered in one place" (Acts 2:1–4), and the Spirit came upon them as wind and tongues of fire. We see here elements lifted quite self-consciously by Luke out of the story of Elijah's ascension and his gift of his own spirit to his disciple Elisha (2 Kings 2).

Then Luke relates Jesus' gift of the Holy Spirit to the expanded power of the Christian community, showing that these Spirit-filled believers can speak in whatever language their hearers understand. The divisions of the Tower of Babel (Gen. 11:1–9) are overcome, and the Spirit creates an inclusive community. This dramatic story reveals clearly how Luke reinterprets the Jewish Festival of Pentecost. In the place in his gospel when Luke needs to provide a single lection to be read on the Sabbath/Sunday nearest the synagogue observance of Pentecost, he uses the story of John the Baptist to presage his Pentecost narrative in Acts. John, he says, baptized with water, but one would come after him "who is greater than I." That one would baptize "with the Holy Spirit and with fire" (3:15–17). Luke was allowing John the Baptist to predict the change in interpreting Pentecost that he would develop in Acts 2.

Luke, like Mark and Matthew, thus keeps the liturgical-year framework, even though he is addressing a bridge community that combines Jews and Gentiles. However, he loosens that framework considerably, and he enhances dramatically the image of Jesus as the incarnation of the theistic God, seeing him as a visiting deity in a human form.

The drive into a supernatural theistic interpretation of Jesus continues at full speed in the last canonical gospel of the Bible, which we call John. Written, at least in its final form, between 95 and 100 of the Christian era, the text of this evangelist takes the theistic interpretation of Jesus to another level.

Interestingly, John appears to have dismissed the virgin-birth story as an inadequate explanation for the God-presence met in Jesus. He even refers to Jesus on two occasions as the son of Joseph (1:45, 6:42). In place of the virgin birth he substitutes a prologue asserting that the preexistence of Jesus is the proper understanding of his supernatural power (1:1–11). Jesus was the word of God, says John—the divine Logos, who was with God from the dawn of creation. He was indeed God's word spoken in creation: "Let there be light." In response to the command of the Logos, there was light (Gen. 1:3). This Logos was then simply enfleshed and dwelt among us, says John. "He came to his own, and his own received him not" (John 1:11).

Throughout the corpus of the Fourth Gospel, the identity forged between Jesus and God is asserted over and over again.

"The Father and I are one" (10:30); "He that has seen me has seen the Father" (14:9); "I go to the Father" (16:10); "Father, glorify me with the glory I had before the world was made" (17:5). John's Jesus can do very Godlike, miraculous things, such as changing water into wine (2:1–11), healing the man who had been born blind (9:1–41), and raising the four-days-dead and already buried Lazarus back to life (11:1–53).

John also has his Jesus claim the name "I am," revealed as God's name at the episode of the burning bush in the book of Exodus (3:14). John's Jesus is made to say such incredible things as "Before Abraham was, I am" (8:58) and "When you have lifted up the Son of Man, then you will know I am" (8:28).[6] He also places what we call the "I am" sayings on Jesus' lips whenever he can. Only John's Jesus is made to say, "I am the bread of life" (6:35), "I am the light of the world" (8:12), "I am the gate" (10:9), "I am the good shepherd" (10:11), and "I am the true vine" (11:51), and "I am the way" (14:6). There is no doubt that in the mind of the fourth evangelist, Jesus is the human enfleshment of the great "I am," the God of the Jews.

John also adds some Passover language to his narrative of Jesus' feeding of the five thousand. In the Jewish Passover liturgy, after the paschal lamb had been slain and its blood ceremonially placed on the doorposts of Jewish homes to dispel the angel of death, the people roasted the Passover lamb and feasted on the flesh of the sacrificial lamb that came to be called the lamb of God. John, who has no last supper in his gospel, puts all of his eucharistic teaching into the episode of the miraculous feeding of the multitude. The Johannine Christ is made to say, "Unless you eat the flesh of the Son of God and drink his blood, you have no life in you" (6:53f.).

John also identifies Jesus early on with the lamb of Yom Kippur. In the exclamation "Behold, the Lamb of God, who takes away the sins of the world," the specific words of Yom Kippur are put on the lips of John the Baptist when Jesus first appears on the scene (1:29, 36). This connection between Jesus and the liturgy of Yom Kippur had already been made by the author of the epistle to the Hebrews. Whether the fourth evangelist knew of that treatise or not, his mind is working in the same general direction. Jesus, says John, is the unblemished young male lamb with no broken bones (19:31–37), who like the lamb of Yom Kippur becomes the offering paid to God to overcome the sins of the world. In another Yom Kippur image, Jesus becomes the scapegoat upon whom the sins of the people are loaded, and thus the sin-bearer who takes away the sins of the people (1:29).

John gives to Mary Magdalene a very prominent role in his story. She is the chief mourner at the tomb (20:1–18), a trusted confidante of both Peter and the beloved disciple (20:2) and an eyewitness to the risen Lord. She is the only one who sees the unascended Jesus, who is said to have admonished her, "Do not hold me, for I have not yet ascended to the Father" (20:17).

When John tells the story of Jesus' resurrection, the full supernatural power of the theistic God incarnate is at work. The risen Jesus appears inside the locked doors and barred windows of the upper room (20:19–23). He does not need access; he can clearly walk through walls. He is also portrayed as possessing such a physically resuscitated body that he can offer the nail prints in his hands and the spear wound in his side for Thomas to touch (20:27). Yet interestingly enough, John suggests that what the disciples see in Jerusalem and later in Galilee is the already-ascended Jesus, who has manifested himself out of heaven. Jesus' primary purpose in departing from them, John says, was to send the Holy Spirit, the comforter, to be with them forever, to lead them into all truth (16:1–15).

As this chapter and the previous one have shown, we can see clearly the progress in the developing supernatural nature of Christ as we follow the evolution of the early Christian scriptures. Paul set the stage for that progress with his movement from his first acclamation that in Christ God was "reconciling the world to himself" (2 Cor. 5:19) to his later interpretation that God had declared Jesus to be God's son, by the Spirit of Holiness, at the time of the resurrection (Rom. 1:1–4). Next Mark declared that God had made Jesus God's son not at the resurrection but at the baptism (Mark 1:1–11). Then Matthew and Luke moved the decisive moment when Jesus was recognized as God to the conception (Matt. 1–2; Luke 1–2). Finally the idea of the enfleshment of the preexistent word or Logos emerged as John's way of portraying the meaning of Jesus' life.

Jesus' humanity faded with each evolutionary step, while his divinity was heightened. His capture by the prevailing God-definition became increasingly accepted. He was God incarnate, man divine, the visiting deity who landed on this planet by virtue of the miracle of virgin birth and who departed from this planet by the miracle of the cosmic ascension. In between he did a series of Godlike things. He was the human form of God as theistically interpreted—that is, God was a being, supernatural in power, living above the sky, periodically invading the world to accomplish the divine will. In Jesus this theistic God lived among us and overcame the fall of the human race.

After completing the supernatural task of rescue, and returning to his external dwelling place with God, Jesus left in place, so the argument went, a structure through which the saving grace of God could continue to work. A hierarchy, beginning with the apostles and coming down through history in valid tactile ordination, in which the apostles' authority was handed over from generation to generation, was established. The authority of this hierarchy guaranteed the infallible truth of the received faith and the valid channels, known as sacraments, through which the theistic God would still act to bring grace to God's people.

After much debate over the first several centuries of Christianity's life, theism's capture of this faith system was made complete. Incarnation was defined. Jesus was the God-Man—perfect in divinity, perfect in humanity. But it was a strange logic that supported this conclusion. How could a human being have the Holy Spirit as his father and still be fully human? How could the pre-existent Logos be enfleshed in Jesus of Nazareth and still be fully human? As doctrine expanded into dogma, these questions were simply ignored. Theism was triumphant. Jesus of Nazareth was clothed with the armor of theism.

As theology developed in the West, Jesus became first the divine Son of God, then the incarnation of the holy God, and finally the second person of the eternal Trinity of three persons in one God. This theistic God still ruled the world, sent the sun and rain, and made invasions to cure a sickness here or lead an army to victory there. If any part of this tightly defined theological system was challenged, excommunication resulted; and if the offense of unbelief was severe enough, death at the stake was demanded, in flames slow enough graciously to allow time for repentance before life was terminated. In the name of security, all doubts were repressed and all ambivalence was denied.

Theism captured Jesus and wrapped him in the garments of supernaturalism. He became the firewall against which the flames of hysteria, born in the trauma of self-consciousness, were banked. He was God in human form. He established the church. He dictated the scriptures. He had the power. He did the miracles. It was a neat system, dogmatically imposed, theistically interpreted, and enormous in power. It managed to still the pain and trauma of self-consciousness and to soothe the shock of nonbeing.

When the church needed to incorporate new truth, it simply proclaimed a new dogma. The pope became infallible in the nineteenth century, in order to buttress the church's flagging authority in the face of the Enlightenment. Mary's virginity was further defined and developed with new proclamations over the centuries. First she became a permanent virgin, which meant that some other explanation had to be developed for Jesus' brother James, mentioned in Galatians, and his brothers James, Joses, Simon, and Judas, as well as his unnamed sisters, mentioned in Mark.

Then Mary became a postpartum virgin—that is, Jesus had been delivered without breaking the sacred hymen. Two biblical texts were advanced to undergird this theological development. In the first, the prophet Ezekiel had said, "This gate shall remain shut; it shall not be opened, and no one shall enter by it, for the Lord, the God of Israel, has entered by it; therefore it shall remain shut" (Ezek. 44:1). In the second, John had told of the resurrected Jesus appearing inside a locked and barred upper room (20:19–23). If the Lord could pass through the closed gates of a city, and the Lord could pass in and out from a locked room, postpartum virginity was no problem; Jesus could also pass through his mother's hymen without rupturing it.

Next Mary was said to have been immaculately conceived, a late-developing doctrine designed to shore up the theological weakness revealed when the world discovered that men were not the only ones who passed on their genetic code to their offspring, meaning that women too passed on the sin of Adam. So for Jesus to be sinless, his mother had to be immaculately conceived. Finally Mary was said to have been bodily assumed into heaven. That strange doctrine was declared in 1950 at the very dawn of the space age.

One wonders how many more defenses must be erected to keep the theistic firewall against hysteria intact. One wonders how long it will be before the whole system shatters. The theistic God-pattern born in human anxiety was not original to Christianity, but it was victorious in Christianity. Can Christianity now throw off theism's chains? So totally has the Christian story been entwined with the theistic definition of God that the collapse of the latter threatens to trigger the collapse of the former.

That is the current dilemma in the Christian church, for theism is dying—perhaps, in fact, it is already dead. Can Christianity then continue to live as theistically understood? I do not think so. But what would a nontheistic Christianity look like? That is the question that lies before the Christian church as the new world dawns.

SEVEN

# CHANGING THE BASIC
# CHRISTIAN MYTH

*Gracious God, when we would make much of that which cannot
matter much to thee, forgive us.*

—RIGHT REV. JOHN ELBRIDGE HINES, presiding bishop of
the Episcopal Church, 1964–1973. Used to open his sermons.

A memorable cartoon, the origins of which have been lost to
me in the passage of time, provides the text for entering the
next phase of this inquiry.

In this cartoon a sophisticated New York urban type in the appropriate Mercedes roadster was parked by a field in a rural setting, staring through his half-glasses at a map. A local resident,
dressed as a rube in bibbed overalls, brogans, a flannel shirt, and a
straw hat, with a bit of hay between his teeth, appeared at the dri-
ver's window. After listening to his urban counterpart try to explain his destination so that he might receive proper directions,

the local, looking quite perplexed, said, "Mister, you just can't get there from here."

Is that the plight, I wonder, of the serious Christian apologist today? Is there no way we can enter the postmodern world of the third millennium wearing the premodern theological clothes of the traditional Christian understandings? If such a way cannot be found, Christianity as we know it is destined to die. But if such a pathway exists, its route is certain to be so circuitous, demanding numerous backtrackings to undo accommodations made to the landscape of a worldview that no longer exists, that many Christians will not recognize the direction traveled as Christian at all. The road these believers in exile[1] will have to travel will look so different that traditionalists will see no continuity. It will be stripped of all those literal things which have given Christianity its primary meaning in the past. The question is thus a good one: Can we get to where we need to go if we must begin from where we are?

We have thus far in this book journeyed at some length through the origins of the Christian story in order to build a base from which to launch this new quest. It is important to document the fact that Christianity, at its inception, was pretheistic and only later and with slow developments was it, along with its Lord, overwhelmed by theistic concepts. That fact rooted in Christianity's past is a crucial insight essential, I am now convinced, to building Christianity's future. The way to accomplish the task of freeing the essential Christian truth from the distortions of yesterday, so that it might live in tomorrow's world, is to return to that original starting place and to begin anew. There is no way I see that will enable us to "get there from here" without a return to our roots.

Clearly there was a profound experience that caused the theistic God-interpretation to be laid upon Jesus. What was it? If we can discover that experience, can we recreate its power or enter it anew? Does anything of value remain in the figure of Jesus once the supernatural context has been stripped away from him? If so, what is it? Can we find a way to assert that the Christ-experience itself is central but that the traditional Christ-explanations are secondary and dismissible? Is that institution called the church, even if it is not eager to do so, capable of giving up all those things in which its claims to power have resided, in order to keep the treasure of its original affirmation that somehow, and in some way, God was in this Christ? These are formidable questions, even fear-inducing questions, but facing them is the absolute requirement of the reformation that is before us.

Unfortunately, the answer to these questions will not be clear until we are well into the process. I can offer no security that will enable seekers to risk this journey with confidence. In fact, the reformation I am proposing *may well kill* Christianity. This is a real and enormous risk. The greater risk which motivates me, however, is the realization that a refusal to enter the reformation *will certainly kill* Christianity. Even though, by traveling the route I am proposing, we may not arrive at a living Christian future, I see no alternative except to begin the journey.

In this chapter, therefore, I shall seek to walk the razor's edge: to remove the interpretations of the ages that have been laid upon Jesus of Nazareth—interpretations requiring that he be viewed as a human manifestation of the theistic deity—but to do so without losing the essence of what I have called the Christ-experience. I will gladly surrender the theistic interpretations of our religious past if I can continue to discover the Christ-experience as a timeless reality, although I am deeply aware that such surrender will eradicate the primary way that Jesus has been traditionally understood throughout Christian history. It will bring hurt and fear to many simple believers—people who, though good and faithful to what they perceive as truth, have nonetheless failed to engage the secular and theological scholarship of the past two hundred years. It will incur the wrath of those who find their faith and, perhaps more important, their power threatened by both my analysis and my proposals.

But if theism is dying, then the theistic overlay that has been placed on Christianity must be shattered. Only when the last shards of that overlay have been removed can we get back to a place where we can begin again. To move forward, I must therefore dismiss the traditional understandings of such doctrinal formulations as the incarnation and the atonement, rejecting them as broken theistic vessels no longer capable of interpreting the original experience. Can I do this, however, without rejecting the meaning that those doctrinal foundations sought to convey? Many people will not see this distinction. I must suggest that these doctrines, which are regarded by Christians as essential and even foundational, are not *wrong*; the problem with them is that as explanatory vehicles they have been rendered inadequate by the explosion of knowledge.

The doctrine of the incarnation, as it has been typically framed, assumes that an external God has been enfleshed in Jesus of Nazareth. This concept was placed by various authors of scripture inside narratives explaining just how it was that this external deity made an entrance into human history. The need for such a clarification explains how the miraculous "doorway" of the virgin birth became part of the Christian story.

But once the theistic God had incarnated the divine presence into human history in this manner, a narrative was also required to provide for this God's exit. For a theistic God, who is by definition external to human life, cannot remain in human history forever. This God invades only for a season or for a particular purpose, so a narrative describing the cosmic ascension of this incarnate deity was developed to serve as the other half of the divine roundtrip ticket.

I have already sought to convey the fact that neither the miraculous entry story nor the miraculous exit story appears to be original to the Christian proclamation. They so obviously represent later developments in the tradition. But now we must face the fact that both of these narratives have also been rendered literally meaningless by new knowledge. I refer not only to knowledge about the scriptures through which we have already journeyed in regard to the birth story, but also to that expansion of human knowledge about how the world operates—historical and scientific knowledge that now makes it impossible for critical-thinking people to entertain either of these concepts any longer.

For example, scholarly research has shown that the dating system employed in these biblical birth stories does not work. Both Matthew (2:1) and Luke (1:5) assert that Jesus was born when Herod was the king of Judea. Luke then goes on to say that the birth occurred when Quirinius was governor of Syria (2:1–8). From secular records, however, we know that Herod died in 4 B.C.E. and that Quirinius did not become governor of Syria until the winter of 6–7 C.E., by which time Jesus would have been ten or eleven years old.

Other details are also contradictory. Matthew believed that the family of Mary and Joseph lived in a house in Bethlehem over which the light of a star could shine (Matt. 2:9). Luke believed that this family lived in Galilee in the town of Nazareth (Luke 2:1–8). Behind this contradiction lie two parts of the early tradition that appear to be irreconcilable. One has to do with the fact that Jesus was called both a Galilean and a Nazarene. The other has to do with the messianic expectation that the promised Christ would be an heir of David and would therefore be born in "the city of David"—that is, Bethlehem of Judea. The obvious Galilean origins of Jesus were, it appears, actually an embarrassment to the early Christians. Nazareth, as a town, was the butt of much coarse humor, some of which is reflected in the gospels. John, for example, observes that "nothing good could come out of Nazareth" (John 1:46).

When birth narratives came into the scriptural tradition, these two conflicting places of origin collided. Each of the two biblical authors of a birth narrative handled the problem in a different way. Luke assumed a Galilean origin for Jesus but then, through the vehicle of the tax enrollment, placed the family in Bethlehem, the city of David, at the time of the holy birth of the Messiah (Luke 2:1–5). Matthew, however, assumed a Bethlehem origin and was therefore required to develop his story in such a way that the young Jesus would move to Nazareth and grow up there, thus accounting for the Galilean part of the narrative of Jesus' life. So Matthew told the story of how Joseph, fearing Herod's brother (who was now in power) and responding to God's instruction in a dream, fled to Galilee and ultimately settled in Nazareth (Matt. 2:19–23).

But as devastating as these bits of knowledge are to the cause of traditional orthodoxy, the deepest problem that the virgin-birth story faces is that it reflects a premodern understanding of the human birth process—an understanding that, because of our expanded knowledge of genetics, biology, and reproduction, educated people today could not possibly believe without closing their minds to vast amounts of data. The early Christians simply did not understand the woman's role in reproduction. They reasoned not from scientific knowledge but from an analogy drawn from their common life. They knew that a farmer planted his seed in the soil of the earth and that Mother Earth nurtured the seed into maturity. This was the analogy that shaped the way the ancient Jews understood human reproduction. The life of any newborn baby was believed to dwell in the seed of the male. The woman's contribution, like that of Mother Earth, was only to provide a nurturing womb. She did not add to the substance of the new life.

Our language up until recently still reflected that mentality. My grandmother used to say, "I've borne my husband's three children," as if she were just a passive receptacle. We still talk this way about racehorses. "The winner of the Kentucky Derby was Secretariat, sired by Bold Ruler," we say, "out of Something Royal [which was the name of the mare]." "Out of" is a phrase that reflects this ancient bit of human ignorance and, I suspect, male prejudice. Given this understanding of reproduction, whenever the mythology of the ancient world wanted to tell the story of a divine origin for a special life, it was not necessary to remove from the equation the human mother, since she added nothing to that life except the warmth of her womb. To assert a divine origin, one had only to replace the human father with some kind of divine agent. Every virgin-birth story—and there were many in the ancient world—made that paternal substitution. In Jesus' case, the male agent was the Holy Spirit.

But in the early years of the eighteenth century, a working hypothesis was finally empirically established: namely, that the woman supplies an egg cell, which contributes fifty percent of the genetic code of every newborn baby. The woman is thus an equal co-creator with the man of every child. From that moment of scientific insight on, the virgin-birth tradition could never again be thought of as producing a divine child in human form. At best this understanding of genetics would produce a strange creature who would be half human and half divine. That is certainly not what the Christian claim has been. Mythology is filled with human-headed, four-legged creatures and with mermaids who have the tail of a fish and the head of a woman. These creatures are considered monsters, neither human nor animal. In like manner, the virgin-birth narrative, literally understood, would produce a creature who was half human and half divine, not one through whose full humanity the fullness of God could be met. A literal virgin birth makes traditional Christology and such concepts as incarnation, literally understood, inoperative.

So the advances in our knowledge of reproduction have obliterated the biological literalness of the miraculous narrative that stands at the front end of the Christian story, to explain how the theistic God entered into human history. That story lies in shambles as a valid explanation of the experience of having met God present in the person of Jesus. It must also be dismissed as literal biology and thus as inappropriate to theology. Not to do so would be to claim that God, theistically understood, miraculously intervened and did a deed that broke all the boundaries of our knowledge of how the universe functions reproductively.

The exit story told on the other side of Jesus' life to explain the theistic departure has fared no better. Realizing that the ascension was not part of the original Christian story, but was woven into the tradition in the ninth decade of the Christian era, is only the first step toward addressing the problems of a literal ascension.

Luke wrote his account of Jesus' ascension against the backdrop of the common conviction that the universe consisted of a three-tiered structure. Heaven, in the mind of first-century people, was located just beyond the sky. It was a sky into which no one in that era had ever flown and out of which people believed that stars literally could fall. To get to heaven, where God dwelt, one simply had to rise, as Jesus did in the ascension story, into the sky. But when Copernicus and Galileo challenged the accuracy of the three-tiered universe, they rendered this possibility null and void.

We have moved far beyond Copernicus and Galileo since their time, but in our transformation to space-age people we have always moved in the direction they set. Our knowledge tells us that the ascension of Jesus, understood literally, is not possible. Indeed, we know today that if one goes up into the sky far enough, one achieves orbit rather than a heavenly destination—or, if one escapes the gravitational pull, one sinks into the incredible depths of a universe so vast that its magnitude cannot be embraced. Neither image—orbit or the desolation of outer space—is spiritually edifying. So the theistic framework surrounding the doctrine of the incarnation on both sides—the divine entry and the divine exit—has become simply inoperative. One wonders how long the doctrine can endure now that all of its underpinnings have been eradicated.

The doctrine of the atonement poses no easier problem. The atonement assumes the accuracy of the primary Christian myth. In this myth God created the world in the beginning. It was complete and perfect. When the creative process was concluded, God pronounced the whole creation to be both finished and good. Then God took a day off and so established the Sabbath. Into that perfect world God placed a perfect man and a perfect woman to live in a perfect Garden of Eden. Then, according to this primary myth, this perfect man and this perfect woman disobeyed God's command and fell into sin, corrupting the whole creation. All human life was hopelessly flawed from then on: human beings were forever after to be punished by death, unable to extricate themselves from the sin into which they had fallen, unable to restore their relationship with God, and unable to save themselves. Even when people finally stopped thinking of Adam and Eve as the literal first man and first woman, it was still said that the Adam and Eve myth captured the essential meaning of human life. We are fallen sinners who are hopelessly lost: this is the definition of human life that underlies the traditional Christian story. It is a strange definition, and ultimately a destructive one.

What would be the effect, we might ask, on an infant's life if that child's parents, seeking to improve their parenting skills, purchased a book on proper childrearing only to read in that book that every day they must inform this child that he or she is a wretched sinner? "You are hopelessly lost," the book might advise telling youngsters; "you are incapable of doing anything about your destiny. You are not even good enough to gather up the crumbs under the family table!" Would that create a healthy adult? Obviously not! Yet that is the message that over the years the people of the church have heard as the "word of God" from pulpits and in prayers, scripture, and hymns.

The early debate in Christian history was about whether the "fall," as embodied in the sin of Adam and Eve, rendered us only partially flawed or meant that we were totally depraved. In either case, the theistic God had to assume the role of rescuing savior and redeemer if this problem was to be solved. Those were the presuppositions that lay behind the traditional doctrine of the atonement, which proposes that God entered human life in the person of Jesus to rescue fallen sinners. The fallen ones that Jesus came to save were, however, not impressed, the story tells us, by this offer, and so they arrested him and crucified him. "He came to his own home and his own people received him not" is the way John's gospel describes it (1:11). Thus Jesus became the designated victim for the sins of fallen men and women. He absorbed their evil, accepted their punishment, paid the price of their sin, and triumphed over the pain of death in his resurrection.

It was through that process that humanity was restored to its state of original goodness, recreating the broken image of God and enabling us to become once more the persons that God had first intended us human beings to be in the good creation. That was the interpretive myth on which Christianity was built.

The church that was then said to have been established by this Jesus proceeded to proclaim the good news of salvation in Christ Jesus and in time to organize its life so that each newborn baby could receive baptism in infancy, in order to cleanse that child from the stain of the original sin that marked all human life. Baptism brought the child into Jesus' redemptive act. Not to be baptized was thus to be hopelessly lost forever.

Then the church shaped its primary liturgical act to be one that recreated the story of Jesus' sacrifice on the cross—a sacrifice that paid the price required by sin and thus enabled people in every generation to appropriate for themselves the salvation wrought by Christ. That liturgy was referred to as "the sacrifice of the mass" or "the eucharist," a term meaning the act of thanksgiving for the saving act of redemption. Christians have thus gathered throughout the ages at the supper of the Lord not just to recall but also to enter this timeless sacrificial meaning of the cross.

The problems with this understanding of atonement are mani-

"WE'VE GONE BEYOND THAT"

fold. First, if it is treated as an accurate portrayal of the human situation—and it is, in Christian churches around the world—it presents us with a strange image of God. This is a deity who acts like a Middle Eastern potentate who cannot forgive until his offended dignity has been satisfied. This deity cannot be moved to embrace God's fallen creatures without the sacrifice of a human being: the blood offering that Jesus willingly provided. To have the story of salvation depend on a divinely required human sacrifice sounds quite strange to modern ears.

Second, this liturgical interpretation of Jesus' death has resulted in a fetish in Christianity connected with the saving blood of Jesus. In the evangelical Protestant segments of the church, hymns are addressed to the wondrous therapeutic character of Jesus' blood. Believers sing of being "washed in the blood" or "saved by the blood" of Jesus. They even sing of "a fountain filled with blood" that Jesus provided, in which they can bathe until their sins are completely removed. I have always found these images to be repulsive.

The Catholic side of the Christian church is perhaps a bit more sophisticated, but no less grotesque in its imagery. In this tradition worshipers participate in Jesus' sacrifice sacramentally by literally eating his flesh and drinking his blood. Thinly disguised liturgical cannibalism is not particularly appealing to this generation either.

The deepest problem created for the doctrine of the atonement, however, is not even this, but the fact that we are post-Darwinian men and women. As post-Darwinians we are in possession of a very different image of the origins of human life; and it is quite obvious that the Darwinian view, not the traditional Christian myth, has prevailed in the life of our civilization.

The Darwinian view says that there never was a perfect and completed creation. The universe is not yet finished. It is still evolving and still expanding. New galaxies continue to be formed. The post-Darwinian world also recognizes that there never was a perfect man or a perfect woman who fell into sin in an act of disobedience. That account is not true either historically or metaphorically. Human beings are *emerging* creatures; they are a work in progress. Neither perfect nor fallen, they are simply *incomplete*. HeResy Does It

These creatures certainly do not need to be rescued by a human sacrifice or saved from a fall that never occurred even mythologically. They cannot be restored to something they have never been. Human beings need rather to be empowered to enter into and to grasp the fullness of their humanity. They need the means to journey beyond their traditional limits. Homo sapiens are the winners of the evolutionary struggle. Our humanity was shaped not by a mythical fall but by a very real battle for survival. We have survived our biological history by our wits and our radical self-centeredness.

The evil we human beings seem prone to do is not a commentary on our fallen nature; it is a manifestation of our dedication to put ourselves first, for that is what our evolutionary history has required of us. So the atoning sacrifice of Jesus on the cross is a divine cure for a human problem that a previous understanding of life postulated but that, from our contemporary perspective, does not now exist, and never did.

Where does that leave us? Since the diagnosis (sinful human nature) was wrong, the prescribed cure (atonement) cannot be right. When that fact is grasped, the entire sacramental and ecclesiastical superstructure, which was based upon a false diagnosis, begins to collapse. Baptism as a sacrament designed to wash away the effects of a fall into sin that never occurred is inappropriate. The eucharist as the reenactment of a sacrifice designed to restore human life to something we have never been becomes theological nonsense. The very lifeline of meaning found in both of these traditional Christian symbols has been severed.

This drives us to what is for traditional believers a devastating realization—namely, that the primary creedal doctrines of the Christian faith were built to address a human condition that is

✱ NOT ONLY SIN — WELCOME

simply not true. There was no good creation followed by a fall into sin that required a divine rescue. There was and is only emerging life, seeking to survive at any cost and yearning to be called beyond its limits into being something more.

What becomes obvious is that these creedal doctrines have captured the life of Jesus inside the symbols of a dying theism. The external God who invaded human history to rescue the fallen sinner, to restore that sinner to God's original purpose in creation, no longer makes contact with the reality of human experience. This discontinuity between the traditional Christian message and the world in which that message is proclaimed is widely recognized today, at least subconsciously. We see it in the unwillingness of the fundamentalist churches to do anything more than to sing their old, old songs louder and louder and to become more and more shrill in attacking all those "secular humanists" who no longer can salute their irrelevant concepts. But their very hysteria reveals their subconscious recognition that the values they espouse are not holding; and when the shouting dies down, the fundamentalist ships will also sink into the vast waters of modernity.

We see this same discontinuity in the rapid decline of the mainline churches, which today might better be called "the sideline churches."[2] Members of these congregations feel the dissonance between what they assume to be true about life and what they hear in their churches, but they do not know how to address that dissonance appropriately. So these churches either avoid the issues or seek other reasons for existence. If that fails they simply whimper their way into oblivion. That is the fate of many congregations today. Most churches will die of boredom long before they die of controversy. They are unwilling to risk death in order to engage the search for truth.

Their demise is seen in the fact that there is an apparent widespread spiritual yearning and hunger abroad in the world at this moment. At the same time, there is an increasing unwillingness on the part of those who still seek after God to think that the institutional Christian church can continue to be a place in which they might appropriately do their seeking. For vast numbers of modern people, including modern religious people, the church is less and less an option.

So Christianity stands today on this boundary. To continue to do what we have always done in the past is to fail to recognize that premodern symbols do not work in a postmodern world. To do nothing is to vote for death. To seek a new way, a totally different way to tell the Christ-story—if it *can* be told in a new way—is our only option. The Christian church thus stands in the early years of this new millennium on the threshold of either extinction or a radically new beginning. No other alternative presents itself as a possibility.

That, in the briefest thumbnail of sketches, is the problem faced today by the Christian church. The vision is so grim that it is no wonder people either recoil from it or actively refuse to gaze at it. It requires that those of us who are Christians place our theistic interpretations of God, Christ, and human life into either the dustbins of our present world or, perhaps more properly, the museums of antiquity as the *first* step toward a radical reformation.

Despite the fact that many will find even this first step so threatening as to be impossible, time will demonstrate that it is only the beginning. The reformation will finally require a restatement in new thought-categories of everything we have ever believed. The success of this reformation will lie in our ability to rescue Jesus from theism without destroying the power of the meaning that was found in his life—a meaning that people understood to be in some way "of God." Once that separation of theistic explanations from the primary Christ-experience has been made, we will be able to ask the questions that might well lead us to a new place—questions such as, Who or what is God? Who is Jesus that Paul could say that God was in him? Who is

God and who is Jesus that early Christians could assert that God had united God's self with this Jesus in a number of ways?

It is not the variety of the ancient explanations that troubles or captivates us today. We know that *all* explanations become inoperative in time. It is the experience that demanded these explanations in the first place that now begs for reexamination. What does it mean to have a God-experience? What was the Christ-experience for the disciples and others who knew Jesus? How can you and I touch it, appropriate it, and enter it today, two thousand years later?

If you have been willing to walk with me to this place, then perhaps you might be ready to take the next step. We must be able to move beyond what we have traditionally said that Jesus is. That now becomes our task.

"Sometimes, a person has to go a long distance out of the way in order to come back a short distance, correctly."

Zoo Story by
Edward Albee

# EIGHT

# JESUS BEYOND INCARNATION:
# A NONTHEISTIC DIVINITY

*Love your enemies is probably the most radical thing Jesus ever said, unless of course one considers the parable of the Samaritan. There the admonition is to let your enemies love you.*[1]

— ROBERT W. FUNK, director of the Jesus Seminar

J esus.

How sweet that name sounds in a believer's ear, one of our hymns proclaims. When I was consecrated to be a bishop in 1976, we entered the cathedral singing the words, "At the name of Jesus, every knee shall bow."

I cannot remember a time when Jesus was not important to me. I was baptized as an infant, acquiring in the process people called godparents who seemed serendipitous to me. I took great delight in going to Sunday school, where I could learn about this Jesus. I sang in a boys' choir, served as an acolyte, and was active in my youth group, because the adults in my life said Jesus was present in all of these activities. As a child I wore around my neck a cross. It was his symbol, I was told, which marked me as "His" person.

In my adult life my stated intention has been to serve this Jesus. I have studied him, written about him, and preached on him. I have probed his life, his meaning, and his power in lectures and books. I do not come to this task of seeking to redefine Jesus easily or lightly. He has always been a part of my life, as the central figure in my faith-story. So it is certainly fair to say that as I approach this subject, I am not an objective bystander. Jesus has been far too important to my life's journey for me to claim that. Indeed, he still is.

Yet I must for my own integrity's sake seek to answer the question which the New Testament suggests that Jesus posed: "Who do you say that I am?" Peter is said to have answered, "You are the Christ, the son of the living God" (Matt. 16:15–16). Is it still possible for me to use these same words? How flexible are they? How open to new meanings? If they are locked into their theistic past, into the meanings by which they have been traditionally understood, then I must set them aside as no longer meaningful.

Is it honest to wrench these words out of that past and to open them to new meanings? I believe that it is. Words change. Perceptions of reality, and even of God, change. Explanations warp truth with the passage of time. So the real question I have to answer is whether I can capture the essence of this Jesus in words that transcend the patterns of yesterday and yet will still be able to affirm, and to invite my world to affirm, the Christ-experience. To put it bluntly, with theism no longer a concept I can salute, can this Jesus still be a God-experience for me? Can he still be for me a doorway into and an expression of the holy? The answers to these questions will determine, quite frankly, whether what I am seeking is a genuine reformation of Christianity or whether I am deluded and in my suppressed fear attempting to hide from or to cover up the death of Christianity. The stakes are thus quite obviously high as I begin this chapter.

If theism is no more, then can the name of Jesus remain sweet in a believer's ear, causing our knees to bend in adoration? If we can no longer with any meaning speak of Jesus as the literal incarnation of the theistic deity or as the literal second person of a divine Trinity, then what can we say of him that is real and that still connects him with the experience that lies beneath these traditional Christian claims? What other words can we use that will enable us to join with Paul in his ecstatic cry: "God was in Christ."

When I begin to explore the life of this Jesus apart from the theistic framework of the Christian past, I am energized and even enchanted as a whole new vision emerges. What I see is a new portrait of Jesus. He is one who was more deeply and fully alive than anyone else I have ever encountered, whether in my lifetime, in history, or in literature. I see him pointing to something he calls the realm (or kingdom) of God, where new possibilities demand to be considered.[2] I see him portrayed as one who was constantly dismantling the barriers that separate people from one another. I see him inviting his followers to join with him, to walk without fear beyond those security boundaries that always prohibit, block, or deny our access to a deeper humanity. Perhaps above all else he is for me a boundary-breaker who enables me to envision the possibility of my own humanity breaking through my human barriers to reach the divinity that his life reveals, indeed that we Christians claim he possesses.

I see Jesus as one who is calling those around him to walk past their tribal fears. In Jesus' day the Jewish people had organized their lives to have as little social contact with Gentiles as possible. That barrier was enormous. The Jews marked themselves as separate from Gentiles through Torah-mandated circumcision and kosher dietary laws. Their separate status was thus assumed to be ordered by God. Yet Jesus is portrayed as inviting people to put their tribal and xenophobic fears aside and to step across this boundary. A new humanity lives on the other side of those fears, he seems to say. I listen to his earliest followers, such as Paul, who, inspired by this Jesus, pronounced that in Christ "there is neither Jew nor Greek" (Gal. 3:28). I note that the author of the first gospel to be written, Mark, has the audacity to place a Gentile centurion at the foot of the cross to interpret the meaning of this life by saying, "Truly this man was the son of God" (15:39). I read Matthew, the most Jewish gospel of all, and listen as he begins his story of Jesus by placing a star in the heavens where it is visible to all the people of the world, obviously including the Gentiles. That star is then said to draw the Gentile world, in the persons of the magi, to come to pay homage to a universal Christ (Matt. 2:2). I can now see with new eyes the power present when this same Matthew, at the conclusion of his story, has the risen Christ say only one thing to his disciples. It is the words we call "the great commission": "Go into all the world"—that is, go to where the Gentiles live—and proclaim God's love for them (28:19). Christianity was clearly, at its origins, designed and intended to be a radical, transforming, boundary-breaking religious system, built on a gospel message identified with Jesus and proclaimed ecstatically through the very being of his life. In the Christ-experience Jew and Gentile could no longer be set against each other. Nor could any other tribal boundary continue to limit anyone's humanity.

Luke, who was probably born a Gentile, though as a Gentile proselyte to Judaism, he surely worshiped in a synagogue for enough years that Jewish liturgical patterns shaped his life, continued to develop this boundary-crossing universality. I refer to the fact that Luke significantly altered the genealogy of Jesus presented in Matthew because that genealogy went back only to Abraham, the father of the Jewish nation. Luke wanted the whole world to be included in his symbols, so he carried his genealogy back to Adam, the symbolic father of the entire human race. His clear message was that the Gentiles are also part of the plan of salvation. Then Luke proceeded to tell the story of how the

Christian movement journeyed from Galilee to Jerusalem to Rome—that is, from the fringes to the heart of the Jewish world, and then beyond that formidable barrier to the very center of the Gentile world. It was and is a radical message. It is no wonder that Jesus provoked the hostility that led to his death since it was clear that he would not allow this vision to be compromised.

Tribal boundaries are powerful dividers of human life. They are the source of some of humanity's most inhumane behavior. Yet in the biblical portrait of Jesus we see him relativizing those dividing lines and calling people to enter the experience of non-tribal humanity. I believe that this is a major step beyond our evolutionary security system, reflecting a call to become that which we human beings have not yet ever been. It is an invitation to enter the "New Being" about which Tillich speaks—a humanity without barriers, a humanity without the defensive claims of tribal fear, a transformed humanity so full and so free that God is perceived to be present within it.

The Bible also portrays Jesus as one who is journeying beyond the barriers of human prejudice. The ultimate symbol of prejudice in first-century Judaism was the Samaritan. The Jews' self-identity and security were invested in the idea that they were pure-blooded, true believers. In their eyes the Samaritans were half-breed heretics, worthy only of being despised. In Jesus' day prejudice against Samaritans had reached the deeply emotional level of visceral loathing. When Jewish pilgrims traveled from Galilee to Jerusalem, they would extend this journey, and their own discomfort, in an acting-out of that prejudice. Crossing the Jordan River to the east, they would travel through the desert, and then recross the Jordan River to enter Jerusalem—all so that they might avoid breathing Samaritan air on their trip.

Prejudices bind human life in such a way as to diminish our humanity. The more prejudiced we are, the less human we are. Prejudice is thus a survival technique required by the self-centeredness of our response to the insecurity of self-consciousness. Yet Jesus is portrayed in the gospels as relativizing this abiding negative passion. Luke tells the story of a Samaritan, one of ten lepers whom Jesus healed, who had the spiritual discernment to know from whom this healing came and to return to acknowledge with gratitude that source of life (Luke 17:16). To make the point of the story even more pronounced, the other lepers—presumably true, believing Jews—did not look back. It was a challenging narrative, not likely to be well received by those listening.

In the parable of the Good Samaritan, the gospel writer has Jesus tell of a man journeying from Jerusalem to Jericho who fell among thieves who left him battered, bleeding, and perhaps unconscious on the side of the road. The Torah, the law of God by which the Jews pledged themselves to live, demanded that human need must take priority over every other concern. Yet in this story, say Jesus, a Levite, a recognized official in Temple worship who was surely cognizant of the requirements of the law to show compassion to those in need, passes by on the other side of the road, ignoring the wounded man. Next comes a priest, a holy man of Israel, ordained, if you will, after becoming proficient in the study of the Torah. He too sees the victim. Perhaps justifying his behavior in typical ordained fashion by countering the text calling for compassion with another text that prohibited one from touching the flesh of a dead man, he refuses even to stop long enough to investigate and passes by on the other side of the road. Then, says Jesus, a half-breed heretic journeys along that way. He is one not schooled in the law and so is perhaps ignorant of the Torah's demands. But he sees a human being in need, and he responds immediately. Going to the wounded man, he pours oil in his wounds and binds them up. He then gives the victim wine and water to drink and takes him on his own donkey to an inn, where he arranges to pay for his continued care and lodging until the healing process is complete.

This story means, says Jesus in his dramatic conclusion, that the one who does what the Torah requires is more deeply a child of Abraham than either the Levite or the priest who, though out-wardly people of religious conviction, did not place meeting human need above every other consideration. Jesus turned the values of his day, by which people lived, upside down. That para-ble was a challenge to the defining prejudice in first-century Ju-daism, and it invited people to step beyond their distorting prejudices, whatever they were, into a new definition of human-ity, a humanity that no longer needed a victim to abuse in order to affirm one's sense of self-worth. Jesus painted a portrait of a new humanity and invited people to step into it. It was a human-ity that emerges beyond the boundaries of our prejudice.

In these stories, through which these ancient writers struggled to capture the meaning of the Christ-experience, Jesus is shown as a God-presence that calls those of us who would be his follow-ers to become more fully human by opening the dark crevices of our souls where our prejudices hide, the place to which we have assigned the Samaritans of our day. Every one of us carries a defining prejudice in our heart of hearts. It may be attached for some of us to those people whose skin color is different from our own, for others to those who worship God in ways we think strange, for still others to those whose sexual orientation is not like ours or even not like the majority. To be Jesus' disciples we are forced to heed his call to surrender all of our killing stereo-types based on external differences and to walk beyond all of our distorting fears into a new prejudice-free humanity. It is another form of the invitation to enter Paul Tillich's "New Being," to enter a humanity without barriers, a humanity without the dis-torting chains of human prejudice.

The portrayal of Jesus' life in the gospels seems also to call those who would be his disciples to put aside all gender and sexual dis-tinctions. His challenge to us all is to see humanity first, and then to watch all differences, such as male and female, gay and straight, white and of color, become only categories into which humanity is divided. These divisions do not reflect brokenness and sin, as our rhetoric of the past has always suggested, but rather the incredible richness of what being fully human means. The portrait of Jesus drawn by the biblical writers shows him violating the sexual boundaries of his day, not once but time after time. John's gospel, for example, says that Jesus engaged the woman at the well in a significant liturgical and theological discussion (4:7–30), even though Jewish males did not converse with women in a public place. Jesus clearly had women disciples, led by the intrepid Magdalene, who was obviously a key person in the Jesus movement, despite the church's later historical trashing of her reputation by turning her into a prostitute without a shred of evidence to support this act of character assassination. That was nothing but a dramatic patriarchal attempt to suppress her flesh-and-blood presence in Jesus' life as a reading of the appropriate biblical texts will affirm.[3]

It also needs to be clearly stated that, despite the homophobic caterwauling that goes on inside the Christian church today, Jesus never said a word in any gospel about homosexuality. This is why no gospel texts can be quoted in this current arena of ecclesiastical debate. Yet the record of this Jesus for standing at the side of marginalized members of his society or the victims of sexual prejudice is clear. If he had had the knowledge that we have today about the nature and origin of homosexuality, there is no doubt where he would have stood or on which side the loving Jesus of Nazareth would have come down. Prejudice, based on either a sense of gender superiority or on differences in sexual orientation, is one more barrier to a full humanity. Jesus steps across that barrier as readily as he does all others. He calls us once more to a new being, to enter a humanity without barriers, without the defensive stereotypes we apply to issues of human sexuality. He is a God-presence who relativizes every barrier that blocks our wholeness and thus our ability to be God-bearers to others.

The biblical portrait drawn of Jesus even calls and empowers his followers to walk beyond our religious differences—differences in which we have consistently and falsely invested something of the ultimacy of God. Beyond these differences we are challenged to cease thinking of people as ritualistically clean or unclean, baptized or unbaptized, right or wrong, orthodox or heterodox, Christian, Jew, Muslim, Buddhist, or Hindu. Jesus' life is portrayed as reaching out again and again to those whom his own religious system rejected. He embraced the lepers whose rotting flesh was condemned as untouchable by his religious tradition. He allowed the touch of the woman with the chronic menstrual discharge who, by the religious laws of his tradition, was declared to be both corrupting and unclean. He set aside the Sabbath-day regimen when it conflicted with human need. He called Levi Matthew, a Jew who worked for the Romans as a tax-collector and was therefore unclean according to Jewish ritual law, to be one of his intimate Twelve. He refused to condemn the woman taken in adultery, as the Torah dictated.

All people seek the path of wholeness into a new humanity. That was the message of Jesus. To empower people to enter into and to grasp that wholeness and to become that new humanity was his apparent purpose.

Jesus understood, as all of us must sooner or later, that God cannot be bound by the limits of our religious systems. When we claim an ultimate truth for our version of God, our revelation, our church, our source of authority, or even our ecclesiastical leaders, we have in fact built another defensive wall around our insecurity. The God beyond theism cannot be bound by human creeds. That realization will enable us to walk into an ecumenical future that will be so dramatically different as to be breathtaking. We will be enabled to see the Ground of Being in Moses, Mohammed, Buddha, and Krishna, as well as in Jesus. This will not be a new version of Baha'i, as noble as that attempt to get beyond religious boundaries is. It will rather be a step beyond every religious symbol. Jesus will become the doorway into the holy for those of us who have been privileged to know his name, but there will be other doorways for other people. The God who is the Ground of Being cannot be bound, not even by our religious claims. Once that is understood, then it becomes apparent that none of us should denigrate the doorways through which others journey in their quest to enter the holy God. Jesus was and is a God-presence through whom we enter the realm of the divine, a realm that transcends every religious boundary.

Jesus understood that the call of every human being is not just to survive but to journey into both the fullness of one's own humanity and into the mystery of God. What most of us do not seem to embrace is that these two journeys are simultaneous, even identical journeys. When, I wonder, will we learn that it is not the road we individually travel, but the destination we seek, that is crucial? To suggest otherwise is to continue to play outdated religious games.

So look with me for just a moment at this Jesus who stands at the center of my faith-tradition. But look with eyes no longer blinded by the theistic patterns of the past—and glimpse a new vision, beyond the theistic patterns we once used to describe him but not beyond a new understanding of divinity.

This human Jesus seems to possess his life so totally that he can give it away without fear. The freedom that marks this man becomes so frightening to those who are not free—and who cannot admit that they are not free—that they rise up in anger to destroy the life-giver. The cross, to me, stands for this destruction, which still goes on in religious disputes. The cross does not represent a sacrifice required by a blood-seeking deity; it rather reveals the ultimate portrait of the threatening power of love that is present in the life of this victim. Even when Jesus walked what later came to be called "the way of the cross," and even when the threat of death became the reality of death, still the bearer of this gift of life discovered that nothing could finally destroy the life he possessed. As this Jesus succumbed to the power of those who could not abide his call to enter "the new being," to grasp a new and radical sense of freedom, he still was able to give his life away. The gospel picture drawn of Jesus portrays him as giving life to others even as he died.

Life cannot be given away until life has been possessed. Yet when life is given away freely and totally, the one who does the giving is not diminished. Indeed, the giving, as depicted in the portrait of Jesus, actually resulted in the explosion of a new and radically different humanity in a world that was still tied to the survival mentality of our evolutionary past. We perceive something new in this Jesus-story, something profoundly moving. As this power touches us, creating new life in us, we are driven to say, "God was in that life," and we stare at this source, this revelation, this God-presence, this Jesus, with a kind of joy and wonder. Jesus thus first reveals the source of life, and then he empowers us to enter it.

Next we observe that there is something expansive and creative about the presence of the boundary-breaking love that we meet in the life of Jesus. When we human beings know love, we seem to grow. Love is present in embryonic forms in all aspects of life. It is seen when subhuman species of life guard the hiding places of their young, when the tongue of the adult feline creature washes the fur of the kitten, when the bird flies forth to gather food for the helpless occupants of the nest, or when two turtledoves couple in a lifelong union. But this kind of life-giving love is even more profoundly seen in the human experience, where it can be entered self-consciously, chosen freely, and appropriated fully. The absence of love in the infancy of the human offspring is as lethal as the presence of a fatal disease. The presence of love is the source of both life and growth.

Love is manifested in the human willingness to venture beyond the boundaries of safety, to risk losing ourselves, and even in the desire to explore the crevices of the unknown. Love creates stability, but not stagnation. Love calls us into being; it expands our lives as it flows through us. If love is ever blocked, it dies. Love has to be shared, or it ceases to be love. Love binds us into larger and larger communities. Love frees us from the pejorative definitions that result in exclusion. Love transcends barriers, unites, and calls. Love enhances life.

So when a human being appears in history with a greater ability to love than we have ever knowingly witnessed before, when this life calls us into a new human unity and refuses to be bound by the rules that rise out of our incompleteness and our fear, then we inevitably look at that life with awe, perhaps even with worship. Love is a presence and power that calls us out of tribal fears for it embraces Jew and Gentile, and out of prejudice-spawning fears for it embraces whoever is our Samaritan. Love has no chosen people, for that implies that some are unchosen. Love bears no malice, seeks no revenge, guards no doorway.

A life defined by love will not seek to protect itself or to justify itself. It will be content simply to be itself and to give itself away with abandon. If denied, love embraces the denier. If betrayed, love embraces the betrayer. If forsaken, love embraces the forsaker. If tortured, love embraces the torturer. If crucified, love embraces the killers. Love never judges. Love simply announces that neither the person you are nor the deeds you have done have erected a barrier which the power of this invincible presence cannot overcome.

If life is holy and if love creates and enhances life, then love is also holy. So I am led to suggest that love and God cannot be separated and that to share love is nothing less than sharing God. For one to abide in love is to abide in God, for one to give love away is to give God away. That is why when one sees a life that loves wastefully, it is said of that person, "God was in that life." That is part of what a nontheistic but still God-centered Jesus means to me.

Love touches something external. When we enter love, we find ourselves caught up in its power. Love lifts us beyond our quest for survival. Love enables us to transcend our limits. Love frees us to give ourselves away.

What human life needs is not a divine rescue. What we need is rather a life so open, so free, so whole, and so loving that when we experience that life, we are called into the reality of love. We are opened to the source of love and enter the empowering presence of love. Such a life then becomes our doorway into the infinite and inexhaustible power of love. I call that love God. I see it in Jesus of Nazareth, and I find myself called into a new being, a boundary-free humanity, and made whole in its presence. So God was in Christ, I say. Jesus thus reveals the source of love, and then he calls us to enter it.

Next, I am forced to recognize that life and love are both manifestations of something that I can only call by that Tillichian word, *being*. Neither life nor love exists apart from being. Being is a strange concept to grasp, so our vocabulary struggles. We talk about a person who has "presence." We cannot define that concept precisely, but we know that it is the opposite of "absence" yet we never say that a person has "absence." We respond positively to the recruiting advertisement of the United States Army because it touches something deep within us: "Be all that you can be. Join the Army." We have immortalized Shakespeare's phrase in which Hamlet conducts his inner debate: "To be or not to be."

Being is a quality we recognize when we see it, and we know its absence when we experience it. We speak about the need for political figures to "define themselves," to project their essential being. When one possesses his or her "being," that person has freedom. "The courage to be" is what Paul Tillich called that freedom.[4] A person who has "the courage to be" is neither enhanced by praise nor diminished by criticism. Being is not something one does. Being is something one is.

So when the human life that we call Jesus enters history—one who appears to possess Being itself—that person is first thought of as memorable. That person, we say, possesses something of great power. When the being of that person is so real that he enhances the being of those around him, then that person is seen as an enabler of life, a source of being for others. Being is always beyond the person who manifests it. It does not originate in any of us; it simply flows through us. It is a gift that comes from beyond ourselves; it is not our possession. Like life, it is found in all the created order. We are rooted in it, grounded in it, recipients of it, bearers of it to others. It relates us beyond ourselves to that which philosophers and theologians through the ages have called the Ground of Being. Following Tillich's lead I use that phrase as another name for God, a God thought of not as a person, but as the source of personhood, the God defined in the book of Acts, in a quotation attributed to the apostle Paul, as that presence or power in which "we live and move, and have our being" (17:28).

Just as I have come to see life and love in Jesus of Nazareth, so now I also see this being in him. I see it when the crowds shouted their hosannas and threw down leafy branches to welcome him to Jerusalem (Mark 11:1–11). There was enormous adulation in that scene; and human praise is a seductive power, a sweet narcotic, almost irresistible to most human beings, including most public figures. But Jesus knew himself. Jesus possessed his being so deeply that his head was not turned and his being was not compromised, even by the praise of the people.

I also see this being in Jesus of Nazareth when he was the victim of crucifixion. When people are unfairly treated, when their lives are being taken away from them brutally and unjustly, the need to survive almost always overwhelms everything else. The typical human response in those circumstances is to plead, to beg, to fight, to weep, to whine, or to curse—whichever response seems to offer some chance of survival. But look once again at the picture of Jesus that greets us in the gospel narratives. There is no clinging to life in that portrait. Instead, we are presented with one whose being is so deeply affirmed that he can give it away freely. He can submit to his outrageous fortune. He can expend his energy in the act of affirming the being of others. To those who per-

HAMLET

petrated the crime upon this Jesus, he is said to have given the gift
of forgiveness (Luke 23:24). To those who shared his fate, he is
said to have given the gift of assurance (Luke 23:39–43). To those
who grieved for themselves at his loss, he is said to have given the
gift of comfort (Luke 23:28–31). To his enemies, those who re-
joiced in his demise, he is said to have given the gift not of resis-
tance, but of quiet resignation (Luke 23:46).

Does it matter whether these are literally accurate photographs
of exactly what occurred on those days between what we later
named Palm Sunday and Good Friday? I do not think so. Indeed,
I argued in an earlier book[5] that even the story of Jesus' passion
from Palm Sunday to the cross was not literal history, but a
midrashic attempt to narrate the drama of Jesus' crucifixion
against the background of such texts as Zechariah 9–14, Psalm 22,
and Isaiah 53. These holy week stories are interpretive history and
liturgical retelling, not eyewitness memories. The gospel writers
are painting a portrait, not using a camera. They are seeking
to capture in their interpretive stories the essence of the being
of this Jesus.

The being in Jesus called those around him into a new and
deeper selfhood. Those who denied him were called into leadership. Cowards who forsook him and fled were called into heroism.
Jews, trapped in their clannishness, were called into inclusiveness.
Women were called into full humanity and full discipleship. Fearful people were called into courageous living. Outcasts were called
into human dignity. Jesus thus reveals the Ground of Being, and
then he calls us to enter it.

I come, therefore, to a new way to speak of this Christ. Please
read carefully and attend closely. Religious words are often misunderstood, because they elicit powerful emotions. I want to
walk a fine line of theological distinction—perhaps even more
important, a fine line of perception and truth.

Is it proper to identify the human Jesus with the Ground of
Being? No. That is not the way I would say it. But one does, I

believe, perceive the Ground of Being through this Jesus. Can Jesus be called the Source of Life? No. I would never make that identification either. But one does, I believe, touch the very depths of life through this Jesus. Is Jesus the ultimate Source of Love? No. I cannot make that claim. But one does, I believe, experience the unconditional quality of love through him. Is the medium, then, the message? No. That, I believe, is to assert more than we should. But the medium is the channel through which the message is received. Jesus is the word of God, not God. That is the argument of the Fourth Gospel's writer, thought to be the evangelist who most powerfully makes the divine claim for Jesus.

But experientially, please let it be noted, there is no essential difference between God and God's word, or between the Ground of Being and Jesus' being, the Source of Love and Jesus' love, the Source of Life and Jesus' life. So in the ecstasy of the Christ-experience, in the transformation and expansion of our humanity, in the moment when love calls us beyond every barrier that has been designed to protect and therefore to thwart our humanity, we first listen to the question posed so long ago, "Who do you say that I am?" Then we respond with new understanding even using the words of antiquity: "You are the Christ, the Son of the living God" (Matt. 16:18). Then we can assert with the Fourth Gospel that those of us who have seen Jesus have also seen God (John 7:09). Finally we can assert that the one we call God, defined theistically in ages past and understood in our patriarchal tradition and prejudices as the creating Father, and the ultimate meaning found in this Jesus are one and the same reality. So we can listen anew as Jesus is heard to say, "I and the Father are One" (John 10:30).

May I suggest that this conclusion, if properly understood, is powerfully orthodox in its essence though it is a long way from the old mythology. It no longer defines God as an external supernatural being who was incarnated into the human Jesus through a miraculous birth. It no longer portrays Jesus as one who did extraordinary things that only God was thought able to do, including walking physically out of his tomb alive three days after death and defying gravity to return to his celestial home in a cosmic ascension after his work was complete. We can set aside once and for all this dying theistic framework without having to abandon the experience that created it. Our hope for reformation and new life lies in that simple distinction.

God is the Source of Life who is worshiped when we live fully. God is the Source of Love who is worshiped when we love wastefully. God is the Ground of Being who is worshiped when we have the courage to be. Jesus is a God-presence, a doorway, an open channel. The fullness of his life reveals the Source of Life, the wastefulness of his love reveals the Source of Love, and the being of his life reveals the Ground of All Being. That is why Jesus continues to stand at the heart of my religious life. That is also why I continue to call him "my Lord" and to call myself a Christian. But I am a Christian who can no longer live inside the exclusive claims of my traditional theistic past.

Let me stretch the boundaries once more. To the extent that the Buddha, Moses, Elijah, Isaiah, Krishna, Mohammed, Confucius, Julian of Norwich, Catherine of Genoa, Hildegard of Bingen, Rosa Parks, Florence Nightingale, Mahatma Gandhi, Martin Buber, Thich Nhat Hahn, Dag Hammarskjöld, or any other holy person brings life, love, and being to another, then to that degree that person is to me the word of God incarnate. No fence can be placed around the Being of God. The suggestion that Jesus is of a different kind of substance and therefore different from every other human being in kind instead of in degree will ultimately have to be abandoned. Then the realization will surely begin to dawn that to perceive Jesus as different from others only in degree is to open all people to the divine potential found in the Christ-figure. It is to invite all people to step into the power of living fully, loving wastefully, and having the courage to be all that any one of us can be—a self whole,

*[handwritten marginal note: "Bad word"]*

*[handwritten marginal note: "QUALITY"]*

free, real, and expanding, a participant in a humanity without boundaries.

Then religious people will have a way, even a means to honor the holy lives in every tradition, for in those lives life is seen, love is experienced, and being is enhanced. Therefore, the presence of God as the source of life, the source of love, and the ground of being can be seen, noted, and honored in them, though we will have to expand that symbol beyond the limits that we now recognize in our own religious tradition. We will then learn to welcome and even to celebrate those differences without allowing them to become ultimate or seeing them as boundaries. Jesus will always be for me the standard by which I measure the God-presence of any other. I can view him in no other way. In that sense, and in that sense only, he remains for me the way, the truth, and the life, the doorway through which I enter the holiness of God. The God I worship will be, however, available from many doorways. For me to claim otherwise is to remain a victim of theism. The God who is life, love, and being itself cannot be bounded by the limits of my tradition. God is beyond Jesus, but Jesus participated in the Being of God, and Jesus is my way into God. These are the claims that will be part of the Christianity of tomorrow. I am hopeful that such a Christianity can be born and that with it an invitation can be offered to all people to step into their own humanity so deeply that they will find it a doorway into God. For that is what the church of the future must proclaim if it wants to live and, I believe, if it wants to be true to the God met in the person of Jesus.

"WAY: NORM FOR FORM"
JACK HIRSCHMAN

# NINE

# ORIGINAL SIN IS OUT;
# THE REALITY OF EVIL IS IN

*We enter a broken and torn and sinful world—that's for sure. But we do not enter as blotches on existence, as sinful creatures, we burst into the world as "original blessings." . . . Creation-centered mystics have always begun their theology with original blessing not original sin.*[1]

—MATTHEW FOX, priest and author

I have now presented the Christ figure in what is at least for me a new light. I see him as a portrait of divinity into which a full humanity inevitably flows, not as the incarnation of a supernatural external deity on a divine mission of rescue. In the preceding chapters, I have laid this radically different perspective before my readers. I know from discussions I have had with people about this new perspective that it will open me to charges on two fronts.

First, there will be those traditionalists who will hear in my Christ-proposal echoes of that nineteenth-century Protestant liberalism that reduced Jesus to the role of teacher and good example. They will argue, and I think rightly, that there is no significant power in such a definition. A good example may be admirable, but it does not empower me to follow the exemplary life. Indeed, good examples tend to exacerbate the human tendency to feel inadequate. I have never known a child's behavior to improve dramatically when the parent encourages him or her by saying, "Why don't you be more like your big brother or big sister?" Such an approach does not recognize the destructive power of comparison present in our survival-oriented humanity.

But to this first charge I respond that I am not portraying Jesus simply as a teacher and example to be followed. I regard teaching as the barest component of my understanding of the Christ-function. So this criticism seems to me to rise out of a deep and significant, perhaps even willful, misrepresentation of what I am trying to develop. Jesus is to me far more than just an example.

My primary vision of Christ is that he is a source of godly empowerment who calls me beyond my boundaries. When I have the courage to accept his invitation, I enter another dimension of humanity that opens new and compelling doors to me. I am drawn by this experience deeper and deeper into life. What I see in the Christ is not an example to follow. It is a vision that compels. Risk and reward are balanced to build a powerful sense of motivation.

Yet it is at this very point that I expect to encounter the second criticism, which is that I have not fully understood the reality of human evil. That is a charge regularly leveled against those of us who dare to move beyond rescue and guilt. I agree with those who say that the biggest weakness in liberal theological thought is that it minimizes the human capacity for evil. I do not want to be guilty of that. I want to make sure that the Christ I have found, and about whom I speak and write, adequately engages life as it is, not life as we might wish it to be.

If I had any illusion that I had dealt with this issue adequately, I was destined to be disabused of such a notion by a letter I received while this book was in progress. The letter writer was a Lutheran pastor who had attended a lecture I delivered in the midwestern part of the United States. In that lecture I had sought to lay the groundwork for this new understanding of Christ. This pastor was clearly not persuaded, however. His letter articulated the weakness that he felt I needed to address if I wanted to present this point of view adequately. These were his words:

> Are you suggesting that evil is not real? That it does not have an existence in and of itself? You do not seem to me to take the reality of evil seriously enough. The old story, that you seem eager to reject, said that evil was so real and so deep that only God could root it out. That story went on to say that even for God it was costly, demanding the death of the divine son. You may well dismiss that story as mythological theistic thinking, but you also appear to have dismissed the reality of human evil. I do not believe that human life can be defined adequately until human evil has been faced.

This cogent and well-phrased criticism compelled me to respond with further amplification. Indeed, it demanded that I return to the theme of evil once more, even on the other side of my chapter on Christ. I clearly had not gone deeply enough into the subject. Perhaps I needed to approach evil from a totally new perspective so that this man (and readers who might share his concern) would hear an answer. If I wanted to develop a new Christianity for a new world—a Christianity that was both whole and authentic—this would be a necessary step.

It is time, I am convinced, to move Christianity beyond that historically inaccurate and psychologically damaging definition of humanity that has resulted in a constant denigration of human life as helpless, depraved, sinful, and in need of divine rescue. The suggestion made by so much of the Christian theology of the past that every baby is born with the stain of original sin distorting his

*Yes !*

or her goodness is abhorrent to me. I admit only that babies are born with a loudspeaker on one end and no sense of responsibility on the other. But I regard both of those traits as morally neutral!

I now regard the traditional Christian interpretation of the account of the fall of humanity, told in the narrative of the Garden of Eden, as the ultimate example of distorted negative thinking. I prefer to look at the wonder of humanity and to celebrate the incredible gift of self-conscious life that has emerged from our earliest living ancestor, which was nothing more or less than a bit of protoplasm constituting a single cell in the midst of the sea. To spend my energy concentrating on the presumed lostness, the moral depravity, or the hopelessness of human beings, so easily called sinners by traditional Christianity, is to fail to appreciate the most incredible product of the whole created order—namely, the human mind. When I look at what human beings have achieved, from great works of art to magnificent symphonies, from architectural wonders to surgical and medical skills that are breathtaking, I stand in awe of human life. A religion that is based on denigrating humanity cannot make sense out of life to me.

In 1999 the New York chapter of a humanist organization presented me with their "Humanist of the Year" award. Almost immediately some of my ecclesiastical critics leaped upon that designation to suggest that I was, as they had long suspected, not really a Christian at all, but a humanist. In their minds being a humanist and being a Christian were mutually exclusive. I was amazed by this rhetoric, because it revealed that in their minds a Christian was one who was defined by a negative view of humanity. In response to this criticism I suggested that they had it all wrong. The opposite of a humanist, I insisted, is not a Christian but either an antihumanist or one who is inhumane. Neither of those latter categories would adequately describe either my personal philosophy or the Christian life. In my opinion, my critics had not embraced the fact that Christianity began with the claim that the reality of God had been experienced through the life of a particular human being. That is a grand and exhilarating claim. Can humanity be so evil, I wondered, if it is through this same humanity that God is revealed? The very way this debate has been shaped is symptomatic of the low estate into which Christianity has fallen in our day.

In the minds of my traditionalist critics, the opposite of humanism is supernaturalism. Since Christianity has been so thoroughly identified with supernaturalism, the very word *humanism* has become a synonym for something evil. Certainly in much of the hymnody and in many of the prayers of the Christian church the identification between humanity and evil is made obvious. To traditional Christians humanism has become a philosophy which suggests that there is an enormous chasm between the human and the divine—a chasm so broad and so deep that we have almost come to think of human and divine as opposites. These traditionalists seem to think that humanism means an elevation of humanity beyond all else. They conclude that I, and others like me, believe that humanity is the highest reality there is; they hear us as saying that there is nothing beyond the limits of the human. In that definition of humanism—a definition to which I certainly do not subscribe—the truth of God is thought to be denied.

Somehow traditional Christians seem to believe that to denigrate humanity as broken, fallen, evil, and sinful makes the reality of the theistic God who is external to life more believable. So part of the church's defense of theism has taken the form of the denigration of the sacredness of human life. Those who define God in supernatural terms look at the human arena and see no grandeur; they see nothing but evil. It is true that evil is not hard to find in human life, but it cannot be the defining and ultimate characteristic of our humanity.

Yet if the Christianity of the future does not take evil seriously, or if it cannot adequately explain the origins or acknowledge the depths of evil, then it will also not finally be an interpreter of human life. For evil is surely a part of our story. But so is human goodness. I suggest that they are intimately linked; that like self-consciousness and theism, evil and goodness are twins (though perhaps not Siamese twins, as the former are), but birthed from the same source, with the seeds of one present in the seeds of the other. YETZER HA-RA + YETZER HA-TOV

In order to focus this discussion, it is necessary first to look at human evil clearly. Only when that aspect of our humanity has been fully embraced can we look beyond it to see the meaning of human glory. My primary concern in this endeavor will be to understand why the church's identification with original sin, and with what we have called "the fall," has such power. The very presence of that preoccupation indicates that when we probe the nature of human evil, we are making contact with something that is real and deep within the human psyche. Thus I will seek to describe evil first, and only then will I seek to understand it.

Evil enters our awareness initially in the recognition, which all people seem to sense, that their lives are not complete, that something is missing. Whatever that missing part is, its absence drives human life toward some fulfillment in the service of which our survival becomes the highest good and thus the overwhelming organizing value of human life. Almost all religious myths are created to make sense out of that drive toward fulfillment. The myths come and go, but the human sense of incompleteness that produces them still begs to be explored and to be understood.

In my retirement I have attempted to visit different kinds of churches in various parts of my nation and the world, seeking always to understand what it is that draws people into each particular worshiping community. Almost always it turns out to be a recognition of this very quality of human incompleteness. In Hollywood, California, I visited a Presbyterian church where during the time of prayer something like confession took place. A young screenwriter, who I was told is the son of a Pentecostal preacher, offered thanks out loud "for exciting things that happened this past week in my personal life." Something had occurred, it seemed, that had made him feel a bit more whole. I learned later that a script he had been working on for a long time had been accepted. He felt that God had in some way brought him to a new sense of completion, at least that week. Then a member of the choir prayed, thanking God for "hanging in with me when I so clearly was not deserving of your love." Finally, an elder in this church talked about his personal battle with alcohol. The congregation was clearly amused, in a loving way, as he held up to ridicule the experiences he had lived through in his drinking past. He invited laughter at things that must at the time have been tragic. The idea of a grown man lying down on the floor of a subway train when inebriated and hoping to be awake at the right stop can, it turns out, be humorously told. He then went on to talk about how God had touched him and what his life in this particular church had meant to him.

Each of these people bore witness to a sense of incompleteness in life that somehow the experience of God alleviated. But how does this incompleteness become evil? Even more important, how does this sense of incompleteness manifest itself as evil? That was the next stage for my exploration. I start with the recognition that the cruelest things we human beings do to each other are direct byproducts of our struggle to survive the evolutionary process, and these actions are what drive us toward the distorted understanding that winning is the road to fulfillment. The deep commitment we have to tribal identity and the massive efforts we make to gain for our tribe the power necessary to be winners and not losers feed the competitive nature of all of our relationships with other people across the world.

So our first vision of evil is seen in the cruelty that one person commits against another in the competitive game we call life. We like to think of these evil acts as being unnatural, the products of our fall, yet even these cruel deeds are direct byproducts of our evolutionary struggle to survive and thus are quite natural to our self-conscious humanity. This innate competitive drive to survive also accounts for the military capability that human beings develop when other less drastic methods of competition do not work. The irrational power that drives even small and poor nations to invest inappropriately in military hardware is incomprehensible apart from this tribal need to survive. That need also accounts for social systems such as slavery, segregation, and apartheid, which are imposed with military might on those tribal members who are the losers in these competitive struggles.

As a child growing up in the southern part of the United States, I became aware early of the heavy militaristic emphasis in the life of my region. This southern military commitment, which originated prior to the American Civil War, rose out of a consuming tribal fear. Militarism to this day continues to mark the emotional and intellectual makeup of most of our southern politicians. This predisposition toward making a virtue out of military readiness is the reason that so many military bases have been built in the South. Military preparatory schools dot the southern landscape, and such institutions as Virginia Military Institute (VMI) and the Citadel (in South Carolina) are held in high romantic esteem across the region.

To understand what created this excessive military emphasis, we need to look at the history of slavery. It began as the fruits of military victory, with the slaves in effect prisoners of war. Likewise, when slavery ended, segregation in the United States and apartheid in South Africa—which were nothing but slavery's bastard stepchildren—were still imposed with superior military strength. To keep such hostile social systems in place required military or paramilitary readiness at all times. So military preparedness became a virtue in the quest for survival, and its justification was quickly supported by turning to tribal religion. Authoritative sources such as the Bible were used to demonstrate that slavery, segregation, and apartheid were consistent with

God's will and thus were well deserved by their victims. Hence the evil that appears in our life as the institutions of slavery, segregation, and apartheid, and the overt racism that accompanies these practices, can be seen as manifestations of an incomplete humanity driven by the primary human value of survival.

The oppression of women in a patriarchal world can also be seen as a survival tactic. Men in the patriarchal period of human history, which is not yet over, had the power to define and to circumscribe the role of the woman. She was to guard the hearth, serve the males sexually, bear and raise the children, feed the young ones first from her breasts and then from the activity of gathering and cultivating, and thus maintain the life of the tribe. Tribal survival depended on women providing these functions, and so they acquiesced to this male-imposed definition. To buttress this survival technique, sexual stereotypes for both the male and the female were enforced with the aid of divine claims written into holy scripture as the tribe's understanding of the "revealed will of God" in creation. These definitions were further reenforced by tribal taboos. The evil that derives from male chauvinistic prejudice thus also grows out of the incompleteness found in our human struggle to survive.

As the human race developed, homosexual people, an identifiable and powerless minority, were perceived to be different enough to be a threat to tribal survival. Homosexual persons appeared not to be interested, for example, in the normal pattern of mating and other reproductive activities on which the life of the tribe depended.

But the threat lay in more than just the differentness of homosexuality: people not understanding the origins of homosexuality feared that it would spread, pulling more and more people out of the all-essential reproductive pool. Because people seem to be on a spectrum of sexual preference from hetero- to homosexual, rather than totally separated into the heterosexual majority and the homosexual minority, there would always be some people who, though defined as heterosexual, would be susceptible to either their fantasies or to the solicitation of other homosexual people. The fear in the noncomprehending early days of human history, then, was that if homosexuality were ever culturally accepted, it might prove attractive to a larger number of people, threatening marriage, weakening society, and thus diminishing the potential for the tribe's survival. To counter this perceived threat, acts of hostility, fear, and oppression were encouraged against homosexual people. It is dangerous to be different when survival is the driving tribal motif. Even today these arguments are still heard from both religious and political leaders as they struggle in their ignorance to justify their blatant homophobia. This is why repression, oppression, controlling, bashing, and even murdering of the different ones were and in many places are still judged to be tribal virtues.

In parts of Africa to this day the presence of homosexuality is vigorously and almost hysterically denied, with some Africans even suggesting that it is the "white man's disease." The perceived threat is so deep that the admission of homosexuality brings death or banishment in some African societies. The denial of its presence is held intact with enormous power.

Homophobia can thus be seen as a survival technique understandable against the background of the deepest of all our motivating human drives—namely, the drive to survive, a gift to us from our evolutionary past.

There is, however, a different but well-documented minority tradition among some ancient tribes which indicates that the way survival was interpreted depended on one's understanding of reality. In these tribes the homosexual person, the transgender person, and that variation in human experience known as cross-dressing were all thought to be not a threat to existence, but a sign of the presence of a higher kind of spirituality.[2] In those tribes, the ones who appeared to possess this special gift were not banished, killed, or oppressed; rather, they were designated as spiritual leaders and healers of the tribe—shamans and medicine men. Most often these were male functions rather than female functions, because the status of women did not allow them to occupy power positions. Female homosexuality was late being recognized in any case, because in ancient societies a girl tended to be mated at puberty and forced to remain a sexual object for the men of her tribe whether she wished it or not.

So our analysis thus far reveals that the evil in human life manifested in tribalism, war, conquest, slavery, apartheid, segregation, the second-class status of women, and the significant hostility toward homosexual people can be accounted for by our evolutionary past. As life emerged into self-consciousness we organized the entire world around the self-centered virtue of our own survival. That is to say that these particular evils in human history are adequately explained by the human sense of incompleteness which roots in the fact of our historical journey from simple to complex forms of life. They are not the result of some fall into sin. They are rather manifestations of a humanity that is still a work in progress. But these categories, enormous as they are, still do not exhaust the experience of human evil.

There is also something evil that manifests itself among human beings when they get caught up in what we might call "the mob spirit." To see a great crowd of people whipped into an emotional frenzy over some issue and then to go on a violent, destructive, and murderous rampage is frightening indeed. As examples one thinks of the Crystal Night that launched Nazi persecution of the Jews, lynch mobs in the old South, and the riots that occasionally occur at sporting matches. In these episodes it is as if rationality disappears and behavior, that the members of the crowd would never contemplate as individuals, emerges in purposeful acts of destruction. Does the quest for survival born in our evolutionary history and rooted in our sense of fragile incompleteness account for this? I think it does, and those who study the psychology of the crowd explain it quite adequately. It is a corporate expression of the individual and social need for power or the recognition of the rightness of a particular cause that reaches a psychotic edge. This evil is thus still the product of our unfinished status bequeathed to us by our evolutionary past.

Next we examine those things that seem counter to our humanity but that afflict only small minorities of human beings. I refer to such psychological disturbances and antisocial behaviors as kleptomania, claustrophobia, acrophobia (a fear of heights), sadism, masochism, and excessive, even murderous, aggression. Can these destructive evils, which produce such obvious pain, be understood as rising out of the drive for completeness and the subsequent installation of survival as the highest human virtue? Once again, to students of inner human drives, it appears that they can.

Kleptomania, for example, is rooted in the desire to possess things in whatever way one can as assets to survival. But there is an irrational quality in the kleptomaniac, in that the things stolen and the person's need of those things in order to survive are simply not related. Kleptomania is therefore an inappropriate, disconnected act of theft. Moving up the ladder of the same drive, stealing—which can be seen as self-conscious and purposeful kleptomania—represents a high-risk attempt at survival on the part of a loner who sets his or her needs above the needs of the tribe. Stealing may be destructive to community life, but unlike kleptomania, it is not purposeless. So both "rational" stealing and irrational kleptomania are grounded in the survival mentality, born in our incompleteness as part of our evolutionary heritage.

Claustrophobia and acrophobia are the neurotic and sometimes even psychotic manifestations of other aspects of our desire to achieve survival. Thus they too are signs of an incomplete humanity. The tactic of not being surrounded or enclosed as a survival technique is well known in times of danger. But when anxiety about being closed in is disconnected from real danger and experienced in every enclosed setting, it becomes claustrophobia, a mental disorder. Put another way, claustrophobia employs a valid survival technique in an inappropriate context. Likewise, acrophobia is a virtue when understood as the urge to avoid risks for the sake of tribal survival. It is a neurosis, however, when it is generalized into a fear that continues even when no danger exists.

Sadism is the identification of one's sexuality with the aggression it takes to survive, and the seeking of that aggression for its own sake as a source of distorted pleasure. A milder and purposeful aggression is found in the willingness to act in ways that serve survival, even though they bring pain to others. I think of everything from disciplinary punishments to surgery in this category.

Masochism is the connection of the passive stance, which is sometimes required of those seeking survival, with sexual pleasure, so that passivity and its consequent subjugation and pain are turned into virtues. These virtues are then cultivated for the neurotic pleasure they provide. Milder forms of masochism appear in people who seem to cultivate the image of victim or loser without the awareness that it serves some inner need.

Murderous aggression may be a form of sadism, but it also may arise from other heretofore unrecognized realities. Recent studies of criminal behavior suggest that aggressiveness may not always be freely chosen; sometimes it may be the result of excessive levels of testosterone, the male hormone, or the presence of a double Y chromosome. So it is natural for some and has survival value. Excessive aggression is also sometimes related to childhood abuse, suggesting that abused children become superaggressive, even murderous adults as a disproportionate tactic of survival.

The explanation that evolutionary human life is driven by a survival mentality that locks self-conscious creatures into a radical self-centeredness thus accounts clearly for many things that society tends to call evil. It indicates that we are not fallen creatures so much as we are incomplete creatures. It also accounts for those things that traditional religious people have tended to think of as acts of our sinful or fallen nature. This analysis frees me to press on with the possibility of identifying the presence of real evil in human life as the product of incompleteness rather than a manifestation of our fall into sin—and thus still affords me a viable doorway into the development of my new Christology. I do take evil seriously. I simply find its origins in a different place than does traditional Christianity.

Yet I continue to confront in human life things that do not, at least at first glance, quite fit my new equation. So I am driven to look more closely at behaviors that appear to be the opposite of survival, namely self-destructive addictive behaviors. I should note that addiction is not a subject on which I am a passive, uninvolved person. My life has been touched by the addiction to alcohol of people very dear to me, one of whom was my father. Addicted people seem bent on destroying everything they hold dear. In my lack of both knowledge about alcoholism and awareness of its power, I initially felt justified in casting blame and expressed moralistic judgment toward addicted people, though my later study of alcoholism has convinced me that the nature of addiction precludes choice. Certainly it has seemed to me, as I have watched the decline of the alcohol-addicted people I have known well, that no rational response could stop the relentless ravaging of that illness.

Survival seemed not to be a consideration. I watched hopelessly and helplessly as addicted people I knew sacrificed career, family, children, future, and reputation in favor of feeding their controlling habit. I have seen in alcoholics a pain so deep that only one more drink could drug it, even when it was obvious to others that this same alcohol had caused much of that pain. I have listened to the vows and promises of these victims of alcohol—vows that I knew had been made in good faith—and I have understood from long and even bitter experience that they would not be kept.

I learned that "lying" was not the proper word to characterize these failed promises. Something far more profound was involved.

There was a deep disconnect with reality that lurked somewhere in the souls of these addicted ones. It was as if they were subject to a—a power over which they had no control. These people were imprisoned inside what was sometimes even interpreted as a destructive demonic spirit, and nothing seemed capable of reaching them, of calling them beyond their boundaries into that new humanity of which I have spoken. Is there not a need at this level of our humanity for an intervening, rescuing, external power? Have I in my proposed theological interpretation jettisoned the only thing that could possibly reach this destructive depth of broken humanity? My view of evil must be expanded to account for this.

I have also watched another member of my family and many others in my ministry fall under the sway of a mental illness that drove them, with their apparent cooperation, out of life. Again the drive to survive seems an inadequate explanation. Rational suggestions that medical treatment, hospitalization, proper drugs, and psychiatric skills could help the mentally ill patient were rejected. In these sicknesses each patient chose instead to live in a world of hiding, preferring unreality over reality and even death over life.

It was as if they too were possessed by something that took them over, lived through them, and would not let them go. All of my calls both as a relative and as a pastor to step beyond tribal fears and protective barriers to embrace new dimensions of humanity fell on apparently deaf or at least unresponsive ears. These lives so clearly needed to be rescued from their bondage. To embrace the empowering love that my Christian understanding suggested had been manifested in the person of Jesus, to enable a completeness of humanity to be born, did not seem to be an option for them. Indeed, they seemed to need the intervention of the theistic deity, for, in the words of our traditional liturgy, they "had no power in themselves to help themselves." My concept of the causes of evil has to account for the reality of that quality of these lives. Incomplete humanity driven by a struggle to survive is simply insufficient. This was once again more like demon possession.

I have known still others who were so bent and twisted by various experiences in life that they were permanently warped, and so they too lived their lives beyond the reach of any healing. No exhortation to enter the Christ-experience was capable of touching the dark places in the souls of these human beings. No invitation to move beyond the boundaries of their fears, no empowerment to be more than they had yet been able to be, could reach these lives. Rescue from outside seemed to be their only hope. Frequently even the doors against such an intervening rescue were tightly locked and barred from inside. It was as if they had identified themselves with their "sweet sicknesses" and now lived only so that they could be destructive both to themselves and to others.

From time to time one of these distorted lives has actually reached a position of high political leadership. The result has been that what is normally only an inner evil in one person becomes externalized, creating hundreds, thousands, and sometimes even millions of innocent victims. One thinks of such people as Rome's Emperor Nero, Russia's Ivan the Terrible and Joseph Stalin, Germany's Adolf Hitler, and Uganda's Idi Amin. The inner evil of these individuals, when combined with power and then externalized, has created some of the darkest epochs in history. At a lesser level one thinks of men such as Republican Senator Joseph McCarthy of Wisconsin, whose own inner needs were projected in the forties and fifties onto those he thought threatened his survival—closeted Communists and what his sick mind called "Communist sympathizers." McCarthy moved to exterminate those he defined with his fears and in the process was responsible for wrecking the careers of many.

That kind of evil does not appear just in secular circles. Early in my career I knew a religious leader who as he got older began to feel himself threatened from all directions. Usually the threat was identified with those who disagreed with him. He first began to defend with great vehemence what he called the "theological center" of his faith. Then he began to attack as heretics anyone who disagreed with his self-imposed definition of that center; finally he identified his own demons with homosexual people and struck out in fury to destroy them. This life became consumed with anger, and he wrote a final sorry chapter to what had once been a bright and promising ecclesiastical career.

It would do no good to discuss issues rationally with this man. He was not open to love, to help, or to any new perspective. He too was a possessed man living under the spell of an irrational power, deeply in pain. Convinced that this pain was being inflicted on him from outside himself, he was highly motivated to seek out and destroy those perceived sources of pain. Though he couched his rhetoric in the sweet words of evangelical piety and sought to portray himself as defending things that many people valued, he actually helped to destroy the things he claimed to be so eager to save. He was "fallen," not free. He did not need to be empowered; he needed to be rescued in a way that my view of the origin of human evil would not appear to allow. My understanding of evil must account for that.

I have also seen this evil in those religious journalists whose passion has been not for truth but for their particular agendas. They were motivated by a desire to destroy those who opposed their version of truth, which they had idolatrously identified with the revealed will of God. So deeply were they in the service of this distortion that they could not see the destructiveness they spewed out. They encouraged prejudice, applauded ignorance, and diminished their lives and those around them while claiming to be servants of Christ.

Please do not misunderstand me: the evil I refer to here is not to be identified with differences of opinion, viewpoint, or perspective. The world can and does honor the integrity of opposing ideas in the search for a truth that ultimately eludes us all. What I speak of is qualitatively different. It is marked by those demonic words, attributed to the satanic one, "Evil, be thou my good; darkness, be thou my light; lies, be thou my truth." I suspect that this journalistic mentality is similar to that which led to the witch-hunt in Salem, Massachusetts, in the seventeenth century. The misplaced religious passion of certain Salem residents resulted in the murder of a number of people who were deemed to be witches, and thus the mouthpieces of a very real Devil.

There is yet another form of destructive behavior that I have experienced that I am not able to explain by reference to the human urge for survival. I recall being the guest speaker at the Metropolitan Community Church's Cathedral of Hope in Dallas, Texas, a mostly gay and lesbian congregation. There I listened to their male choral group, "The Positive Singers," perform memorably and masterfully. The name of this group comes from the fact that every one of its members is HIV-positive, victimized by a potent virus that has terrorized the homosexual community. From whence comes this evil? It surely cannot be located in our human incompleteness. Everything I know about both science and medicine tells me that these young gay adults did not choose their sexual orientation, and yet because they dared to practice their being in what was for them a natural way, they now live under a cloud that may ultimately be a death sentence. What sense does life make when what is a natural drive for people toward fulfillment or wholeness becomes the avenue of death for some?

These are the experiences, the realities that make evil real and yet do not fit easily into my definition, which locates evil primarily in the incompleteness of humanity. I must find a way to incorporate addiction to alcohol and drugs, mental disorders, those who destroy others in the service of their convictions, and those who, seeking love in what is for them a natural way, find only death. These are the issues that confront me as an observer of life and force me to seek a Christ-function that would not just empower and call to a new humanity, but would also rescue people from these kinds of brokenness.

If evil is the distortion of love, then I have surely seen evil, and history has witnessed evil in these places. Not evil people, mind you, but people in the throes of an evil power over which they appear to have no control. There seems to me to be a different dimension of reality that is present here. One cannot bring completion and wholeness to those whose brokenness is so total that they do not even know that they are broken. Salvation in such experiences is not a matter of calling people to step beyond their limits into a new humanity, because the victims of these kinds of brokenness are incapable of recognizing how twisted their own view of reality is or how simply being who they are opens them to being victimized by their very quest for wholeness. Is there then a rescuing function that can be located in the post-theistic God or a saving power that can be identified with a Christ who is beyond the theistic myth of incarnation?

My understanding of human life is no longer described adequately or accurately by the theological story of a fall into sin. It rather is described as the product of a struggle for survival that has left the scars of self-centeredness writ large upon our psyches. It is a humanity that stands in need of a power that will lift us beyond these scars into a new being. I believe that definition must now be expanded to embrace these self-destructive elements, which are surely a real part of our humanity. How do we understand these things that seem to attack even our survival?

These data force me to continue this journey into both my assumptions about life and the resources of my faith-tradition, seeking a fuller explanation of what it means to be human and asking if there is an aspect to our God-experience that can address and finally make sense out of these aspects of our humanity.

I have no final answers. That is the first thing I need to say. Perhaps there will someday be a completely adequate explanation for evil, but we have not yet found it. We do, however, have hints found in the depths of our internal probe that might offer a new direction, and so to these hints we turn.

Carl Jung suggested that a part of every person's humanity was something he called our "shadow." This "shadow" is defined as that aspect of our being which is feared, repressed, denied, coped with, and in some cases even transformed to serve the well-being of the person. However, Jung argued that one's shadow is never healed until it has been brought into the self-consciousness of the person whose dark side it is. Healing, for Jung, comes with the embrace of our shadow, the acceptance of our evil. Evil too is part of God, Jung suggested, because it too is a part of Being.

Jung even went so far as to say that in the realm of symbols, there had to be two sons of God: Jesus and the Devil. In his mind they were not divided beings. Each was the reverse side of the other's coin. In his famous book *The Answer to Job*, Jung argued for the need to have the Devil, along with Mary the mother of Jesus, and thus the embodiment of the feminine principle, assumed into heaven and recognized as part of what God is. When the concept of God reflects not only male and female, but also Christ and Satan, said Jung, then God will be complete.

Until evil is symbolically taken into God, he argued, it cannot be taken into ourselves, and thus wholeness cannot come to human life. If we are made in God's image, then good and evil must be lifted into consciousness in both God and ourselves. That, Jung argued, is the doorway into the fullness of our being. It was and is a startling concept, one not easily absorbed. Yet I believe that it is a concept begging to be incorporated into the Christianity that is struggling to be born in the twenty-first century.

This Christianity must be, I have suggested, one that presents a picture of a deity who is beyond the definition of theism but not beyond the reality of God. It must portray a Christ who is beyond incarnation but not beyond the divine. It must reflect life as it is. So evil needs to be embraced and transformed as part of our quest for wholeness.

This troublesome aspect of the human experience thus finally drives me back to the role of the community that calls itself the body of Christ and that lives to be a symbol of the kingdom of God, that is the realm of God being born and living as a presence within human history.

This community must be able to incorporate all of our human reality into itself. It must be able to allow God and Satan to come together in each of us. It must allow light and darkness to be united. It must bind good and evil into one. It must unite Christ with Anti-Christ, Jesus with Judas, male with female, heterosexual with homosexual. For the Christian story to be complete, the body of Christ—the community of believers—must play the redemptive role in transforming life inside human history.

That radically new Christian vocation is begun, I believe, when theism dies and God, as a being external to life, disappears from our consciousness and our vocabulary. We have begun the reformation of Christianity, I believe, by walking beyond that marker. But the reformation will not be complete until the Devil, the satanic figure, also dies as something external to life and thus also disappears from our consciousness and our vocabulary. That is the revolution that is needed to complete the picture. Human life is not perfectible: evil cannot be removed from our being because it is part of our being.

Remember the parable of the wheat and the tares (Matt. 13:24–30) they must grow together, Jesus said, until the harvest. We cannot remove the tares without destroying the wheat. Evil, like the tares, is part of the Ground of Being, the nature of reality, the meaning of God. My being is always light and darkness, love and hate, God and Satan, life and death, being and nonbeing—all in dynamic tension. I cannot split off part of who I am, confess it, be absolved of it, and seek to try again. I cannot pretend that I am made in God's image until I own as part of my being the shadow side of my life, which reflects the shadow side of God. That is why evil is always present in the holy; that is why evil is perceived as relentless and inescapable; that is why Jesus and Judas have been symbolically bound together since the dawn of time. The Johannine myth was not wrong in suggesting that Jesus was the preexisting word of God who was enfleshed into human history. That is a very accurate conception of an ultimate truth. But it is not complete. Judas Iscariot was also mythically present in God at the dawn of creation, and he too was enfleshed in the drama played out in Judea in the first century.

The mythical themes are woven together time after time. God and Satan, life and death, good and evil, sacrifice and freedom, light and darkness, Jesus and Judas—are all inextricably bound up with one another. I cannot finally step into the new being without bringing my own dark shadow with me. Many times in human experience those who cannot deal with their shadow finally have that very shadow become their possessing reality. One's shadow can consume one's being, and when it does we become possessed people, addicted people. That then constitutes the missing dimension in my definition of evil. Incompleteness is thus augmented by a fuller view of the complexity of human life. This then is that part of human life that cries out for a rescuing act, for this person has no power to save himself or herself. The theistic God invading life is, however, not the proper source of that rescue. That is rather the role of the people of God.

The role of the church must be to become the place where the disparate parts of our humanity can be bound together and then kept from being separated again. The church must never pretend that it has the ability to separate good from evil or even God from sin.

So in this sense it is the church, not the Jesus figure, that must itself play the role of the rescuer reaching out to those who appear to be the possessed ones, whether that possession be to alcohol, to drugs, to mental illness, or to obsessive negativity. These things are but the symptoms of the ultimate need in human life for a redemptive process to occur. People who are addicted to anything are not free to be until they have accepted the shadow side of their lives as an essential part of who they are. That shadow side is finally a stark and overt counterpoint to our being. The healing power that can address our shadow is not absolution—the declaration of the forgiveness of our sins, as if somehow our evil deeds were separate from our being. The healing power is the love that accepts us as we are, shadow included, and says that every part of who we are is made in the image of God.

So the call of Christ to the life of discipleship and the message of the rescuing community is simply to grasp our own being—all of it, light and darkness—and to practice wholeness. The ability to step into wholeness is that act of empowerment, which I now conclude can happen only in a community in which all sorts of human beings, whatever their condition, are members. That is why a community called the church must be part of the future of Christianity. Human beings cannot incorporate all that we are into wholeness by ourselves. That does not occur even in the intense counseling relationship of therapist and patient. We have to build a community so deep and so real that good and evil, God and shadow, might dwell together. Those whose being seems possessed by some alien power must therefore be present in that community as loved and valued parts of the whole. They stand as symbols of the need for redemption. They remind us of our own shadows, which are part of our own being.

The primary task of a faith-community is to assist in the creation of wholeness—not goodness, but wholeness. That community's raison d'être is to be the place where each person can be nurtured into being. This wholeness we seek, the wholeness that comes to us only in community, includes our shadow, which is never separated from our being. Some of us need to be rescued from our goodness to be made whole, while some of us need to be rescued from our evil. But none of us can be made whole until good and evil are bound together inside one being. That, I believe, is a community function. That, I believe, is the work of the church. That is why the church is called "the body of Christ."

It is at this point that I rejoice in the unfinished nature of evolution. For what we are is light and shadow. The shadow represents not only our drive to survive but also our distortions, which allow destructiveness to control some part of our being. But the processes of life go on, and we find in them the hints of a new being that is always struggling to emerge in our lives. That new being is the dimension of our humanity that escapes the drive to survive and literally gives itself away to enhance the lives of others. This is not a neurotic giving, a death wish, a martyr complex, but a manifestation of selfless love.

We see it in relationships we characterize as shared by those who are in love. True lovers are motivated not by survival but by the desire to serve the well-being of the beloved. They have come to the point where they can live for another, where not even selfishness, demonic possession, neurotic attachment, or psychotic destruction distorts their ability to love. That sort of selfless love represents, I believe, the next stage in evolutionary human development. The Christ figure to me is an image, a sign, and indeed a promise of that birth of a new humanity.

That is why I still rest my hope in a God who is beyond theism but not beyond the divine, and in a Christ who is beyond the incarnation but whose humanity is so whole that it fades into divinity. That is the "new being" to which we are destined and through which God is seen and experienced as present.

# TEN

# Beyond Evangelism and World Mission to a Post-Theistic Universalism

*A nation is a group of people united by a mistaken view of the past and a hatred of their neighbors.*[1]

— ERNEST RENAN, French philosopher

When the theistic deity of the past is abandoned, the power-claims made in the name of that deity will also have to be dismissed. The primary political purpose that these claims serve is to enable a particular institution to assert that it alone possesses the truth and to suggest that those who are not part of that particular community of faith are lost in the darkness of their own errors. These power-claims increase the pressure for conversion to the life of the institution in question by offering would-be converts the reward of a salvation that is not available to anyone who is not a "true believer" or part of the "true church." This system makes it clear to all who bother to look, just who is "in" and who is "out." It produces a mentality that tends to focus the message of the institution's belief system until it reaches a kind of white-hot intensity. It feeds a sectarian and separatist tradition that enables one's religion to minister to one's sense of incompleteness. These exclusive claims made for "my God and my tradition" have marked every expansionist and missionary religious system throughout the world. All of them will have to go in the new reformation.

This tribal and human mentality also transcends the content of every religious system. In Judaism these claims were written into the essence of the Torah in the Ten Commandments: "I am the Lord your God who brought you out of the land of Egypt, out of the house of bondage. You shall have no other gods before me" (Exod. 20:2). The punishment prescribed in the law for worshiping a God other than Yahweh is death (Deut. 8:19).

In Islam this exclusive claim is asserted in the sacred Muslim chant: "There is but one God [Allah] and Mohammed is his prophet." The Koran undergirds this claim by justifying negative behavior against non-Muslims as consistent with the word of God. *Jihad* is their name for it.

The exclusive claims of Christianity have most often been attached to a text in the Fourth Gospel where Jesus is quoted as having said, "I am the way, and the truth and the life, no one comes to the Father but by me" (John 14:6). This imperialism and the pain that has flowed from that single verse is so great it would be hard to measure.

This mentality is again present in the assertion made by the more Catholic side of Christianity that the reception of certain Christian sacraments is "necessary for salvation." Apart from those sacraments, presumably one is lost, a fate that obviously applies to the whole non-Christian world. The destiny of the unbaptized ones has been debated in this tradition throughout Christian history, but no one in this debate has advocated inclusion of those unbaptized and therefore lost ones in the kingdom. It is the varying degrees of exclusion that have constituted the boundaries of the discussion. "There is no salvation outside the church" is yet another phrase heard in these same ecclesiastical circles. "Church" in this phrase clearly means the Roman Catholic Church, not the church catholic. It is a power claim.

On the more Protestant side of Christianity, where baptism is frequently postponed to serve as the outward sign of conversion, different but still exclusive claims are often made. Salvation in this tradition requires "accepting Jesus as one's personal savior," for example. Heaven is thus reserved for those who can assert that this kind of conversion is part of their personal story. Lostness awaits all others.

The unbaptized and those who do not know Jesus as their personal savior face the ultimate penalty of spending eternity apart from God or inside the reality of hell. Hell ranged from a place of ultimate meaninglessness to a place of eternal suffering. Evangelical Protestants still sing hymns designed to place the burden of these lost souls on the consciousness of the true believers: they ask themselves, "Can we whose souls are lighted with wisdom from on high, to those with souls benighted, the lamp of life deny?"[2] Christians have also envisioned the church as an army out to conquer the world. Such popular hymns as "Onward Christian Soldiers" and "Lead on, O King Eternal, the Day of March Has Come" are illustrative of this. In addition, there are demands placed on believers to make Christ known to the entire world that also involves their certainty of being among the elect or the saved. They are exhorted to "fling out the banner, let it furl" and to "stand up, stand up for Jesus." All of these ideas are rooted in an imperialistic theism that has been wrapped around the gospel, and as theism dies, so too will these ideas.

This is the mentality that has marked Christianity in previous centuries. It still marks the rhetoric of conservative churches, both Catholic and Protestant. It was the duty of those Christians whose faith was defined by this mentality to be witnesses for Christ to all nonbelievers. It was their solemn obligation to support foreign and domestic missionaries who in the name of the church carried the saving message of Christ to "the heathen," as the non-Christians of the world tended to be called. Not to do this was evidence that the believer did not love Christ sufficiently or that the believer did not love the lost ones sufficiently.

In previous eras there was enormous romance connected with this missionary activity in the sponsoring Christian circles. Missionaries on "furlough" regaled believers with tales of their successes and with statistics of souls won for Christ. They also passed the hat to enlist support for their efforts in those more "primitive" parts of the world, where as one hymn suggested, "apes swing to and fro."[3] It was once considered almost a denial of Christianity itself not to support these expansionist efforts. But a closer and less romantic look at the missionary enterprise of the church reveals the darker side of these religious convictions, which has not even yet been faced fully by the Christian church. Facing that darker side is unavoidable, however, when we begin to walk beyond theism into a post-theistic religious scene.

Kenneth Scott Latourette, the foremost historian of Christian expansion, called the nineteenth century "the great missionary century."[4] But surely it does not escape our notice that it was also the great century of European colonial conquest. Seeking the natural resources of the world to enhance their wealth, the major European powers dominated the underdeveloped lands of this planet, making them part of various European empires or, at the very least, part of their "spheres of influence."

England, France, Holland, and Spain were the original winners of North America before the English influence finally prevailed everywhere except in Quebec and Mexico. Spain and Portugal divided Central and South America. After Germany was driven from Africa, that continent became French in northern Africa and on the west coast, English in central Africa, and even Belgium in the Congo. In southern Africa the Dutch and the English vied for power, with the English finally winning in the Boer War. The Portuguese kept an African foothold in Angola and Mozambique.

Great Britain was the major power in the Middle East, with the Suez Canal anchoring that control. Asia was split up among the French in Southeast Asia, the Portuguese on the Island of Macao, and the British in Malaysia, Singapore, and Hong Kong. The British also had Australia and New Zealand, while the Dutch dominated the islands that today are tenuously united into the nation of Indonesia. When the United States got into the expansionist mode in the nineteenth and twentieth centuries, the province called Louisiana, which was far larger than the state that today bears this name, was purchased from the French, and its nomadic native population was then both decimated and Christianized. About a half-century later, in 1867, Alaska was purchased from the Russians; and still later Puerto Rico and the Philippine Islands were added as the trophies of the Spanish American War (1898). The Hawaiian Islands were then annexed, and by supporting its American-inspired bid for independence from Colombia, Panama was also added to our "sphere of influence" so that "our" canal could be built.

Much of the justification for these colonial acts of conquest was explained by the rhetoric of religion. The Western nations were not hostile conquerors, it was said; they were rather bringing "civilization and Christianity" to the uncivilized lost people in these unenlightened parts of the world. Even the kidnapping and subsequent enslavement of Africans to work the fields in the agricultural southland of the United States was justified by citing these same virtuous motives. The world watched the strange anomaly of Christians sending missionaries to Africa to convert the natives even as these same natives were being kidnapped and enslaved by the nations in which the white Christians lived.

Yet the fact remains that all of this missionary activity, buttressed by the economic and political power of the colonial nations, was still relatively unsuccessful. Wherever there was a strong, unified religious tradition, such as that which marked India, China, and Japan, for example, the Christian inroads were minimal. Islam, though it got a much later start than Christianity, quickly established itself as a significant religious force, becoming the dominant religion not only in the Middle East but as far away as Pakistan and Indonesia. It even involved Europe at its edges— in Spain and in the area of the continent between Greece and Italy, known variously as Yugoslavia, Macedonia, Croatia, and Serbia. Hinduism still is the dominant religion of the Asian subcontinent, and Buddhism, the child of Hinduism, dominates China and Southeast Asia to this day. Christians enjoyed little missionary success in these places despite massive efforts.

Africa is the only continent that in the last analysis provided missionary success for Christians, and even there, with the exception of Africa's southern tip, Christianity had to compete mightily with Islam. The reasons for Christianity's relative success there were unique to Africa. In that continent there was no unifying, widely held religious system. Instead, African religious practices tended to be local and animistic. The primary missionary voices in Africa were also English-speaking evangelicals, who brought a fundamentalist mentality to their conversion work that appeared to meet African needs for religious certainty in a significant way. That evangelical religion, when filtered through the African ethos, tended to make the converts as moralistic, Victorian, and oblivious to developing biblical scholarship as their evangelical mentors had been. That assessment was a general truth but not a universal reality.

The southern tip of Africa became strongly Christian, but what happened there occurred almost in spite of missionary efforts. In what is now the Republic of South Africa, the energies of the dominant society were drained first by the tensions between black Africans and white Europeans and later by the tensions that divided the Europeans into Dutch Christians and English Christians. When the Dutch won back politically the power they had lost in the Boer War, a program was adopted of separating the races in the system of apartheid. This evil was actually blessed by the Dutch Reformed Church in South Africa. Some other Christians, however, offered a counterpoint and helped to create an authentic and indigenous African Christianity that, in time, indeed after many generations, would produce such voices as Desmond Tutu, Lawrence Zulu, and Nelson Mandela who played major roles in bringing down apartheid. Their activity made it clear, finally, that black Africans do have a part in the Christianity of that land. The post-apartheid experience in South Africa handled so graciously by retired Archbishop Tutu stamped this land with a unique spirit.

In the rest of Africa, however, Christians faced the appeal and power of Islam that was rooted in part in its independence from the colonial process. It also claimed a prophet, Mohammed, whose skin was not white. In time, this anticolonial spirit made contact with the descendants of African slaves in the United States. Black sports figures such as Cassius Clay and Lew Alcindor became known by their Muslim names—Muhammad Ali and Kareem Abdul Jabbar—and thus began to give visibility to a growing willingness on the part of African-Americans to go back to a religious system that in their minds was more indigenous to their ancestral roots than Christianity was. Islam, sometimes in very aggressive forms, began at that point to make significant inroads into the United States.

These are the data that make it very clear that the Christian goal of converting the world to Christ has been a significant failure everywhere, missionary rhetoric not to the contrary withstanding. In fact, the world has a smaller percentage of Christians in it today than it did earlier in its history.

I submit that these expansionist efforts were flawed from the beginning, because they were nothing more than an ill-disguised quest for power born out of the self-centeredness that is our heritage from evolution. They were strategies adopted in the service of a tribal theistic deity and confused with the gospel imperative.

Evangelistic efforts and missionary enterprises are thus compromised by a lack of integrity and filled, despite the veneer of virtuous religious jargon, with manifestations of hostility. I think the Christian Church should abandon these tactics forthwith as unworthy of the Christ figure. I want no part of a "decade of evangelism," or those perennial misguided Christian attempts to convert the Jews. That activity grows out of a sense that one tradition possesses the sole route to God. It reflects a tribal mentality that cannot be part of our post-theistic world.

Thomas Harris, an American doctor and student of social history writing more than a generation ago, described various human interactions in his popular book, *I'm OK, You're OK*. One of those interactions was what he called "I'm OK, you're not OK," which carried with it the implication that you will not be okay until you become like me.[5] Surely we recognize that this is the posture of all conversion and missionary enterprise activities. It is quite obviously the stance of the superior to the inferior. It is judgmental, rejecting, and hostile. Surely the story of Jesus, as the love of God, cannot be told amid judgment and hostility. That remains true, I believe, despite the fact that some beautiful and sensitive people with the best of intentions have, over the years of Christian history, given themselves to missionary enterprises. We now must see those activities as base-born, rejecting, negative, and yes, I would even say evil.

It is fascinating to note that without raising the issues involved here to full consciousness, foreign missionary work has in the main line churches been reduced to time-limited self-help projects.

If Christians of the twenty-first century are courageous enough to let those missionary activities rooted in a premodern theism die a natural death with no weeping, wailing, or attempts at artificial respiration, we will discover that beyond them lies something that I regard as far more appealing.

We recognize first that we are shedding only the survival, security-seeking instincts developed by our fearful, newly self-conscious ancestors. We are laying aside a religious content that was crafted to satisfy the ancient fears of these ancestors and to make human beings feel safe. It was a content that kept people dependent, childlike, and comfortable in not seeking maturity. As such, it does not serve the purpose of enhancing our humanity.

The theistic thinking that undergirded conversion activities is dead. We Christians today know that we possess neither certainty nor eternal truth. We know that we do not possess the sole pathway to God, for there is no sole pathway.

If God is not a being but the Ground of All Being, the source of life and the source of love, then God surely cannot be contained in any religious system, nor can any people continue to live as if God were the tribal deity of their particular nation or group. Being, life, and love transcend all boundaries. No sacred scripture of any religious tradition can any longer claim that in its pages the fullness of God has been captured. Exclusive religious propaganda can no longer be sustained. The idea that Jesus is the only way to God or that only those who have been washed in the blood of Christ are ever to be listed among the saved, has become anathema and even dangerous in our shrinking world.

That is not all. To discover a God beyond theism is also to acknowledge that ecclesiastical creeds can also never *capture* the truth of God, all they can do is point to it. That is true whether the creed is the original three-word affirmation "Jesus is Lord [Messiah]" or the increasingly complex versions we call the Apostles' Creed, the Nicene Creed, and the Athanasian Creed, each of which marked another stage in the theistic development of the Christian church. There can be no ultimately defining, and thus limiting, creeds in the post-theistic Christianity that is now struggling to be born. We will rather see our theistic creedal past as a necessary stage through which we had to walk. That past can no longer bind us as we break into a limitless post-theistic experience.

The same thing is true of the Bible. The new reformation will not require Christians to abandon the Bible, but it will require that we remove from the Bible the tribal claims and the literalness that have so often been attached to Scripture. The Bible is a doorway into God, but when I enter that domain of God, I discover that all of the Bible's word pictures and word symbols must be broken open so that the word of God can speak to us in new accents calling us to new meanings.

As the years and decades pass, we will finally begin to understand that none of these sacrifices required by the death of theism causes us to lose that essential experience of God that Christians believe we have met in Jesus. Rather, all they do is to challenge the idolatry of our claims that the holy, mysterious, wondrous experience of God could ever be captured in any human religious system or be made to serve any institution's power-needs. Disarming excessive claims never invalidates personal religious experience.

I am now, and always will be, a person who has come to experience God inside the Western tribal religion known as Christianity. That religious system will remain my doorway into God. At the center of that tradition I confront the person of Jesus of Nazareth, in whom first-century people believed they experienced the presence of God. Their experience of the divine in Jesus is what required the explanations that we find today in both the scriptures and the creeds.

I start here, then, affirming the ecstatic experience that was the first response to this God-presence called Jesus, and then I begin to understand without a compelling necessity to literalize it, the explanation employed by the author of the Fourth Gospel, who wrote that if you have seen Christ, you have seen God (John 10:30, 14:9).

So this Christ remains my doorway into God. It is not, perhaps, a doorway that everyone can use, and it is certainly not the *only* doorway; but it is *my* doorway. But once I have entered that particular doorway, I discover that there is a whole, perhaps even an infinite, faith-tradition to explore that breaks all of the limits of the past. I am not required to reject this part of my religious past; I am only required to relativize its exclusive claims.

So my pathway into God allows me and even encourages me to sink myself deeply into the content of my tradition. I cannot begin at a point where I am not; I must begin where I am. So I scale the heights and plumb the depths of my own faith-system. I open the symbols of my faith-story and allow them to escape the molds of antiquity. I try quite deliberately to move beyond my scriptures, my creeds, my liturgies, my hymns, and my traditional devotions, recognizing each of these as containing the explanations of a particular time and place, but allowing none of them to continue to claim that they can do anything more than point to a truth they cannot capture. I remove from these things any sense of their completeness, their unchangeability, their infallible possibilities, their stance of being closed to new understandings, and then I seek to explore the experience that caused these artifacts to be created.

I become aware of how much the passing of time and the particular journey in history through which the Christian faith has passed have bent Christianity, distorted it, and perhaps even destroyed its original meaning. I begin to embrace how these secondary considerations have been invested with a sanctity that they do not deserve. I see how political divisions in Western Europe found expression in the church's life. I recognize that church people have historically made much of those divisions that are part of our tribal mentality. Is not the primary difference that separates the Episcopalian (Anglican), the Lutheran, the Presbyterian, and the Roman Catholic related most closely to which part of Europe was the filter through which that person's version of Christianity was received? But is it not also true that Jesus knew nothing of England, Germany and Scandinavia, Scotland, or Italy, Ireland, and Southern Europe? My responsibility as a Christian in this twenty-first century is to separate the wheat from the chaff of my tradition in order to discover the essence and to grasp the treasure of its ultimate insight into the meaning of God. Then, escaping the limits of my own tradition by breaking out of its boundaries at its very depths, I will be prepared to share its purified treasure with all the world.

My hope is that my brothers and sisters who find Judaism, Islam, Hinduism, or Buddhism as their point of entry, based upon their time and place in history, will also explore their pathway into God in a similar manner, until they too can escape the limits of their tradition at its depths and, grasping the essence of their system's religious insights, move on to share that essence with me and all the world. Then each of us, clinging to the truth, the pearl of great price if you will, that we have found in the spiritual wells from which we have drunk, can reach across the once insuperable barriers to share as both givers and receivers in the riches present in all human sacred traditions. A new day will thus be born, and Jesus—who crossed every boundary of tribe, prejudice, gender, and religion—will be honored by those of us who, as his disciples, have transcended the boundaries of even the religious system that was created to honor him.

The fulfillment of that vision is a dream that I will rejoice to see appear. I have prepared for it by going beyond the imperialistic claims and barrier-erecting prejudices of my tradition to meet deeply spiritual people in faith-communities different not just from my perspective as an Anglican, but from my perspective as a Christian—people raised apart from the Jesus who is my doorway into the holiness of God.

I recall my 1974 dialogue in Richmond, Virginia, with a rabbi, Jack Spiro, and the people of Temple Beth Ahabah—beautiful people who showed me holiness that was shaped apart from Jesus but not apart from God. It was a distinction I could not have made before that experience. I recall another moment, this time in 1984, in the little town of Kottayam in the state of Kerala in the vast nation of India, where I engaged in a dialogue with three Hindu scholars who revealed to me a holiness that had emerged from this noble religious system of India. They had not been shaped by the one I call Christ, but I did not doubt that they had been shaped by the God that I have met in Christ. Finally, I recall my time listening, observing, and praying at a Buddhist temple in the New Territories in China in 1988, and the rich dialogue I enjoyed with two Buddhist monks—the Reverend Kok Kwong and the Reverend Yuen Quing—as we explored the origins and goals of our respective faith-traditions and looked for points of contact not so much in the answers we offered as in the questions we raised. Kok Kwong and Yuen Quing had met my Christ only as a weapon of oppression in the hands of a conquering colonial power. I wanted them to know my Christ through the gentle love I could offer them that day. But God they clearly knew as transcendent, holy, and filled with wonder, and that God so obviously lived in them and through them. The God-presence assumes so many different forms in human history.[6]

In a recent book, my admired friend and fellow priest Matthew Fox suggested groundwater as an analogy by which we might think of God in this post-theistic world. I find that image quite compelling.[7] Groundwater flows beneath the surface of the earth, ultimately sustaining all living things. Periodically it erupts in different ways and in different places. Sometimes that eruption occurs naturally, in the form of a spring or a lake. That spring or lake may become the source of a river; or, if it appears in an isolated desert spot, may remain an oasis. Sometimes people dig wells deep enough into the earth to tap this liquid treasure. Some of these wells are simple mudholes; others are tiled and as complex as modern technology can produce. Out of these wells whole communities are sometimes served.

The springs, rivers, lakes, oases, and wells are viewed in a wide array of explanatory descriptions, each arising out of the faith, the scientific knowledge, the cultures, the values, and the needs of the people who are sustained by that particular source of water. Yet no matter how differently it tastes from one location to another, and no matter how the water is used, it still comes from the same source, and it is ultimately connected in a radical oneness. Perhaps that is not different from the relationship of God to the various religious traditions that seek to interpret the God-presence they have experienced in a particular group of people living in a particular time and place on this planet.

God is, for me, the Ground of Being seen in the being of every living thing, the source of love found in the ability to love present in every creature and the source of life calling everyone everywhere into the fullness of life. This is the God I see through the lens of my time and place in history, the God I believe I have met in Jesus of Nazareth. That is why he is Lord for me. So as theism passes into post-theism, we experience the same God, but in the accents of a new century. I believe that this expanded consciousness, this rejection of theism, this openness to what lies beyond theism, is finally a better way to honor the Christ who is called by those of us who seek God inside the Christian perspective "the Son of God."

# ELEVEN

# BUT WHAT ABOUT PRAYER?

*Not as in the old days I pray,*
*God. My life is not what it was . . .*
*Once I would have asked for healing*
*I go now to be doctored,*
*I would have knelt long, wrestling with you*
*Wearing you down. Hear my prayer, Lord hear*
*my prayer. As though you were deaf, myriads*
*of mortals have kept up their shrill*
*cry, explaining your stillness by*
*their unfitness.*

*It begins to appear this is not what prayer is about.*
*It is the annihilation of differences,*
*the consciousness of myself in you,*
*of you in me; the emerging*
*from the adolescence of nature*
*into the adult geometry*
*of the mind. . . .*
*Circular as our way*
*is, it leads not back to that snake haunted*
*garden, but onward to the tall city*
*of glass that is the laboratory of the spirit.*[1]

— R. S. THOMAS, Twentieth-century Welsh poet

A national news story circulated by the Associated Press[2] recently told of a student athlete at a college—defined in that story as a "Christian Bible school" in Tennessee—who had had both of her legs amputated below the knees as a result of a disease known as meningococcal meningitis. It was a heartrending and tragic event, but life is full of such things, and they do not become front page media narratives. This one, however, touched a strange and different chord.

The unique drama in this particular account was not the tragedy itself, but rather the tension between this tragedy and the concept of God and faith as believed and practiced at this conservative religious institution. It seems that these students expected the promises of God that they read in scripture to be taken literally not just by them, but, more important, also by God. The apostle Paul had directed his readers to "pray without ceasing" (1 Thess. 5:17), and so these young adults did exactly that. Upon hearing of their fellow student's rare diagnosis, they organized around-the-clock prayer vigils so that at no moment of any day or night were the gates of heaven not stormed by a member of that student body on behalf of the endangered classmate.

These believing young people also reminded one another that Jesus had said, "Ask and it will be given to you" (Matt. 7:7), and so these students asked, making their requests known to God relentlessly, constantly. If God has the ability to hear, there is no doubt that God heard their endless petitions.

They told one another, furthermore, that their Christ had assured them in the gospels that "all things are possible" (Mark 9:23) and that prayer can produce miracles, moving mountains if need be (Mark 11:23; Matt. 17:20). They saw this apparent tragedy in the life of their classmate as a test designed to verify the truth of that assurance. They were, they said, simply taking

God at God's word, and they expected God to do God's part, which was nothing more or less than to fulfill the divine promises of scripture. "God does not lie," they assured one another.

But despite all that they believed and all that they did, this disease relentlessly progressed, taking its dramatic toll: this fellow student, an eighteen-year-old female basketball dynamo, was forced to endure a double amputation, losing her ability ever to run or play her favorite sport again. The winner in this struggle was not God, but rather the nonpersonal, amoral, theologically neutral process of a particularly destructive and deadly bacterium. The focus of the wire-service story was therefore not the tragedy that affected this young woman, but the ensuing crisis of faith that embraced the praying students. The story was about their manner of reconciling the ways of God to the reality experienced by these sincere and devout human beings. The nonbeliever's cliché, so filled with hostile satire, which suggests that "Nothing fails to work better than prayer," was the experience that this community endured.

Some students, according to this story, defensively saved the basic assumption of their faith by moving from the task of praying for specific things to the far more passive and dependent stance of praying only "thy will be done." These students did not seem to embrace the fact that this shift rendered the promises they quoted from scripture to be null and void. Yet this is a familiar place of retreat for religious people when reality fails to affirm piety. In this retreat, whatever happens, no matter how tragic or evil, must be accepted as God's will. Thus faithfulness merely requires people to accept as God's will whatever happens in their lives.

That stance presents us with a strange deity who wills such things as the amputation of a young person's legs and the loss of life for countless infants and children to crib death, leukemia, gunshot, and more. This pious, but woefully inadequate, fallback position also means we must conclude that those who are killed in war, as well as those who manage to survive, somehow die or live according to the will of a deity who controls the world. It is not an easy concept to uphold rationally. It does not seem fair. The theistic God pointed to in this mindset appears to be manipulative, vindictive, and even cruel.

Other students at this same school had as their primary concern the fact that their victimized fellow student might turn her wrath on God and blame the deity for her fate. If God had the power to save her legs and did not do so, then God was surely guilty of blameworthy malevolence. That conclusion, so obvious in this kind of thinking was, according to these classmates, fraught with peril for her soul. If she, as the victim, adopted such a stance, it would, in the minds of her fellow students, constitute blasphemy. The great danger of blasphemy is that the blasphemer runs the risk of incurring, once again, the divine wrath. If God had on this first occasion struck her in anger, what might God do if she were to return the divine anger with her own? God might just strike again, and even more terribly! This scenario, contemplated with fear by these young believers, presents us with a picture of theism at its immoral worst. God is now portrayed as a vindictive demon.

Another student offered yet another theory that further reveals the inadequacies of all theistic thinking. This tragedy in his classmate's life was, he asserted, simply part of another more complex divine plan that God had in mind for her. Neither the student offering the explanation nor the victim herself could see that plan from their place in time, he argued, but someday, if they trusted God deeply enough, it would be revealed. At that later moment the purpose of this tragedy would be fully understood. God's will would then be clear, and the people would be able to see that what they had believed all along was still true.

The beauty of this rationalization was that God would be vindicated eventually. Then, this student suggested, the victim would give thanks that this experience, so apparently purposeless initially, had been part of God's grand plan. The loss of her legs, he suggested, was actually just a necessary stepping stone into a greater opportunity that God would reveal to her. God apparently had some need for a legless young adult. God would still be God once the vindication was complete, and the unspoken but very real questions that now plagued the minds of those whose view of God was being tested, would be satisfactorily answered without their theistic images ever being disturbed. This too is a familiar religious defensive position, one employed by human beings for centuries.

People do learn to cope with tragedy. People who lose their eyesight develop new levels of compensatory sensory and intuitive awareness. A paraplegic's heroic struggles do inspire others to greater efforts that affect the quality of many people's lives. People do die nobly or bear grief creatively and thus help many to find a deeper way to live and a new commitment to use the time in life available to them in a more dedicated, less self-centered manner. But can any of us honestly argue that these benefits are the divine reasons that such tragic events occur? Is there a divine plan worked out by a theistic God who has the whole world in the divine hands and who pulls this string here and that string there but who is clearly always in full control? Is it only that the total picture of this God is never fully revealed, so mortals must trust God's ultimate benevolence and learn to "walk by faith"—faith that there is such a plan and faith that God really is like that which we have constructed God to be? Or is such faith nothing more than delusional theistic thinking, so false that it needs to be dismissed?

Some of the students who attended this Bible college with the ailing basketball player said that the experience of trying to make sense out of this tragedy in the light of their view of God would remain with them forever; they expected it to be among the most enduring of their college memories. The experience had galvanized the whole student body. Praying together around the clock had been a dramatic community-building event. Projects designed to raise money to cover the enormous medical bills their classmate faced even spilled over into the entire community and gave the students an enormous sense of purpose, of doing something worthwhile, of standing on the God-human boundary, and of breathing in an atmosphere that projected them onto those edges of life's mysteriousness that few people encounter on a regular basis.

This story, however, raised for me a host of questions that regularly come my way as I struggle to think of God in nontheistic patterns while I continue to be a praying, worshiping Christian. When I am doing public lectures designed to call people beyond the boundaries of theism, the questions that come first when the lecture is complete are generally focused more on the subject of prayer than on any other subject. These questions seek to retain the meaning found in both individual prayer and the corporate prayers that form a part of the liturgy of the church. Questions about life after death are a distant second. That pattern is so consistent that I have come to expect it.

Somehow prayer and liturgy are the places where the nontheistic God-concept most obviously collides with the religious security system erected by the worshipers of the theistic God. _To whom do we pray?_ is at the heart of questions asked by those considering abandonment of theism. A gripping sense of aloneness lies barely beneath the surface of their words: _Are you saying that there is no parent God in the sky?_ they wonder anxiously. _If there is no supernatural being outside the world who directs the affairs of human life in an intensely personal way and who answers our prayers, why bother with Christianity at all or with the Christian God?_ they seem to be saying. I get the impression that many believers think of prayers as adult letters to Santa Claus. The ability of their God to respond to their prayers becomes the point for them at which faith lives or dies. So it was and is an appropriate question that requires an appropriate response.

What does prayer mean? To whom does one pray? How does prayer work? That is the way prayer questions are usually framed. Yet when the questions are asked in words such as these, the questions themselves have the effect of defining prayer inside traditional concepts. The assumptions that underlie such questions are that prayers consist of petitions and intercessions addressed to the deity, that the deity is external to this world, and that the deity can intervene to assist the one praying in a personal crisis or in a crisis in the life of his or her society.

As such, prayer is a direct descendant of the behavior of those first self-conscious ancestors of our humanity. Traumatized at the feeling of helplessness and hopelessness, those ancestors met their anxiety by postulating the existence of a protector more powerful than the forces that threatened them. Prayer has thus traditionally been an attempt to seek the aid of that protector or to form an alliance with that supernatural being. The assumption has been that this supernatural being is able to do more for us than we can do for ourselves. Prayer consequently perpetuates the primary illusion of theism—namely, that we are not alone, that there is a personal power somewhere, which is greater than the limited power of humanity; and that this personal power can effectively deal with all of those issues that lie beyond human competence to solve. Prayer began as, and continues to be, a primary attempt to exercise control in those arenas of life where we sense ourselves to be out of control, ineffective, weak, victimized.

The traditional understanding and definition of prayer, then, is finally nothing more than an attempt to control the impact experienced in the trauma of self-consciousness or in the shock of nonbeing. Thus prayer, please recognize, is the way a human being plays the trump card of theism. When that card ceases to work, however, the praying person must discover a way to live with the loss of the protector and thus with the inadequacy of theism. So as theism dies, the human understanding of God's behavior begins to express itself in more and more convoluted explanations. The students at the Bible college in the story at the beginning of this chapter used every one of these explanations.

The theistic God must be protected from the irrationality that seems to surround the deity. This God must be shown to be in control, no matter what the evidence suggests to the contrary. Some divine or benevolent purpose must be discovered that serves to explain the irrationality of life or the suffering that appears so undeserved and so shocking. But those explanations are no longer adequate, because theism is dead.

Sickness and tragedy are not punishments; sickness and tragedy are facts of life. Viruses attack. Wars kill. Tumors are formed. Leukemia strikes. Blood vessels wear out and rupture. Innocent people are killed by drunk drivers and by psychotic people acting out a drama that makes sense only within their sick minds. Accidents occur. Alcohol distorts. Children are killed playing with guns.

These are the facts of existence. There is no theistic God directing these processes of cause and effect to whom we can appeal. There is no divine plan that we must either seek to know or await its unfolding patiently. That is neither the way life is nor the way God is. The belief that God is at the helm is only the modern-day remnant of the theistic system that our forebears developed at the dawn of self-consciousness in order to still human angst, to enable them to survive the trauma of self-consciousness. Today that theistic system is dying the slow death of irrelevance. Theism is a truth no longer saluted. But theism is also a security blanket with which we are loathe to part. Like all security blankets, theism may make us better able to pretend that we are competent to cope with life. But when the crisis comes, theism and security blankets both prove inadequate to deliver what they so loudly promise.

So does this mean that prayer must also cease when theism dies? I do not believe so! I, as a post-theistic Christian, still pray. I pray daily. I pray as one who believes that God is real. I pray in the confidence that this activity is still in touch with meaning. I pray in the awareness of a relatedness found in all of life and especially among those of us who share the glory and the anxiety of self-conscious humanity.

But how do I pray? To whom do I pray? One cannot simply assert the validity of this experience without a further explanation.

I begin my answer by recommending that we face the limitations of our language and seek first to find a new word to describe the activity we have tended in the past to call prayer. I do that because the word *prayer* is so shaped by the theistic understanding that it is almost useless in our post-theistic world. I propose instead that we substitute words that have over the centuries been identified with the mystical disciplines of spiritual development—words such as *meditation* and *contemplation*. I hear people today talk of something they call "centering prayer." I hear them refer to breathing exercises that are designed to heighten self-awareness. These words and concepts help to begin the task of creating a new definition of prayer.

Next, I seek to find some experience inside my life that might correspond to that which drove our ancestors in faith into the activity they called prayer. I discover in my own depths a spiritual desire, an internal yearning, to be more deeply the person I am and thus to become one who is more capable of giving myself to others. Sometimes this desire inside me is all but overwhelming. It is, I believe, nothing less than an inner quest for being which in my understanding is identical with the human desire for God. It is that restlessness about which Augustine spoke that remains unresolved until we rest in God.[3] That is a description of the desire, the reality that calls a new language of prayer out of me.

In this experience I discover a new sense of what it means to be fully human. This new humanity almost totally counters the way of life that my evolutionary history has created in me—namely, the human propensity to make survival our highest good. My life teaches me that when I can give my being away to another, without any anticipation of being compensated with any gift in return, not only do I experience no diminution of my selfhood, but

I become an enhancer of the life of another, the expander of the love present in that other. I sense that this makes me nothing less than an agent of God.

Why would anyone ever think that this was not a worthwhile enterprise in and of itself? Why do people presume that if there is no payoff for goodness, there will be no motivating force? Is not the presumed reward nothing but a means of keeping my self-centered anxiety in full control? Is goodness not good for its own sake? If prayer does not bring results, does it lose all its worth? Why can we not surrender the need to manipulate and control God by receiving a payoff? When Paul said, "Pray without ceasing," was he not referring to a way of living rather than to a specific act of doing? *BOTH*

Has it never occurred to the followers of the God met in Jesus that when Jesus promised a "second coming" he might have been speaking not of his own mythological return in the clouds of a theistic heaven, but rather of the second coming of the God who is present in each of us? Is it not the same God who was present in Jesus who comes again to our world in us and through us? Is the imagery of the second coming of Jesus that has dominated traditional Christian thinking not simply an attempt to rescue the traditional image of messiahship that in fact failed to be accomplished in Jesus' life—an image that Christians were forced by history to relegate to his second coming? Can we dare to embrace the possibility that we ourselves might be the second coming of Christ?[4] Does the grandiosity of that suggestion discredit it in our minds?

The time is right to explore even unheard-of dimensions. These possibilities offer us a new way to think about and even to enter the activity we tend to call prayer. We know that the theological perspective, suggesting that our frail humanity is always in need of a divine protector, does not work. It presents us with a deity that we must please, placate, flatter, and beg, one whose power is so overwhelming that we are reduced to a childlike dependency. Contrast that with a theological perspective that affirms God's power present at the center of our lives—a power that calls us more deeply into the mystery of Being and into a fuller humanity! Do we need any longer an external, invasive, miracle-working deity who must be implored to come to our aid? Would we not do better to seek from within ourselves a God-presence that would enable us to embrace the fragility of our humanity and to step boldly into the experience of living fully, loving wastefully, and entering courageously into the depths of being?

If we reject the theistic deity beyond the sky, the deity who was supposed to take care of us, do we have to reject also the depth of life present within each of us and within the gathered human community that sustains us and propels us beyond our limits? Is not that depth of life what God is? As we grow into maturity, we begin to entertain the possibility that to discover the fullness of our being is also to discover the meaning of prayer. It is our *shared* being that binds us powerfully into a human community.

While teaching at Harvard, I listened to one student present a paper dealing with the massive difficulties present in the health-care system now available to the citizens of the United States.[5] At his conclusion he noted that the only thing Christians really have to bring to health care, as it is presently practiced, is neither prayers nor lobbying activities, but the gift of community. As the health-care system becomes more impersonal, the community must be present to personalize the life of the one who is sick. No one should be sick alone. No one should die alone. No one should seek high-tech solutions to medical problems without a community to provide a high-touch environment of love.

It is not that these intensely human things will stop sickness, bring about cures, or postpone the inevitability of death, but rather that these things will enhance life, expand love, and enable a deeper being to emerge in both the giver and the receiver. But the suggestion that through this process comes a healing that is the result of human petition or intercession turns God into a being who does our will. That is a strange idea indeed. Prayer is rather the activity that enables each of us to be givers to and receivers from one another of the deepest meaning of life—a meaning I call God.

In the more traditional and theistic phase of my life, I developed a habit of spending the first two hours of the day—from six to eight—in my office at home in prayer and study. I would pray first for those nearest and dearest to me, easily crossing the boundary of death that today separates me from my parents, my first wife, my brother-in-law, and some very precious friends. I would use various calendars, such as the Anglican Cycle of Prayer, the House of Bishops' Prayer List, and the Diocesan Prayer Cycle, each of which would serve to link me by prayer to that Christian community in which I lived.

Then I would go through the world's trouble-spots, praying for peace and for the end of suffering in war-torn lands. I must say prayer was particularly meaningful to me when someone I knew well was in the eye of a particular storm: Desmond and Leah Tutu in the struggle to end apartheid in South Africa or Bob and Lance Moody[6] in Oklahoma at the time of the bombing of the government building in Oklahoma City. Finally, I would go over the things I had to do that day, bringing both people and events into my prayer focus.

All of this was within the context of what the church once called "matins" or "morning prayer," which included lectionary scripture readings, chants of praise, and other worship elements. That format also provided a period for a homily which, in the privacy of those early hours, I turned into the discipline of reading a major theological book systematically over an entire year.[7] My assumption at that time was that this was for me the holy time of being in touch with God each day. Robert Schuller might have called this my "hour of power."[8] My image then was that power ignited by my prayers flowed outward to all of these recipients of my concern. I was meeting the expectations of both my religion and my profession.

As I moved beyond theism into a post-theistic understanding of God, I discovered that my commitment to starting my day with this focused two-hour time slot did not change, but my understanding of what I was doing did—and dramatically. It made perhaps a 180-degree turn. The primary shift came in what I thought the prayer part of my day was. It ceased to be identified with these first two hours each morning and shifted to embrace the balance of the day. My actions, my engagement with people, the facing of concrete issues—all these became for me the real time of prayer. My prayer came to be identified with my living, my loving, my being, my meeting, my confronting, my struggles for justice, my desire to be an agent of the world's transformation. That was where I met and communed with God. God was no longer found for me in the quiet places of retreat; now God was in the hurly-burly of a busy and sometimes troubling life. God was found not in the stable rocks but in the rushing rapids.

If prayer is the act of engaging God and if God is the source of life, then my prayer time became my time of engaging life. The monastic prayer pattern created by a theism that located God outside of life, an understanding that suggested that one must withdraw from life to pray or to be holy, was turned upside down. Prayer became for me the way I lived, loved, and struggled, the way I dared to be. Preparation for prayer was the time I spent in my office each morning recalling who I am, remembering where God is and how God can be met. So my definitions of what prayer is and what life is shifted totally, while the way I organized my life remained the same. To this day that early-morning time of two hours remains an enormous part of who I am.

Does that God-activity which I do each morning change the patterns of history? Since I no longer think of prayer as invoking the presence of an external deity, would it make any objective difference in my world if I were to cease this discipline of a lifetime? Well, I no longer expect to change the mind or the will of the theistic deity. That is a clear conclusion. I no longer expect God to act in human life in some way different from the normal course of cause and effect. I no longer believe that my uttered prayers will alter the progress of a disease or change a hurricane's wind or even deter the mind of a military adventurer. I remain skeptical of the claims religious people have made in history for their prayers. I do not deny that love shared or concern expressed creates positive energy. I do not deny that positive energy has therapeutic power, that positive energy enhances life and being just as negative energy diminishes and drains life and being. But I make no claims beyond that.

I do believe that my early-morning time prepares me more adequately to be a God-bearer—a source of life, love, and being to others. I also claim that this private time equips me to do that task more fully, more adequately, and more completely. I know that I am changed, opened, sensitized, and strengthened to act by setting aside this preparation time each day. But I no longer think of that as *prayer* time. Prayer for me is *living*. Preparation time is a time of discovering who I am and who God is within me, so that I can live my life out of that knowledge. That is what enables me to "pray without ceasing"—that is, to live without counting the costs or seeking to preserve my strength. As noted earlier, today I find words such as *meditation* and *contemplation*—words that do not suggest that I am seeking to change anything more than myself—to be preferable to the word *prayer*, with its connotation of petitioning the theistic deity to intercede in order to force a new solution on history that might not be possible if such intercessions were not offered. PRAY-ER...

When someone suggests, as my religious critics insist on doing, that I no longer pray, what they are really suggesting is that I no longer understand and practice prayer as they do. I no longer expect a theistic deity to work for me, but I do expect to spend my days working for the expansion of life, for the fullness of love, for the enhancement of being. That is, I expect to do the work of God—a God I believe is real. I no longer seek to define this God in terms of a supernatural person. I do believe, however, that I experience this God when I am an agent of life, love, and being to another. For the God I worship, the God I see in Jesus of Nazareth, is revealed in the personhood of everyone. This God is present in the love of everyone. This God is encountered in the being of everyone. This God calls me constantly to be the incarnation of this God's love, a witness to the reality of this God's life. I do these things by working to enhance the humanity of every person, to free the life present in every person, to increase the love available to every person, and to celebrate the being of every person. It is in those actions that I discern the very presence of the divine footprints and know that God has been in this place before me and sometimes because of me.

I am also experientially ready to affirm that the power of prayer is very clear in the profound way that my times of meditation and contemplation have, in fact, changed *me*. They have helped me to face more honestly who I am and how I impact others. Is that somehow different from confession? Yet there is nothing left of that image of a groveling sinner seeking mercy from a divine judge.

My times of prayer and meditation have convinced me in a radically new way that I am not alone. Rather, I am bound together in a community that could indeed be described as a "great cloud of witnesses" (Heb. 12:1). I am both a lover of others and one beloved by others. The giving and receiving of love are intimately bound together. There is life-changing power in that realization. I wonder, is that experience somehow different from intercession?

My early-morning hours of focused meditation have enabled me time after time to solve problems, step across barriers, move beyond my prejudices and fears, and enter a new being, a barrier-free humanity. I wonder, is this somehow different from petition?

Finally, I find great energy in these preparatory times. For here visions are born that later, in fact, do change the world as I am experiencing it. I am empowered to be someone I have not been before and to do some things I have never been able to do before. Change in who I am brings change in what I can do. Sometimes that change is minuscule, sometimes it is massive, but change always occurs. I stand in awe of that reality. I wonder, is that any different from adoration and praise?

I am part of that change process because I am part of who God is. That is my startling conclusion. Incarnation is not just a fact about Jesus. It is a symbol of how God, who is the source of life, love, and being, operates. God was in Christ, reconciling. God is in me. God is in you, reconciling, healing, restoring, making whole. Prayer is thus the conscious recognition of that reality.

So I pray. I pray constantly, but I pray nontheistically. My goal in life is to pray without ceasing, which means that I seek to be a God-presence in every relationship I enter. I could not live this way without simultaneously affirming the living reality of the God that my life serves and without the necessity of having my life centered in that God and connected to that God in all that I am and do. That is the first and the personal part of my answer to the question of prayer.

TWELVE

# THE ECCLESIA OF TOMORROW

*The whole earth must become resanctified in our eyes: the holy colour must change from heavenly purple to earthly green. The imperative to care must take precedence over lesser loyalties and over all differences of race, nationality, gender and personal beliefs. It is the kind of love which is ready to sacrifice individual self-interest for the greater good of the whole. ... This calls for the kind of self-sacrificing love which has long been affirmed in the Christian tradition and symbolised as the way of the cross.*[1]

— LLOYD G. GEERING, theologian, New Zealand

**P**rayer is not just an individual activity. It is also a corporate phenomenon. Worshipers gather in spaces that have been consecrated, both officially and by a constant and holy usage, to offer their prayers to God. Liturgy is the name we give to the various forms that this corporate worship activity takes. Typically, the liturgies of the churches are even more infected with theistic images than are individual prayers, and these images endure in their corporate setting far longer than they do in individualistic settings. Indeed, the last place where change tends to make its presence felt is in the corporate liturgies of well-established churches.

Yet even there change is inevitable. The Roman Catholic mass has abandoned its classical Latin. The Anglican *Book of Common Prayer* is periodically revised. The books of worship of every other liturgical church are always undergoing modification. In the "free churches"—that is, those using congregational polity— the liturgy is even more amenable to change, because it is normally designed by the resident pastor and thus tends to reflect his or her theological convictions.

In a previous book[2] I cited various changes that, while barely noticed by congregations, are noteworthy—such changes as moving the altar from the back wall of our sanctuaries and placing the priest or celebrant behind that altar facing the people. This shift has become almost universal in liturgical churches during the last fifty years. Though it seems a minor change and has been defended by proponents in a variety of ways, it signifies to me a gradual realization of the death of theism. The priest or pastor with his or her back to the people is addressing the theistic God out there beyond the sky. The priest facing the people is addressing the God present in the midst of creation. That is a significant transition.

Simultaneously, there have been other changes to which I have previously referred—the decline in the practice of kneeling, for example, the verbal modifications, and even the specially printed handouts, that enable the use of inclusive language. There is an increasing discomfort with the kingly vestments that bishops in particular wear, with the parental titles that clergy use, and with the entourage of lesser orders needed to support the principle liturgical leader.

Yet the language of hymns, prayers, and other parts of the liturgy is still predominantly shaped by the traditional concepts of this lingering theism. God is defined as an external other in most of our liturgies. As such this God is praised, flattered, placated, beseeched, entreated, and begged in both spoken and sung words. The concept of the fall into an original corrupting sin, previously noted as both an inaccurate and dated concept in our post-Darwinian world, still underlies the words of many prayers. I recall one prayer from an official ecclesiastical worship book that refers to human life as worthless, weak, ignorant, and helpless inside the space of five lines.

This sense of universal evil into which presumably all are born still underlies the sacrament of baptism as I have also previously noted. In recent revisions of the baptismal liturgy, churches have tended to blunt the rhetorical excesses of this negativity, but they have not removed them. Once the liturgy renounced in a rather straightforward way the world, the flesh, and the Devil. Now we speak a bit more metaphorically of the corrupting powers of this world, the forces of evil that draw us from the love of God, and the sinful desires of the flesh. The language of being made clean in the waters of baptism, of being washed from all our sins, and the implied threat that apart from baptism there is no salvation, however, are still present in most liturgies.

The idea of Jesus' death on the cross as a human sacrifice offered to God and understood as a payment, or a ransom, for the sins of the world is still found in the heart of the service of holy communion. The primary message in the liturgical reenactment of the sacrifice of Jesus on the cross is that we were incapable of saving ourselves so Jesus did it for us, at the cost of his life. We are supposed to be the grateful yet passive recipients of this act of salvation. We seek to blunt the message of human sacrifice or divine child abuse found in the eucharist, or mass, or Lord's supper, yet both are present in the literal words that our liturgies use, which are at best uncomfortable and at worst repelling.

I am frequently asked how I can continue to do liturgical events in ecclesiastical settings when I am calling into question the ultimate meanings expressed in the traditional language of liturgy. That is a fair question.

Perhaps it does not bother me as much as it should. I welcome the changes as they come, but I have learned not to literalize liturgical words. I treat them as poetry, symbols, or illuminating phrases used by our forebears in faith to articulate their deepest yearnings. I see the words extolling the theistic God's great power as a way we articulate the human call to move beyond our weaknesses into a new humanity. I see the breast-beating words of human failure not to be the response of a naughty child before a judging parent, but to be an act of self-analysis: we enumerate our failures to become aware of those internal realities that block us from ourselves, one another, and the source of life itself. I see praises and elaborate accolades offered to God as nothing but laudatory activity designed to call us beyond our boundaries into the greatness of being the body of Christ. I celebrate those sacrificial elements of our liturgies as the way our ancestors in faith treated their yearning for atonement, a way to overcome their sense of alienation and separation from their deepest identity as God-bearers.

Clearly, I find some prayers more primitive than others and tend to avoid them. I also find some hymns more gauche than others and refuse to sing them.[3] I experience some liturgies as being more sentimentally subjective and maudlin than others and would not welcome a steady diet of them. None of these things, however, blocks me from worship. So while I call for radical reformation, I continue to worship under the discipline of a prayer book that still reflects, in apparently literal language, some things that I cannot literally say with any personal integrity.

Perhaps this is nothing more than the schizophrenia brought about by a lifetime of familiarity with or a love of the words of antiquity. Perhaps it even represents a failure of nerve. But I do not think so. I treat the language of worship like I treat the language of love. It is primitive, excessive, flowery, poetic, evocative. No one really believes it literally. When I say to my wife that she is the most wonderful and beautiful person in the world, no one thinks I have conducted a global poll to ascertain the literal truth of that statement. Likewise, I do not say or sing the words of liturgy to express a literal truth.

What I seek to do in public liturgy is to enable all of the participants to begin the journey that will carry them into meanings that liturgical words can never capture. Indeed, my experience is that liturgical words are inevitably primitive and that the more deeply one enters into what I call the God-experience, the more all words fade as vehicles of meaning. At the center of that God-experience, the worshiper is reduced to silence before the awe, the mystery, and the wonder of the divine. Thus dated words and archaic practices are not the burden to me that they might be to others. I rejoice in that, but I do not seek to hide in that conclusion from the task of reformation.

I am deeply aware that people who do not have a lifetime of living inside the liturgies of the church find them to be everything from mentally and emotionally disturbing to piously nonsensical. I am aware that for many, hearing liturgy is like listening to a language that the worshiper can neither speak nor understand. For others, liturgy presents the gymnastic task of twisting their minds into theological pretzels in order to utter meaningless sounds that do not seem to connect them with any reality whatsoever. I must look at new ways the church can worship with meaning as we live beyond the exile, purged by the reformation that is upon us, and redefined as the body of Christ in what will surely be a death and resurrection experience. What will that church and its liturgy look like, and what are the steps we will have to take and the path we will have to follow to get from where we are now to what the church must be in the future?

My guess is that our journey into that future will not be marked with abrupt transitions. We will rather tend to move experientially into tomorrow. We cannot grasp with our rational faculties something that our minds cannot yet envision or our words capture. Nonetheless, I think that those of us who at least pretend that we can perceive what lies ahead have a responsibility to hold that vision up high for all to see. With the caveat that this is all I am trying to offer clearly stated, and with a tip of my hat to that rescuing role of the community of faith about which I have already spoken, I dare to plunge into this task.

What purpose will be found in our post-theistic world that will cause people to gather together on some regular basis to engage in an act that could be described as worship? I begin this analysis by stating first what that purpose will *not* be. It will *not* be to sing the praises of a theistic deity. It will *not* be to confess our sins or shortcomings to a parental judge in order to wipe our particular slate clean so that we might try again. It will *not* be to count on the power of the community's prayers in directing the course of world history, the weather, or the life-and-death issues of any individual. It will *not* be to cleanse babies through baptism of the sinful and fallen humanity into which they were born, nor will it be to reenact liturgically the divine sacrifice made on the cross of Calvary to secure our rescue from a presumed hopeless state of original sin. It will *not* be to have our eyes and our minds lifted upward by Gothic arches and pointed windows to contemplate the God who lives above the sky. No, all of these are images that come out of our dying theistic world. That world is no longer well or alive.

Yet I believe that there will still be a need for a place where we might gather to worship and that worship will continue to be a function of whatever the church becomes in the post-theistic future. We may not even call that new post-theistic institution a church. Other names are available and probably ought to be considered—mosque, temple, synagogue, holy place, or ecclesia. I tend to support the latter—a transliterated Greek word—as the preferred name for the post-theistic religious institution of the future, because it means "those called out."

I see this new church or ecclesia as the community of those who have been called out of limits, out of prejudices, out of brokenness, out of self-centeredness. But one cannot be called *out* of anything without also being called *into* something. So I also see the ecclesia as a community of people called into life, called into love, called into being, called into wholeness, called into God. This community will, I believe, continue to gather on a regular basis to remember and to celebrate who they are, what it means to be human, and how they can be agents of life.

Part of the liturgy of the future will be the recollection and re-hearsal of our sacred stories, our past. But we must go far beyond those moments now celebrated as the beginnings of our faith-story. By that I mean that we must go beyond such things as Abraham's journey from Ur of the Chaldeans to found a new people, the exodus of Moses and the Hebrew people into the promised land, and even Jesus' journey to the hill called Calvary, which brought the Christian church into being. Our liturgy of the future must celebrate the long human journey from the first form of life in a single cell to the complexity of our modern, fearful, human self-consciousness. That celebration must help us to recognize, and then to remember our connectedness with all living things in both the plant and animal worlds—a connectedness that the dis-covery of DNA and of the human genome has revealed to be very close. That celebration must enable us to see the mutuality of life and to be cognizant that one can be neither human, nor a living being of any kind, alone. Liturgies of the future may thus bring us a renewed understanding that each of us is able to live only because of our interdependence so powerfully expressed in the realization that every species feeds on another in the endless cycle of life.

We will also learn to honor in our worship the gift of self-con-sciousness—that major step which enhanced the meaning of life dramatically—even as we recognize how fearful a thing it is to be aware of our finitude, our mortality, and the fragile nature of our life. One of the goals of worship in the ecclesia of tomorrow will be to help those who gather in community to enhance their self-awareness, to grasp the incredible dignity of being fully human, and to live more deeply, richly, and completely than any of us have yet been able to do. This worship will be postulated on the conviction that the pathway into the divine must go through the development of a fuller humanity.

Worshipers will also face those aspects of our journey through our vast evolutionary history that still scar our humanity. I refer once more, but this time liturgically, to that radical self-centeredness created in the evolutionary struggle that I have suggested elevated survival to be our highest value. This self-centeredness has served our survival needs well in our evolving years, enabling us to succeed in the struggle for life. But that same gift, now casts a dark shadow across our continued capacity to endure the anxieties of our existence.

We have evolved faster technologically than we have as the responsible masters of that technology, which means that we have the capacity to destroy all consciousness by a technological accident or an environmental disaster. Yet we, in our self-centeredness, do not appear to have the wisdom to deal with that danger competently. This is what the strange tribal behavior reveals when every nation on this tiny planet wants to own or build armaments capable of killing every human being in the world some twenty times. Rationality would suggest that one death per person would be sufficient!

Shortsighted, self-centered tribal behavior is also visible in our unwillingness to cease the pollution of our environment even though we have the power to do so. We act out of the conviction that the effects of pollution are unlikely to be devastating in our particular lifetimes, so we passively allow them to worsen rather than striving mightily to reverse them. We clearly put our needs, our comfort, and our economic well-being above the needs of future generations. The worship of the church in the future must therefore assist us to grow beyond these limits until we arrive at a place where it is not personal or tribal survival, but the making of corporate decisions for the welfare of the whole human race, that becomes the highest human virtue. That will mean such things as limiting, by commitment or by law, the spiraling birthrate and making responsible family planning a universally saluted value. Those who cannot or will not help to rein in the birthrate must be named immoral and be penalized severely for their disregard of corporate responsibility for this prerequisite of survival.

Worship must also be the means whereby we challenge and alter radically our excessive ways of living in the developed parts of the world. That means that it will call us to act in such a way as to begin to level the gap between rich and poor. It will also address the task of removing the scars that our prejudices in the past have inflicted on our victims. It will celebrate the oneness of humanity as self-conscious creatures who are now asked to be the co-creators of whatever life lies ahead of us. In activities of this nature we will find something reminiscent of, but yet quite different from, confession, absolution, and the vow to live a redeemed life.

In the ecclesia of tomorrow we will obviously continue to have ritual acts that are designed to mark human transitions. Life seems to demand that. There will surely always be a ritual to welcome a newborn baby into the life of the community, for example, because that is the way life is renewed. That ritual act might well even continue to use water as a symbol, since it is in the breaking of the maternal waters that life is born. Furthermore, our evolutionary history has taught us that water was the original home of life itself. A ceremony of water baptism might continue to remind us of that. But baptism, to survive, must shed its negativity and concentrate on the wonder and hope of life, not the depravity and sin of life.

Other moments in life that cry out for a liturgical observance and that have traditionally been observed include puberty, marriage, childbirth, parenthood, sickness, aging, and death. Such observances will surely find continuation, even as their content will be transformed by our deepening understanding of life itself. Puberty, for example, is not something unclean. Marriage is not a compromise with sin. Childbirth does not require the ceremonial cleansing of the mother. Parenthood involves both parents equally. Sickness is not punishment for sin. Aging and death are not unnatural. The liturgies of the ecclesia of tomorrow will make all of these adjustments.

All people develop a way to celebrate their particular faith-story, which has for them defined humanity. But in the ecclesia of tomorrow, none of these faith-stories will be allowed to condemn or denigrate another. All will be honored as pathways into the wonder of the divine. The people of the ecclesia will share in that expanded identity.

But that does not mean that Christians will be required to abandon the Christ-story—the particular and treasured pathway of those of us whose faith came out of Judea through the Western world. We will continue to walk this pathway that has led us to God and to the meaning of life itself. The Christ-figure will continue to be our central icon, the gift we have to offer the world. That Christ-life will be seen as the one that helps us know who we are now, that holds before us a vision of who we can become in the future, and that defines for us what life is finally all about. We will therefore continue to lift this life up liturgically, enabling the Christ to stand in some defining way before the evolving ecclesia.

That is the way liturgy works; it helps us connect with the divine by rehearsing divinity as it was revealed in the Christ. The moment that this Christ-life entered history will thus continue to be celebrated with appropriate birth stories and festivities. In the northern hemisphere it will be associated with the return of light at the winter solstice, as it has been for centuries. Perhaps the Christian part of the southern hemisphere will someday free itself from the European-imposed liturgical connection of the birth of Jesus with December 25 (a date that is totally meaningless in the actual life of Jesus) and begin to celebrate his birth as light coming into the world's darkness in late June, which would be *its* winter solstice.

The climax of the Christ-story, the moment that this Christ-life transformed and transcended human history, will continue to be observed with proper somberness and perhaps even with penitence for the human response to that life, for that is what the crucifixion means theologically. We could not endure either the vision or the maturity to which he called us, and he would not compromise his vision; so we killed him. But then we will also observe with great celebration his relentless call to enter the realm of God, as he has done, for that is the meaning of the Easter story; that is what it means to break the barrier of death.

In the northern hemisphere that remembrance is now celebrated coterminously with the emerging life returning each spring to conquer the deadness of winter. The southern hemisphere needs to find the freedom to move that celebration into the September-October phase of their year, which for them is the time of the emergence of new life, for that is what the resurrection symbolizes. To keep the celebration of Easter in April in New Zealand, when the trees are shedding their leaves and the harvest is complete, is to be bound to a mindless literalism.

The events that marked that Christ-life as revelatory of some ultimate meaning—those epiphanous moments when the heavens seemed to open to reveal in Jesus the meaning of life itself—will be ceremonially reenacted in the worship of the ecclesia. Worship will be a compelling drama, drawing the whole world to that which this life reveals, as if we were all magi following our stars. The task of worship is not to compel devotion to an external God who has invaded our world, but to hold before the world on a regular basis the eternal meaning that we have found in the special life of Jesus, the new being that was revealed through this Christ figure as he endured the climactic events in his life.

Perhaps the drama that has traditionally defined this Christ-life in the liturgies of the past will continue to be reenacted corporately in the context of a shared meal, but surely the focus of our new celebration will be quite different. Food is such a powerful symbol. Love and food are intimately connected in human experience, from that first moment of life when the new baby nurses at his or her mother's breast while cradled in her arms. Perhaps the major liturgical event in the life of the ecclesia will continue to be a liturgical meal—a new eucharist if you will—that calls to mind the ultimate power of love about which we have learned from the Christ-life that stands at the center of our faith-story. It will not, however, focus on sacrifice and rescue, but on a call to move in response to love, as this Christ did, beyond our self-imposed barriers into a new humanity.

In liturgy we need to be led to recognize that while survival was the driving value that enabled self-conscious human beings to win the evolutionary struggle, it will not be the value that moves us into a new humanity. A new humanity depends on our ability to move beyond the self-centered mentality of survival and into the kind of being that has developed a capacity to love others beyond our own needs—indeed, beyond our own limits. So one of the goals of the ecclesia will be to organize its worship life in such a way as to encourage this selfless love. That is the compelling reason why Jesus will continue, I believe, to stand at the center of our liturgy as the empowering example of one who could live fully, love wastefully, and be all that he was capable of being. In his life we can point to a moment in history when humanity was opened to divinity, when human life became the vehicle for the experience of divine life, when human love was expanded until people saw it as the vessel bearing divine love, and when the Ground of All Being was revealed in a particular being. If the word *Christ* stands for that moment or that person through whom the word of God is spoken and the will of God is lived out, then we might actually say of that life in our liturgy, "Jesus, you are the Christ, the Son of the living God." For it is in these ways that this life has opened to us the doors of transcendence and has enabled us to see the meaning of our lives when they are related to the reality of God.

We will of necessity remove from this life all of those traditional words implying that this life was the incarnation of a theistic deity. We will cease portraying this person as one who came to rescue us, by dying, as if some despotic deity actually required such a blood offering. No, the defining life around which the liturgy of the future will be organized is that of a Christ who can help us to see that when we are fully human, we become the channel for that which is fully divine, that love which expands life and consciousness and being. So this Christ-life, newly defined, will continue to be at the heart of our liturgy; it will be the focal point, the interpretive clue around which worship in the ecclesia of tomorrow will be organized.

Guilt will no longer be a weapon of control and oppression in this emerging ecclesia. To make people feel guilty is not to enhance humanity. The task of tomorrow's worship will be to call people beyond those limitations out of which their guilt arises. Worship in the ecclesia will not be aimed at controlling or repressing behavior, as it has so often been in the past; rather, it will focus on calling people into that state of life where control and repression are no longer necessary. It will celebrate life, enhance humanity, call people into being, free people to be themselves, and invite people into a new humanity and a new maturity.

We will then be able to read with new understanding the story of our ancestors in faith as they walked through history. We will never literalize their story or say that the way they understood reality is the way we must understand reality. We will treasure the sacred book of our religious tradition as a guide, but we will open that book so that it might be supplemented by more contemporary readings from those who, living since the time we closed the Bible, might be a bridge for us to our biblical past. These people are part of that communion of saints who in their day bore their witness with integrity. I think of people like Valentinus, Origen, Francis of Assisi, Meister Eckhart, Aelred, and Bernard of Clairvaux. We will also no longer act as if we believe that the world is now closed and can never receive new revelations. We will read the words of such contemporary religious heroes as Desmond Tutu, John Hines,

Karen Armstrong, John A. T. Robinson, Martin Luther King Jr., Pope John XXIII, Mother Teresa, and many others, and we will "hear what the spirit is saying to the church."[4]

The ecclesia of the future will exhibit a renewed dedication to the search for truth. It will never claim that it already possesses truth by divine revelation. It will seek to enlighten people by honoring their questions. It will not seek to propagandize people by claiming that it has all the answers. To have the ecclesia be the recognized center of learning where truth from every human branch of knowledge, even that truth that challenges previous religious presuppositions, will be its primary source of both appreciation and power. SHANGRI-LA

The ecclesia will also be a center of caring. It will help people to walk through the difficult times of life without being alone—those times of trouble, sorrow, need, sickness, or any of the other adversities that afflict all of us. We may not be able to take the sting out of life, but we can take the loneliness out of the sting—and that is no small accomplishment.

The new ecclesia will also offer opportunities for people to grow into a new being—a being not bounded by tribal claims, superiority claims, gender claims, or even religious claims. Having surrendered the security-producing tribal claims which suggest that our way is the only way, we will be freed to recognize that we do not have to say to another person that his or her way into the holy is wrong. Those who once called themselves Catholic and Protestant, orthodox and heretic, liberal and evangelical, Jew and Muslim, Buddhist and Hindu, will all find a place in the ecclesia of the future. There being and nonbeing, substance and shadow, can be accepted—no, even celebrated.

There we will walk together into the meaning of God—the joy, the wonder, the mystery of God—a God not bounded by our formulas, our creeds, our doctrines, our liturgies, or even our Bible, but still real, infinitely real. BOUND BY NEW ONE

In the ecclesia of tomorrow we will also find a way to take note of other special moments in life that have not in the past been thought of in the same breath as liturgy. I think of the decision, difficult as it surely is, to abort a fetus[5] or to terminate a life on artificial support systems. I believe that both of these human decisions, when made responsibly, should be the subject of a liturgical act. So should the many other moments in life that cry out for a liturgical rite to wrap them into the meaning of worship. These would include such things as the adoption of a child, the trauma of a divorce, or the loss of one's employment (for which the English use the terrifying phrase "to be made redundant"). I think of job changes and even retirement moments that cry out for liturgical observances. Any time a faith community can help a person walk beyond a once fearful dividing barrier into what lies beyond, that community serves as an agent of life to that person. That is, I believe, what the holy gathering together of the people of God in the future will be designed to achieve. Yes, there will be a need for an ecclesia in post-theistic Christianity.

Will this body have trained leaders? Yes, I believe it will, because we will value what the ecclesia can do for us so much that we will not want it to be without responsible and guiding enablers. But people in leadership positions will not be portrayed, as they have been in the past, as all-knowing parents relating to their immature children, or as royalty sitting on a throne waiting to receive the homage of the people. No, there will be no privilege of rank, status, or authority in the leadership role of tomorrow's ecclesia, and no claim that the holy can be mediated only by those who are trained or ordained. That is the carryover of the theism of the past. The liturgies of the new ecclesia, from baptism to the meal that reenacts and recalls the defining life or the significant moment in the history of this faith-tradition, will not be the privilege of the leader. That authority will rather be among the possessions of *all* the people. A lay presidency of the eucharist is inevitable.[6] The institutional head of the ecclesia of the future will be part of a hierarchy of *service*, not a hierarchy of *power*.

That is my vision, sketchy of necessity, but I am convinced that this vision is our future. For as the theistic God fades from view, the worshiping community that has been tied to this theistic view of God will also disappear. Many people will feel bereft. Father God and Mother Church will be no more. But human beings will always worship, seek the Holy together in community, and gather as a family might to remember who they are, to recall their origins, and to seek help in becoming all that they can be. It will be in the doing of these things that the church of the future will be born.

Will the ecclesia that emerges in the tomorrow of our lives be in touch with and know itself to be the post-theistic heir of the church that we have known in the past? Will it be recognized as the descendant of the church of the theistic God that once dominated the life of the whole society? That is not my judgment to make. I can only hope that it will, for I began to dream of the birth of this new ecclesia only because I had so deeply loved the church of my past. Will the nontheistic Jesus of tomorrow be in touch with the triumphal Christ who was once thought to reign in victory from his throne on the cross? I believe he will, for it is not the explanation of either God or Jesus that is eternal. It is the experience of the holy that is eternal, always crying out for explanation.

"God was in Christ" is the ecstatic exclamation that the apostle Paul made long before he first tried to explain how it was that God had been met in this Jesus. The Christians of the theistic past and the Christians of the post-theistic future will be united not by their explanations, but by their experiences, which are finally all that we have of the divine.

Explanations are *human* creations. Explanations result from our opening our eyes to the trauma of self-consciousness, from seeing ourselves as separate from and defined against the world itself, from engaging the shock of nonbeing, and from asserting that we live, love, and have the courage to be because only through such living, loving, and being can we make sense out of our experience of the divine. Living, loving, and being thus ultimately relates us to the holy God.

That is the gospel which will create the ecclesia of the future. It is also the message to which I believe Jesus was referring when he said, "Go into all the world and preach the gospel." That is, I believe, what the Johannine writer understood when he had Jesus say, "I have come that you might have life and have it abundantly" (John 10:10). That is what I mean when I call myself a Christian. That is my dream when I try to envision the church of tomorrow.

THIRTEEN

# WHY DOES IT MATTER?:
# THE PUBLIC FACE OF THE ECCLESIA

*The Kingdom [realm] of God is a power which although it is en-
tirely future, wholly determines the present.*[1]

—RUDOLF BULTMANN

He was an animated presence following my lecture, eagerly
waving his hand to be recognized and then actually strain-
ing to control himself as he spoke. His challenge was straightforward, commanding attention. His words, direct and incisive, got
immediately to the point: "Suppose you finally get God defined
to your liking, then what have you achieved? If your new God-
concept doesn't affect the world in some positive way, then who
cares?" His bottom line was *Why does it matter?* Or, *So what?*

The audience waited quietly for my response.

Speakers and writers sometimes fail to make the necessary
connection between the cause they espouse and the effects that
the cause might have on the body politic. Until that connection is

made, however, the communication is incomplete. It is not unlike a conversation I had with my nine-year-old grandson about the effects of too much candy on the permanence of his teeth. Unable to see a connection between the candy he loved now and the teeth he might lose in sixty years or so, he responded, "Who cares?" My words simply did not seem germane to his young, vigorous, and present-moment-oriented life. Certainly the vague threat of a toothless old age did not seem to him to be sufficiently real to counter the present sensation of satisfying sweetness.

Similarly, my questioner at that lecture was demanding that I show effects sufficiently compelling to enable him to entertain my God-propositions. If there were none, or none that appeared to him to be substantial, then he was quite prepared to dismiss me as a theological dilettante and my work to redefine God for today as of no great import. He wanted to know what difference it would make in the life of our world if we ceased to define God in theistic terms. What would be the specific implications for the secular society of developing a nontheistic way to speak about God? He wanted me to go beyond the ecclesiastical boundaries of the church's life and speak to the differences that this view of God would make in what he called "the real life of the real world." If I could not answer that, he clearly had no interest in entering the scary realm into which I had invited the audience—a realm that might require him to lay down his traditional God-images in order to embrace new ideas that, in his mind, had not been tested and might not lead him anywhere. It was a legitimate challenge to which my own integrity demanded that I find an appropriate response. I doubt that I answered him satisfactorily that night, but his question continued to haunt me, forcing me to put my own confusion on these issues into order.

My first concern was to avoid the pitfalls of the past. Religious people throughout recorded history have tried to claim far too much for their view of God and to make the effects of this view far too demanding on the world at large. It is one thing to assert that what one believes about God matters and should shape the public's perception of reality. It is quite another to suggest that a particular view of God must be imposed upon the entire secular order. History reveals that such attempts at imposition have been carried out by the church repeatedly, and not infrequently in cruel and inhumane ways.

I thought, for example, of that period of medieval history when the church believed that the articulation of its doctrinal faith required a universal allegiance. Disagreement was simply not allowed. That was the mentality which produced the crusades, the inquisition, and the burning of heretics at the stake. Religious leaders of that period had no problem demonstrating that their particular view of God made enormous differences in the life of the world. The imperialistic imposition of their well-defined theological view of God on the life of the entire public showed why that view mattered, to be sure; but that very conviction gave us a Christianity at its demonic worst. I would never want to see the church walk down *that* path again. If that were the only way that I, as a Christian, could respond to the concerns of my questioner, then I would have to keep silent and live with my own subjective God and this God's social irrelevance. The question is this, then: Can one develop a particular perspective on the divine in such a way as to demonstrate why it matters publicly without falling into the religious trap that has plagued the God-talk of the Christian church since its creedal birth as the established religion of the Western world?

A search through history did not reveal for me any successful illustrations. I thought first of Giordano Bruno, who was burned at the stake on orders from the leadership of the Christian church on February 17, 1600. His crime was that he no longer believed that the earth was the center of the universe around which the sun rotated. His view of the universe was not therefore compatible with the church's understanding of God. Certainly the understanding of God espoused by the church made a difference: it was not a privately held conviction, but a premise upon which the life of the whole social order was erected! People of that day could have immediately answered my critic's question, "What does it matter?" Because the church would not allow the new understanding that Bruno espoused—an understanding that he based on the relatively recent insights of Copernicus, Kepler, and Galileo—to challenge the church's "truth," he perished, a martyr to human hysteria expressed ecclesiastically. The church's successful attempt at silencing Bruno did not make Bruno wrong, as history has clearly demonstrated, but it did make Bruno dead!

Periodically, the leadership of the church confesses its sins. On the first Sunday of Lent in the year 2000, Pope John Paul II officially stated not that his church had been wrong, but that some of his church's "sons and daughters" had made serious mistakes. It was probably as close to an admission of guilt as a church can come when it has confused its own understanding of the world with the mind of the theistic God. However, Giordano Bruno was not mentioned. He waits still for his apology from the church for snuffing out his creative life. Regrettably, he is not alone in that wait.

Next I thought of David Friedrich Strauss, the great nineteenth-century German New Testament scholar. At age twenty-seven he published a book entitled *The Life of Jesus Critically Reviewed*, dealing with issues of biblical criticism and interpretation that are today commonplace and routine in the Christian academy. But in 1835 Strauss was breaking new ground, raising questions that clearly eroded the pillars upon which ecclesiastical power had been erected; and so he, like Bruno, felt the wrath of a threatened church. The world had perhaps grown a bit kinder and gentler by the nineteenth century, as there was no effort to burn Strauss at the stake. A better explanation for this absence of violence, however, might be that the church of the nineteenth century simply did not possess life-and-death authority any longer. Weakened by the Reformation and by the necessity of absorbing wave after wave of new insights derived from the knowledge revolution, the church had been sapped of both strength and power.

That, however, did not mean that the church, which still controlled the educational centers of the Western world, was powerless to do Strauss harm: David Friedrich Strauss was summarily removed from his university appointment and never again allowed to teach anywhere. He died many years later, a broken man living in poverty. His insights, however, were destined not only to live, but in time to become mainstream and then later even to be thought of as tame and conservative.

The view of God prevailing in the church of Strauss's day clearly made a difference in the public arena. Is that what a new and challenging view of God must accomplish in order to gain credibility today? I knew, as I wrestled with this public question, that I was not willing to fight on this turf in order to demonstrate that my view of God might also make a difference. Yet the church seems to acknowledge no God-definition that lies between that which is imperialistically imposed and which thus makes all the difference in the world, and that which is relegated to a benign irrelevance that matters only to the one who holds that idea. If I could not accept the first category of definition for my nontheistic God, was it destined to be relegated to the second?

That troubling agenda all but immobilized me as I sought to frame a response to my critic's "So what?" charge. Did my view of God matter? Could I make it matter? If I could not, why was I bothering? If I succeeded, would my God-concept fall into the same imperialistic trap that has marked so much of Christian history? No matter which way I turned, the only thing I saw was a flashing warning light that seemed to say, "Don't travel this route!"[2]

It was a modern Roman Catholic scholar, John Dominic Crossan, who provided me with a way to step beyond the sterile choices that boxed me into these inadequate alternatives. Perhaps the fact that Crossan is not generally appreciated by his own hierarchy gave him the freedom to peer beyond traditional limits and thus to be of help to me.

In a memorable and attention-grabbing essay, Crossan forced his readers to define their religious concerns inside unusual parameters.[3] He accomplished this by posing the provocative question, "Is Christianity more like sex or politics?" He juxtaposed sex and politics because both, in his view, are profoundly human, and both have been invested with sanctity and lifted into "worship." In other words, is Christianity more about *individual* belief and practice or *corporate* belief and practice? If we cannot avoid religious imperialism in the corporate arena, Crossan went on to ask, should we reduce religion to the private sphere?

Crossan's questions gave me a way to approach the difficult relevance issue. If my concept of God, redefined in nontheistic terms, was to win the day, I asked myself, would its sphere of influence be more like that of sex, something that occurs in private, or more like that of politics, something that occurs in public? If it were the latter, could it avoid the sins of the church's past and still be effective in the secular world? At least now I had a framework inside which I could search for an answer.

Certainly it must be acknowledged that religion and worship can be like sex—that is, an individual activity practiced in the privacy of one's own home. Perhaps, as Crossan suggested, private houses of the future could be built with "a God room in them."[4] I have known people who have done just that: they have created a meditation room in their home, equipping it with prayer rugs, incense holders, and evocative icons. Would it not be better if the Christianity of tomorrow were modeled after that image? The institutional power-claims and the cruel and destructive excesses of the church throughout history would thus be avoided.

So I played with that private image for a while, but it would not work. There is nothing about Christianity that enables it to be contained inside the response of an individual. Christianity is not a private activity. Something located deep within the meaning of God refuses to allow us to acknowledge that boundary. Whatever Christianity is, it cannot be relegated to an individual activity.

But if Christianity has to be expressed politically, where are the safeguards that will protect our religiously pluralistic and increasingly secular world from the excessive claims of our own sectarian religious leaders? While this book was being written, the Vatican made this issue quite existential by releasing, with the approval of the pope, a document called *Dominus Iesus*. This document revived in the twenty-first century the mentality of the inquisition, not in deeds but in attitudes; and the heresy hunts of the tribal history of yesteryear loomed once more on our horizon. This document asserted that Christianity is the only true religion and that the Roman Catholic Church is the only true church within Christianity. That church thus must be acknowledged as the sole pathway to God. Ecumenicity and interfaith hopes died as Rome went so far as to warn its own bishops against referring to other Christian bodies as "sister churches," for fear that this language might be misunderstood to confer some degree of legitimacy on these bodies. It was a present-day expression of the very dangers I had feared from the past, a shot across the bow of rationality.

Undaunted by these newly revived fears, I nonetheless pressed on at Crossan's invitation. The reason one enters politics, Crossan argued, is to get things done. After all, there is no effective politician without an effective organization, an effective party, and an effective program. Society can be changed only by corporate action.

Jesus spoke of a corporate response when he used the phrase "the realm of God" (traditionally translated with the sexist rendition of "the kingdom of God"). He portrayed himself as the sign of that realm's arrival, the announcer of its presence. Jesus even juxtaposed his understanding of the realm of God against the realm of Caesar. He called people into purposeful community. The Christian message had to be communal not individual, public not private. That was a clear first conclusion.

Yet Jesus never suggested that the task of God's people was to impose its talk, its creeds, or its teaching on the populace. In two of the gospels he went so far as to say that anyone who was not specifically against his movement should be counted as supportive (Mark 9:40; Luke 9:50). Jesus' call was rather to point to the realm of God, to invite people to enter that realm as members in order to bear a corporate witness to the values of justice that define that realm. 3 1 FLAVORS

We need to face the fact that the agenda of the church in history has quite often been antithetical to the agenda of God's realm. The church has frequently resisted justice, for example, and has justified and implemented dehumanizing practices toward racial minorities, women, homosexuals, the mentally ill, left-handed people, and socially and intellectually searching people. Rather than hearing from the church the invitation to enter and to share in what the realm of God is all about, the world has witnessed repeated Christian attempts to impose the agenda of the church upon it.

We can avoid reliving these destructive and demonic moments of shame in Christian history by keeping our focus off the church and its needs, concentrating instead on the task of proclaiming and expanding the realm of God. It is the vocation of God's realm to bring life not death, love not oppression, being not the diminishment of humanity, to the secular society. To concentrate in new and effective ways on the realm of God separated from the power-needs of any human beings or any ecclesiastical institutions is to discover the true vocation of the ecclesia of tomorrow. It is to follow the Jesus who talked of a universal God, not a tribal or a sectarian deity. Jesus' God caused "the sun to rise on the bad and the good" and sent "rain to fall on the just and the unjust" (Matt. 5:45). The realm of

God will thus move against all ecclesiastical boundaries, whether they be theological, doctrinal, or political, that have been suggested as limits within which God will operate. The acceptance of such limitations is the source of imperialism. The realm of God is its exact opposite.

The God beyond theism is also the God beyond every ecclesiastical claim to possess ultimate truth, and thus beyond every religious judgment that places any limitations on the invitation of the ecclesia to the world to enter the realm of God.

God, I have suggested, is experienced as life. No one owns or sets limits on life. Representatives of all human and religious traditions *participate* in life. Hence any public agenda, corporately engaged, that has as its goal the enhancement of life is a sign of God's realm. That same goal is what must be the result of the public witness of the ecclesia of the future. Working for the enhancement of life is very different from saying, "This is what the true faith is, and this is what you must do about it."

If the ecclesia of the future is dedicated to expanding the realm of God, what will its activity look like? The realm of God is identified with life so it will confront the racism that diminishes the life of people of color. It will confront the entrenched patriarchy that diminishes the lives of women. It will confront the conscious and unconscious homophobia that diminishes the lives of gay, lesbian, bisexual, and transgender[5] people. It will confront the economically powerful in the name of the economically deprived. It will demonstrate that when one human being treats another human being as if that other one is of little value, the humanity and the life of both is violated and diminished; the victim by hostility, the perpetrator by insensitivity.

The ecclesia of the future must act decisively, not for a religious agenda, but for the agenda of life. That is where the realm of God is identified. The Johannine Jesus says that his purpose is to bring life abundantly (John 10:10). That same goal—abundant life for all—must be the focus of the ecclesia of the future.

The realm of God is also identified with the presence of love. Can anyone imagine love that is bounded or conditional, or love that stops to count the cost? Jesus understood as the sign of God's realm breaking into history, espoused a radical love that would extend beyond those barriers that our fears erect to protect our insecurities. "Love your enemies and pray for your persecutors" (Matt. 5:44), he said. Paul, a disciple of this Jesus, understood his call and wrote, "Bless those who persecute you, bless and curse not" (Rom. 12:14).

This radical call is that which must be the message of the ecclesia of the future, even though it flies in the face of the church's witness in history. Time after time the church has in fact tried to kill its enemies and those who have threatened its power. The church has also sought to silence, reject, or marginalize its criticss. It has persecuted its challengers, sometimes even going to war against them, demanding conformity to the truth the church has claimed to posse   These are not acts of love. These are not the marks of God's realm. To serve the God who is the source of love is to find the pathway that leads me not beyond public witness but beyond the imperialistic ecclesiastical violence that has so often accompanied that witness.

The realm of God expands love's call. Love unites even the lion and the lamb, to say nothing of the Jew and the Gentile, the slave and the free. To spread the power of love, to push back the power of hate, is to enter the realm of God.

Yet please notice that the agenda of the realm of God is not an agenda of words or creeds. It is an agenda of action. To expand the presence of love is to do the work of the kingdom. A messiah who will not confront the claims of life and love on all humanity and thus work for justice is no messiah at all. To enter the realm of God to which Jesus invites us is to stand against those who still seek to extend the church's authority and power in order to divide rather than to unite the world. As Robert Funk has observed, "The messiah we need [today] is some random act of kindness, some bold proposal to close the hole in the ozone, some discrete move to introduce candor into politics, some new intensive care for the planet. Perhaps the messiah will come when we have broken bread with our enemies."[6] The only agenda love has is to create wholeness. That agenda must be the agenda of the ecclesia of the future—an ecclesia that lives only to enhance the love that is present in life. For, as Saint John has written, "God is love, and the one who abides in love, abides in God" (I John 4:16).

The realm of God is also seen when being is enhanced. *Being* is yet another of those words that has no boundaries. The realm of God will confront whatever represses being and will support whatever enhances being. To be able to say, "I am," is to affirm being. To be able to say, "We are and we shall be," is to affirm being and thus to set a new goal for the action of the ecclesia. For Jesus to be remembered or even to be interpreted as having said, "I am bread," is to assert a conviction that he came to satisfy the deepest human hunger for meaning. When people reported him as having said, "I am living water," their conviction was that he would satisfy the human thirst for truth. "I am the vine" speaks to the human need to belong. "I am the door" speaks to the human need to find an entryway into God. "I am the resurrection" speaks to the human yearning to escape the limits of humanity and touch the infinite wells of God.[7] None of those goals is designed to enhance power or to impose anyone's meaning upon another as if there were an exclusive truth.

To enhance life, to enhance love, to enhance being is to do the work of God's realm. That is the work Jesus was about. That is the power I vest in the God beyond theism. Jesus did not write creeds or set rules or develop tests of orthodoxy to determine who the true believers were. He only suggested a criterion by which people could recognize his disciples: "that you love one another" (John 13:35).

The work of the ecclesia of the future is to expand the arena of life, to enhance the capacity to love, and to develop in every person the courage to be, for these are the marks of God's realm, the God who is beyond the definition of theism. These things are also pointers to a universality of faith and practice that will recognize no boundary between Christian and non-Christian, Protestant and Catholic, true believer and heretic, conservative and liberal, educated and illiterate, male and female, Caucasian and person of color, homosexual and heterosexual, for all are creatures in whom the source of life, the source of love, and the Ground of Being find expression.

Thus the agenda of the future ecclesia is not to impose its "truth" on anyone, but to work for the realm of God in every arena, to enhance the life of all, to expand the love for all, and to encourage the being of all. Working toward that agenda will give us a strategy, a focus for the future, a sense of what we are to do as citizens of the realm of God, and it will help to ensure that we never again have another dark chapter of religious imperialism or intolerance.

So why does it matter that we reformulate the tenets of traditional Christianity or attempt to redefine God in nontheistic terms? What is the answer to the "So what?" question from my critical listener?

We reimage God to keep the world from enduring the pain of a continuing reliance on a theistic deity. The same paternalistic, protective God who offers feeble humanity comfort in theism is the deity alleged to have supported burning critics at the stake or fighting brutal wars to impose a particular version of divinity on other people. That same theistic God is quoted by people who want to impose their definitions of homosexuality or their values in the right-to-life movement on everyone else. So it matters how one thinks of God.

We need a reformation in our thinking about God not to give people a comfortable God-figure that they can keep in the God-room of their home—a room that they enter periodically to do "God-things." No, we need a reformation so that the ecclesia of the future will invite people into the realm of God, where they can act corporately to enhance life, to expand love, and to encourage being.

It matters. God matters. The realm of God matters. The ecclesia matters. The reformation matters. When someone next asks me to respond to the "So what?" question, I shall be prepared.

# FOURTEEN

# The Courage to
# Move into the Future

*The creed has become for me an unlivable place.*

—KATHRIN FORD, graduate student, Harvard Divinity School

Sometimes travelers walking on uncharted paths see a vision that guides their journey, causing them to rejoice greatly in its discovery. Such was my experience when one of my students at Harvard Divinity School became the light that guided me to the conclusions of this study which I now seek to articulate. This student was quite unique and incredibly perceptive. Her name was Kathrin Ford. Her friends called her Katie. She was seeking a master of divinity degree, but because she was alienated from her patriarchal church, she was not sure that she wanted to be ordained. She possessed a skillful capacity with words, and she was an ardent feminist. As such, she was not sure that the church, as she had experienced it, would ever be open to the direction she felt compelled to travel. Yet she was still committed enough to continue to walk the path that normally leads to ordination.

In one of her sermons in a class on "Issues in Public Preaching," Katie spelled out these compelling themes in her life quite powerfully. She stood before us quite still, quite silent, then she began. Slowly at first, she painted with words the picture of a town facing a major flood. The rains came with such relentlessness and over such a long period of time that the river rose dangerously. The people formed sandbag brigades to protect the things they valued. The sandbag walls rose, but the floodwaters rose faster. Soon water covered their fields, drowning first the wheat, then the canola, then the onions. The people, seeking safety inside their homes, watched with a sense of helplessness as their livelihoods were destroyed before their eyes. They wanted to flee, but their roots were too deeply planted; they were so totally attached to the values enshrined in their farms and town that they felt they could not leave.

Still the river kept rising. It now covered the first floor of their homes. As they watched their family photographs—symbols of their past—curl up and float away on the water, they felt they were losing the very meaning of their lives. Soon their physical sustenance was also endangered: the floodwaters covering their town began to seep into the ground, contaminating their groundwater.[1] Their homes were becoming unlivable. If they stayed in this place, they would surely die. Yet something powerful and relentless inside themselves continued to urge them to remain where they were. *Rationally* they knew they had to leave, but *emotionally* they were immobilized.

Katie Ford described this scene with evocative images that kept her classmates raptly attentive. Yet they had no idea where she was going with this image or this theme, nor did I. Then, with all of us caught up in her symbolic description of a killing flood, she began to speak the words of the Christian creed, beginning with the phrase, "I believe in God, the Father almighty."

This creed, she said, like that flooded town, "has become for me an unlivable place." She then described the history of creedal formation. The creeds were "a response to debate," she said, "designed to tell who was an insider in the Christian faith and who was not. A creed is a border-maker," she added, fashioning her developing definition.

No Christian creed is "a full statement of faith," she continued. It is only the Christian community's ecclesiastical "response to arguments." All the undebated issues, she said, have been left out. That is why in the creeds "there is no mention of love, no mention of the teachings of Jesus, no mention of the kingdom of God being present in our bodies and souls, no mention of God as the ground of life."

The creeds have fallen on us, she asserted, like the rain over the centuries. They have been repeated endlessly, shaping our minds and our souls to the point where we cannot think of God outside the forms they affirm, or the boxes they create. They have permeated our land, shaped our values, and yes, even entered the intimate assumptions of our living space. "Drop by drop," she said, our religion, as it came to be embodied in our creeds, has given us "a profoundly dangerous doctrine of God." It has covered our fields, she said, and destroyed the very crops that Christians are supposed to harvest as their livelihood. It has contaminated our groundwater. "We have been drinking in the Father God our whole life."

"This creed," she argued, "has, like that flood, rendered our traditional religious dwelling places no longer habitable." Yet this creed, and the definitions that arise from it, are so powerfully present in our emotions that even when we judge it to be a destructive document that is killing our very souls, still it whispers, "You cannot leave. You will be lost if you wander. You must stay where you are." But we cannot stay. The price is too high. These creeds have given us a God, she said, "who caused the death of his son, the damnation of disbelievers, the subordination of women, the bloody massacre of the crusades, the terror of judgment, the wrath toward homosexuals, the justification of slavery."

She further delineated that God of history: "The Father almighty God embodied in the creeds is a deity who chooses some of the world's children while rejecting others. He is the father who needs a blood sacrifice, the father of wrath, the father of patriarchal marriage, the father of male ordination and female submission, the father of heterosexual privilege, the father of literal and spiritual slavery."

She examined and dismissed the ways various church people have tried to address the "unlivability" of the creeds, the no-longer-believable quality of the Father God as traditionally defined. Some do it, she said, by nibbling or tinkering around the edges of reform. Making God-language less masculine and more inclusive is a positive step, she conceded, but it does not go deep enough. The real issue, she continued, "is that God is not a person. God is not a being. God is Being itself." There was stunned silence in the room as Katie drove her conclusion home. This God, who is "Being itself, is not the father of life," she countered. "This God *is* life." Our creeds, she concluded, have now made it impossible for us Christians to continue to live in the place to which these very creeds have taken us.

I listened to this gifted, God-filled young woman with awe and wonder. With her powerful words she had so perceptively captured the essence of the church's present-day dilemma. Not only had she perceived the realities, but she had also shaped them into a compelling vision. She was, as one of her classmates said, that rare combination of "prophet and poet." She knew where she wanted to go, who she wanted to be, and what she wanted the church to be. Her only question was whether the church would allow her to live within its structures if she raised the issues that she felt compelled to raise. She had no confidence that what she was seeking to say could be heard by church traditionalists, or whether the church, as she had known it, could ever embrace her vision. She did not discern in her church any ability to walk away from those creeds that, in her view, were "contaminating" the church's "groundwater," that were making the Christian faith-system unlivable for her and many others. She saw no questing search going on in the church that might enable it to find a new place toward which she and that faith-community might move.

Katie Ford, in her relatively brief but profoundly perceptive student sermon, captured all of the questions that I set out to address in this book. Indeed, she captured my own autobiographical experience.

I have tried for a lifetime to live faithfully, if not always comfortably, within the confining boundaries of this institution called the church. That church has conferred on me gifts of honor, position, leadership, and influence. I have loved my life as one of the church's ordained servants. I have never wished the church harm. But I no longer believe that this institution—or the Christian faith as this church has traditionally proclaimed it—can continue to live without dramatic change in our post-theistic world. Somewhere along the way we Christians appear to have lost our ability to initiate effective self-reformation. We have warned others against idolatry but have not listened to our own warning. We have acted time after time as if the God we have experienced could be or has been captured in and bound by the words of our scriptures, our creeds, and our doctrines. Throughout Christian history we have acted as if God had to be protected and defended by those in possession of the infinite truth of the divine being. We have presumed that the doorway to God is in our hands. Proclaiming that God can be approached only through our symbols, we have excluded those human beings who do not use our words or refuse to bow before our altars erected in the community of "the saved."

Yet we human beings cannot *know* God; we can only *experience* God. Thus there is no way that we can say God *is* anything. When we talk about God, we can say only that the experience of

God is "as if ___," adding whatever human words we can find to characterize our experience. But, as Katie Ford noted, we Christians have tended to replace "as if" with "is." We have pretended that we can actually say "God is ___," arrogantly filling in the blank with our concepts.

I live at this moment inside a powerful experience of the divine, the holy. I call the content of that experience God. I trust its reality. The God that my life has encountered and engaged is most profoundly present for me in the portrait painted by the early church of the man called Jesus of Nazareth. Jesus is thus for me the doorway into this God. His life reflects the life that I call God. His love reflects the love that I call God. His being reveals the Ground of Being that I call God. The God that I have met in Jesus calls me to live fully, to love wastefully, and to be all that I can be. When I do all these things, I believe that I make God visible and real for others.

It is not simply as an individual that I experience this God, but rather as a part of a community. The church to me is a community of people bound together by their willingness to journey into the meaning and the mystery of this God. That journey must take us away from that place where the preservation of the institution determines our ultimate values and witness, and where we assert that we either have defined or could define God in our ecclesiastical or doctrinal words. We have lived in that place so long that we do not recognize that even our groundwater has now been polluted by the rising tides of negativity, sterility, ignorance, and oppression. We are not able to discern that the religious place in which our lives are grounded is no longer a livable place; it has become a place where to remain is to die.

These are the realizations that force me to action. I believe that I must now leave the political and ethical compromises that have corrupted the faith of this Jesus. I believe that I must leave the stifling theology, the patriarchal structure, the enduring prejudices based on any of the givens of our humanity, such as skin color, gender, or sexual orientation. I must leave the mentality that encourages anyone to think that our doctrines are unchangeable or our sacred texts are without error. I must leave the God of miracle and magic, the God of supernatural, invasive power. I must leave the promises of certainty, the illusion of possessing the true faith, the excessive claims of being the recipient of an unchallengeable revelation, and even the neurotic religious desire to know that I am right. But I can never leave the God-experience, nor can I ever walk away from that doorway into the divine that I believe I have found in the one I call the Christ and acknowledge as "my Lord."

I will never again assert that my Christ is the only way to God, for that is an ultimate act of human folly. I will say, however, that Christ is the only way *for me*, for that is my experience. I will never again feed my ego with the familiar Christian claim that every other pathway to God, such as the paths that wind through Hindu India, Buddhist China, Tibet, and Burma, the Islamic Middle East, or the Jewish state of Israel, on which millions of human lives have walked with integrity in their search for the holy, is inadequate, or even second-rate. I will certainly never call these pathways false.

I will move from my familiar creeds and faith-symbols into the exile where all seems lost, hoping that together we who are exiled can find a new place where once again we can sing the Lord's song. What I can no longer do is stay in an unlivable place. No matter how difficult moving is, it is nonetheless the only option I have; and so move I must, to a place where my faith-tradition can be revived and live on.

That is the road I have traveled in this book. I have moved into dangerous and religiously threatening places. I have walked beyond theism, but not beyond God. I have allowed theism to die, recognizing it for what it is—a human explanation of the God-experience—not a description of who or what God actually is. The old debate between theism and atheism becomes, for me, not wrong but sterile, vapid, and inept. So I walk deliberately beyond it. I transcend it; and when I do, I begin a search for the words that will enable me to talk of a post-theistic God, the God who is not a person but the source of that power that nurtures person-hood, not a being but the Ground of Being, the source from which all being flows.

I have now moved to this new place, and I challenge the church to move with me. I do so not because I reject the church, but because I am convinced that if we stay where the church now is, the faith that we profess as Christians will surely die. The floods of creedal distortion have destroyed our fields, contami-nated our groundwater, and made our faith-assertions of yester-day unlivable places for us today. No matter how deeply we fear to move, there is no alternative. Being delusional about our situa-tion will not help: our constant attempts to deny reality are ulti-mately ineffective. Shouting loudly while pretending that we still believe will not help either: fundamentalism will finally result in even greater disillusionment. Nor will it be sufficient to reshape the church into something that has more recognized status, more cachet: liberal solutions that focus the church on social action, self-help counseling, and efforts at spiritual direction are as dead as is fundamentalist hysteria. Liberals are reaction people, defin-ing themselves as "not fundamentalists." They are unable to say what they are because there is no ground left under their feet.

With all other options inadequate, our only alternative is to move. No matter how deep the tugs, how fearful and insistent the inner voices that tell of the danger of moving, we still have to move, for the danger of staying is mortality itself.

Katie Ford was right. The central issue is that "God is not a per-son. God is not a being. God is Being itself." When we move into that radical, but not new, understanding of God, all else changes, and it changes dramatically. Indeed, for some people it changes vi-olently. If God is not a being, supernatural in power, then Jesus cannot be the incarnation of that being. So Jesus must now be de-fined as differing from you and me in degree but not in kind. In that assertion most of the Christology of the ages collapses. Yet that assertion has been present among Christian people as a kind of minority report since the fourteenth century. If God is not a being, then no human hierarchy can claim to be the chosen receptor for this being's revelation, the guardian of this being's truth, or the dispenser of this being's grace. In that assertion all ecclesiastical power-claims disappear, feeding religious insecurity. The pope becomes unemployed, and so do all of the cardinals, the archbishops, the bishops, the priests, and all of us who have pretended that we are the divinely commissioned and ordained servants of this theistic deity or the vicars of this incarnate Christ on earth. Those people who have placed their confidence in such things will also become islands of radical insecurity. The church, the body of Christ, must thus be reconstructed from the bottom up.

When we shift our definition of God away from supernatural theism, then all the claims we have made for prayer become inoperative and prayer must either be dispensed with or redefined. More than that, all the claims that ecclesiastical hierarchies have made for their ability to interpret the ways of God to men and women have to be relinquished, and all the power that we once placed in the prayers, masses, and assertions of the ordained will quickly disappear.

It is easy to understand why we resist this shift so adamantly and fear it so deeply. During the shift we will be terribly lost, lonely, and anxious. Yet if we look closely, we can see beyond our personal needs to the place where the positive results of moving on can be discerned. Once the shift has taken place, we will be free of unrealistic expectations. Once we have moved to a new place with a view of God radically redefined, we will learn to pray again, not as children imploring the protection of a heavenly parent, but as adults in touch with and empowered by the source of life itself. How the ecclesia will help us to do that is part of what lies ahead.

When our understanding of God shifts, so will the moral ground underneath our feet. The traditional basis for ethics will disappear. For if there is no theistic being who rules the universe, then there is also no law-giver, no dispenser of eternal ethical principles, no fiery finger that inscribed the Ten Commandments on tablets of stone or wrote unchanging laws into the texts of holy scripture. So all those claims must also be abandoned. Those who have simply quoted the Bible to solve ethical problems will discover that their moral compass is askew, and rampant anxiety will result.

Many people will be gripped by the fear of moral anarchy as we shift to a new view of God. But we already know that the moral claims of the past are no longer operative. Those claims, which evolved as coping devices to deal with the trauma of self-consciousness, no longer keep our fears under control. There simply is no theistic deity whose will we must seek to obey in order to gain divine protection. There is no heavenly parent whose goodwill and blessing we must seek through virtuous living, who will reward our frightened, fragile, yet obedient lives. So the ethical debate must find a new ground to which it can be moved and a new context in which it can be viewed.

If the Ground of Being is holy, then those actions that diminish the being of another are nothing less than expressions of sin. So a new definition of morality emerges, grounded in the very being of God. In this new morality mindless prejudices can no longer be affirmed by quoting sacred sources. Black is beautiful for it enhances being, while racism is evil because it diminishes being. Feminism is of God for it enhances being, while chauvinism and patriarchy are evil because they deny being. Gay pride is the sign of the divine in human life for it enhances being, while homophobia is evil because it oppresses being. The persistent theological search for truth is of God for it expands life, while religious claims to possess exclusive truth are sinful because they thwart truth itself and allege that God can be boxed inside our thought-forms.

The defensive hostility exhibited by various religious groups does not enhance being; rather, it diminishes it and is therefore sinful. Likewise, missionary efforts to convert people to our way of believing are evil, because they deny the presence of truth incarnate in other people and in other traditions. Attempts to convert others because our way is the only way are nothing less than marks of our radical insecurity, signs of our self-centered, survival-oriented humanity. They are thus pathways toward death. Sharing faith-stories as equals, on the other hand, is a way into the very life of God.

In this book I have tried to move in these new directions. I conclude this book as I began it, with a statement of my faith. I am still a believer. God is infinitely real to me. I am a Christian. Jesus is for me not only a God-presence but the doorway into the reality of God who is beyond my capacity to understand. I am a person of prayer, which for me means contemplating the meaning of God as life, love, and being and acting that meaning out. I am a person with deep ethical commitments, which for me means becoming an agent of life, love, and being to every other person through both individual and corporate behavior. The mark of the faith I strive for is self-possessed maturity, not childlike dependence. My hope of heaven lies in the ability to share in the eternity of God who is the source of life and love and the Ground of Being.

In this new understanding of God toward which the death of theism directs us, churches will cease being behavior-controlling institutions and become institutions dedicated to the empowerment and expansion of life. Worship will become the celebration of the power of God, who is present in the heart of life. Christian education will become the search for truth rather than the indoctrination of the faithful with a particular form of religious propaganda. Life in community will be important because it will help free us to live fully, love wastefully, and be all that we are capable of being.

Thus Christianity becomes not something to be *believed* but a faith into which we must *live*, a vision that stands before us, inviting us to enter. I proclaim a God beyond creeds, a Christ beyond incarnation, a way of life that dares us to grasp the insecurities of our being and move beyond the boxes created by the security-producing churches of yesterday. To be ready to move into this not fully clear vision is to face honestly the recognition that that place where the church, with its binding creeds and closed scriptures, has traditionally dwelt is no longer a livable place. If we vote to stay, we are voting to die. As Katie Ford observed, our produce has been destroyed, and our groundwater is contaminated. The fears that whisper, "Stay, stay," are no longer rational. They are the voices of a dawning hysteria that recognizes its own doom. Like most people and most institutions, we deny the reality of death until we have a vision that carries us beyond its limits into something new.

I have tried to sketch out that vision of something new, hint at the goals of tomorrow, and cite the directions in which we must walk to reach those goals. Is this discussion adequate? Hardly. Is it complete? Of course not. Is it real? I believe it is. Will it work? Only time will tell. Will churches see the vision and respond to it? Some will; most will not. Many churches would, if given the choice, choose to die rather than change. LEFT, RIGHT AND MIDDLE

Will the church, then, in its institutional form, die? That is what the process will look like initially, but that is not what will occur. The few individuals who see, respond to, and move toward a new place will be the leaven in the lump, the salt in the soup, the light in the darkness, ultimately leading the reformation. They will be sources of new life that will feed individual communities of faith within dying worldwide churches and denominations. This leavening presence, this embryo of new life, will be criticized, threatened, and harassed by fearful ecclesiastical leaders. Nonetheless it will survive, for truth will be on the side of the few communities of faith that embrace the vision.

Such communities are present in our midst today as tiny signs of hope. They do not claim to themselves or others that they have the answers. They do not traffic in a security that they know they cannot provide. They do not make excessive claims for their message or even for their Christ. They are open to truth no matter what its source. They are also open to the rich diversity of human life. They know that in the God who is the Ground of Being, and in the Christ who manifested that gift of being, there is neither east nor west, tribe nor ethnicity, male nor female, gay nor straight, true believer nor heretic, Christian nor Jew, Muslim, Hindu, or Buddhist. There is only a God-filled humanity, wonderfully diverse, yearning to live, eager to love, daring to be, and wanting to journey in community into the wonder and mystery of the God who is Being itself.

These faith-communities will emerge, I am confident, inside our existing structures. They will ultimately separate themselves from the pack. They will float freely, taking a wide variety of forms. They will attract the restless, the hungry, the alienated, the marginalized, the open, the honest, the doubters, the seekers. In time they will recognize kinship with one another, allowing them to coalesce and to build a new consensus.

The resulting ecclesia will be based on the experience of people, not on the desires of the hierarchy. It will cross all denominational lines and then all faith lines. A thousand years from now, people will make a judgment as to whether or not the community that this new reformation has built in the intervening millennium is the descendent of the Christian church that is dying in our generation.

I think that the answer will be yes, but the assessment is not mine to make. My task is simply to engage this process. I intend to walk beyond the boundaries of my faith as a believer, not as a nonbeliever; as one who loves the church that has shaped me, not as one who wishes to deny it or to harm it. Knowing that when a place becomes unlivable people must either move or die, I have chosen to move. I invite others to move with me—to enter the exile as believers, to enable a radical reformation of the Christian church to occur, and then to find a new place where faith can live and where God can be experienced.

I welcome the reformation. I hope that I have been one of its enablers. I yearn for it to succeed so that my grandchildren can say, "God is real to me, and Jesus is my doorway into this reality."

# Notes

Preface

1. Dietrich Bonhoeffer, in a letter to Eberhard Bethge dated July 16, 1944, from his book *Letters and Papers from Prison*, p. 219.
2. Archbishop Ramsey later acknowledged his negative reaction to John Robinson as one of the major mistakes of his primacy.
3. The theses were published in the appendix to my autobiography, *Here I Stand: My Struggle for a Christianity of Integrity, Love, and Equality.*
4. I was happy to have this experience challenged by a conference I led at St. Deiniol's Library in Hawarden, Wales, in October of 2000. The audience was over eighty percent clergy and included priests (and even bishops) from England, Ireland, Wales, Australia, the Virgin Islands, and the United States. It was an intense conference of five days during which I delivered eight lectures. Much of the tone of this conference, including its positive engagement with the material found in this book, was set by the warden, the Reverend Peter Francis. I was thrilled to have this conference suggest that there are some clergy willing to risk, to venture, and to engage the future. I stand in gratitude to St. Deiniol's.
5. From the opening line of a hymn by Augustus Montague Toplady, 1776, which appears in many hymnals.
6. *The Bishop's Voice.*
7. Between the final editing and the publication of this book, our one surviving parent, Ina Bridger, died.

Chapter One

1. A. C. Dixon and R. A. Torrey, eds., *The Fundamentals.*
2. The five fundamentals as presented here are adapted from a book by Lawrence Meredith, entitled *Life Before Death*, p. 31.

3. I treated these issues in more detail in a book entitled *Why Christianity Must Change or Die: A Bishop Speaks to Believers in Exile.*

4. I treated all of these themes earlier in a book entitled *Born of a Woman: A Bishop Rethinks the Virgin Birth and the Treatment of Women in a Male-Dominated Church.*

5. I treated these themes earlier in a book entitled *Resurrection: Myth or Reality? A Bishop Rethinks the Meaning of Easter.*

6. For fuller treatment of these ideas, see my *Why Christianity Must Change or Die: A Bishop Speaks to Believers in Exile,* chap. 6.

7. I addressed these themes in an earlier book entitled *Living in Sin?: A Bishop Rethinks Human Sexuality.*

8. I chronicled this life conviction in a book entitled *Here I Stand: My Struggle for a Christianity of Integrity, Love, and Equality.*

9. This is a phrase from a poem by James Russell Lowell in the hymn "Once to Every Man and Nation Comes the Moment to Decide," found in the 1940 Episcopal hymnal, #519.

10. Richard Holloway, primus of the Episcopal Church in Scotland, addressed these themes in a book entitled *Godless Morality,* which was totally misunderstood by his ecclesiastical detractors, led by the archbishop of Canterbury.

11. I spoke far more intensely on this subject in a book entitled *Rescuing the Bible from Fundamentalism: A Bishop Rethinks the Meaning of Scripture.*

12. Davies is the author of *God and the New Physics* and *The Mind of God.* These comments, however, were made to me personally at a conference in 1984 at Georgetown University.

13. Words attributed to Professor Pheme Perkins, a Roman Catholic scripture scholar at Boston College, when she was asked to comment on one of the controversies engendered by one of my books, which she had not yet read.

14. From the baptismal vows in the Episcopal *Book of Common Prayer,* 1979.

CHAPTER TWO

1. David Hare, *Racing Demons,* p. 1. This opening soliloquy from Hare's play about faith and life in the Church of England is spoken by a priest.

2. Edward Edinger, *The New God Image: A Study of Jung's Key Letters Concerning the Evolution of the Western God Image,* p. 129, 143.

3. Friedrich W. Nietzsche, *Thus Spake Zarathustra.*

4. I think of such authors as Thomas J. J. Altizer, William Hamilton, and Paul Van Buren, all of whom were identified with the death-of-God movement.

5. I refer my readers to Don Cupitt's book, *The Sea of Faith*.

6. These issues were publicly raised in the primary campaign for the presidency of the United States in the year 2000 by a visit of Republican candidate Governor George W. Bush of Texas to the campus of Bob Jones University in South Carolina. This fundamentalist and evangelical school had prohibited interracial dating and pronounced the pope to be the Anti-Christ.

## CHAPTER THREE

1. Excerpted from the poem "God's Funeral" published in *The Collected Poems of Thomas Hardy*. I first was introduced to this poem in a book by A. N. Wilson, also entitled *God's Funeral*.

2. There are some examples in subhuman life that look like ethnic cleansing, but they are related more to biological drives than to self-conscious evil. Jane Goodall, in her book *Reason for Hope*, says that she has observed something that looks like ethnic cleansing among chimpanzees.

3. Dating the origins of this planet is not an exact science, as this range indicates. There are some scientists who would suggest a date even earlier than five billion years ago. I have used two major sources in arriving at the dates cited here: one is the *Encyclopedia Britannica*, and the other is Robert Jastrow's *The Enchanted Loom*. Jastrow is a professor at Columbia University.

4. Fossil evidence points to the existence of bacteria in this period of history known as Precambrian time.

5. The *Encyclopedia Britannica* dates this division between five hundred million and one billion years ago.

6. The age of the dinosaurs extended, according to the *Encyclopedia Britannica*, from 250 million to 65 million years ago.

7. Louis Pasteur, a pioneer in the study of microbes, was a nineteenth-century figure.

8. I made reference to this material in *Why Christianity Must Change or Die*. I repeat it here because it is essential to the development of the argument and because I intend to draw different and, I believe, more significant conclusions from it.

9. There is still debate among anthropologists about this, but the data do appear to support the idea that the theistic deity moved through a

phase in which God was identified with the feminine. Whether that
enabled women to achieve more power in the tribe is not as certain.

10. This is a phrase I have heard Professor Goulder use in public dis-
course. It is also a theme in his co-authored book (with John Hick),
*Why Believe in God?*

## CHAPTER FOUR

1. From the essay "From Divinity to Infinity," published in the book
*The Once and Future Jesus*, p. 28, edited by Gregory Jenks.

2. Tillich discusses this concept in a book by the same name.

3. *Why Christianity Must Change or Die.*

4. Compare Exod. 33:23 in the KJV and in the RSV or NRSV.

5. This person was Kathy Ganin, an active member of All Saints'
Church, Hoboken.

6. The theme echoes repeatedly in selected writings of both Meister
Eckhart and Julian of Norwich. For those who do not know Julian
of Norwich, it is worth noting that despite her masculine name,
Julian was a woman.

7. This phrase serves as the title of one of Tillich's major books.

## CHAPTER FIVE

1. Robert W. Funk, "The Once and Future Jesus," the lead essay in
*The Once and Future Jesus*, p. 7, Gregory Jenks, ed. The Jesus Seminar is a think tank of modern Christian scholars who have dedicated
more than a decade to their attempt to recreate the authentic sayings and deeds of Jesus. Major publications of this group include
*The Five Gospels* and *The Acts of Jesus.*

2. Walter Russell Bowie served as rector of St. Paul's Church in Richmond and Grace Church in New York City in the early part of the
twentieth century. He also taught homiletics at Union Seminary in
New York and at Virginia Theological Seminary in Alexandria. The
author of numerous books—including his best-selling *The Story of the
Bible*, which he wrote for children—Dr. Bowie also wrote the popular
hymn "Lord Christ When First Thou Camest to Earth," found in
the Episcopal hymnal. He was what came to be called a nineteenth-
century Protestant liberal. His title for Jesus, "the Master," reflected
the liberal point of view of his day, which suggested that Jesus' beautiful and noble human life reflected the divine presence.

3. For fuller documentation, I refer my readers to Michael D. Goulder, *Luke: A New Paradigm*, and my own book based on Goulder's
thought, *Liberating the Gospels: Reading the Bible with Jewish Eyes.*

4. In *Liberating the Gospels*, see especially chap. 7.
5. Joachim Jeremias, *The Central Message of the New Testament*, p. 17.
6. Robert Funk, *Honest to Jesus: Jesus for a New Millennium.*
7. Burton Mack, *The Lost Gospel: The Book of Q and Christian Origins.*
8. D. R. Catchpole, *The Quest for Q.*
9. Arland D. Jacobsen, *The First Gospel: An Introduction to Q*; A.J.B. Higgins, ed., *The Original Order of Q: Essays in Memory of T. W. Manson.*
10. The Jesus Seminar entertains a date in the fifties. I am not convinced.
11. Robert Funk et al., eds., *The Five Gospels.*
12. I am not personally persuaded either by the Q hypothesis or by the early dating of *Thomas*. I do, however, have to admit that the majority of New Testament scholars accept the Q hypothesis as the basis of their work, though there might be more debate as to the actual time of its composition. There is less consensus in New Testament circles about both the early dating of *Thomas* and the inclusion of *Thomas* into the canon of the New Testament. I follow at this point the thought of English New Testament scholar Michael D. Goulder of the University of Birmingham (emeritus), who believes that Matthew is the author of the so-called Q material and that he wrote it as a kind of commentary on and expansion of Mark. This Goulder theory assumes that Luke had access to Matthew as well as to Mark and that Luke preferred Mark undiluted but used Matthew's expansion of Mark whenever it served his literary purposes. This theory would, if accepted, invalidate Q as an early source and would date it in the early eighties.

 Goulder offers his critique of the Q hypothesis in the long preface to his monumental two-volume work on the gospel of Luke, entitled *Luke: A New Paradigm*. He also hinted at this view in earlier books that are now out of print (and have been in part disavowed by their author): *Midrash and Lection in Matthew* and *The Evangelists' Calendar*.

 At a seminar held at Johns Hopkins University in Baltimore in early 2000, Goulder defended his festival calendar theory of the synoptic gospels and his opposition to the Q hypothesis against a panel of both critics and supporters. The papers from that seminar are available from Johns Hopkins and will shortly be published by Trinity Publishing Co. in New York.
13. See note 19.
14. I refer my readers to chapters 7 and 8 on Paul in my book *Rescuing the Bible from Fundamentalism*, where this exercise is more fully worked out.

15. The tomb appears to be important to Luke in the book of Acts, where he has Peter compare Jesus to David, whose tomb is "with us to this day" (Acts 2:29–36). It seems clear that the early Christians sought to prohibit the sense of a shrine developing around the tomb of Jesus, a place at which people could recall the deceased hero. That became a bit more difficult when the empty-tomb stories entered the tradition.

16. See chapter 14 on Judas in *Liberating the Gospels: Reading the Bible with Jewish Eyes*. See also chapters 14 and 15 in that same book on the midrashic content and the liturgical style of the passion narratives.

17. Dr. Chris Rollston, of the faculty of Johns Hopkins University, has made a study of apocalyptic symbols in the New Testament. Darkness and three days are certainly among them. When the kingdom of God descends out of the sky to inaugurate the reign of God, that day is called in the apocalyptic tradition the first day of the new creation.

18. They are both carried in the footnotes of the NRSV.

19. I see in Mark's story of the transfiguration the suggestion that Jesus has replaced the Temple, a notion that I suggest would not have developed until after the Temple had been destroyed in 70 C.E. I seek to document this idea more fully in *Liberating the Gospels: Reading the Bible with Jewish Eyes*. That is why I date Mark in the early seventies.

## CHAPTER SIX

1. Adolf Harnack, *What Is Christianity?* p. 193.

2. I went into this Isaiah text both in its Hebrew original and its Greek translation, some verses of which Matthew employed, in chapter 7 of my book *Born of a Woman: A Bishop Rethinks the Virgin Birth and the Role of Women in a Male-Dominated Church*.

3. See Michael D. Goulder, *Midrash and Lection in Matthew*, or my book *Liberating the Gospels: Reading the Bible with Jewish Eyes* (chaps. 6 and 7), for a more elaborate description of this process.

4. Dating any book of the Bible is an inexact science. There are some scholars, including Burton Mack, who date Luke and Acts well into the second century. The timespan 88–95 covers the majority range of scholarly consensus.

5. See Michael D. Goulder, *Luke: A New Paradigm*, for further amplification of this process.

6. Even the translators missed this "I am" reference, for in the RSV they translate this line, "Then you will know that I am *He*."

## CHAPTER SEVEN

1. The designation "believers in exile" was developed in my previous book *Why Christianity Must Change or Die: A Bishop Speaks to Believers in Exile.*
2. I first heard this phrase from the theologian John Cobb.

## CHAPTER EIGHT

1. Robert W. Funk, "The Once and Future Jesus," the lead essay in *The Once and Future Jesus*, p. 16, Gregory Jenks, ed.
2. When seeking to avoid the patriarchal connotation of the word *kingdom*, modern scholars use the word *realm* to translate *kingdom*.
3. See Mark 15:40–41; Matt. 27:55–56; Luke 23:55. The trashing of Magdalene begins in Luke 8:2, where this evangelist introduces a heretofore unknown bit of data: Jesus had cleansed Mary Magdalene of seven demons. By the middle of the second century of this common era, she had been transformed into a world-class prostitute. Later popes would identify her with the woman taken in adultery and with the woman of the street who washed Jesus' feet with her tears and wiped them with her hair. There is no biblical evidence to support this later development, though it continues to be reflected in plays, hymns, theater pieces, and television shows.
4. Tillich used this phrase as the title of one of his books.
5. *Liberating the Gospels: Reading the Bible with Jewish Eyes.* I still think that this is the best book I have ever written.

## CHAPTER NINE

1. Matthew Fox, *Original Blessing*, pp. 47, 48.
2. One of my Harvard students, Mark Strickler, did some primary research on this subject for one of his papers, which I draw on here.

## CHAPTER TEN

1. Quoted from a *New York Times* op-ed piece by William Sloan Coffin, 2000, following the close U.S. election.
2. From the hymn "From Greenland's Icy Mountains," written by Reginald Heber in 1819, found in the 1940 Episcopal hymnal, #254.
3. From the hymn "Remember All the People," written by Percy Deamer in 1929, found in the 1940 Episcopal hymnal, #262.
4. Kenneth Scott Latourette, *The History of Christianity*.
5. Thomas A. Harris, *I'm Okay, You're Okay*, pp. 72, 73.

6. I described this dialogue in an essay entitled "A Dialogue in a Buddhist Temple," published in *The Bishop's Voice: Selected Essays*, compiled and edited by Christine M. Spong.
7. This image was developed by Fox in his latest book, *One River, Many Wells*.

## CHAPTER ELEVEN

1. R. S. Thomas, "Emerging," *Collected Poems, 1945–1990*, p. 263.
2. This story ran in the Portland newspaper, *The Oregonian*, March 11, 2000.
3. Found in Augustine, *The Confessions*, chap. 1.
4. That idea was first brought to my consciousness by one of my students, Jamie Washam, at Harvard Divinity School.
5. This particular student was James Pratt.
6. The Episcopal bishop of Oklahoma and his wife.
7. Such books as Gerhard Von Rad's *Genesis: A Commentary*, Ernst Haenchen's *The Acts of the Apostles*, Edward Schillebeeckx's *Jesus: An Experiment in Christology* and *Christ: The Christian Experience in the Modern World*, Hans Küng's *On Being a Christian*, Thomas Aquinas's *Summa Theologica*, and even Paul Tillich's *Systematic Theology*, vols. 1–3.
8. Schuller is the minister of the Crystal Cathedral in Orange County, California.

## CHAPTER TWELVE

1. Lloyd G. Geering, *Tomorrow's God: How We Create Our Worlds*, p. 235. Lloyd Geering taught theology in New Zealand for years and is the best-known religious voice in that country.
2. *Why Christianity Must Change or Die: A Bishop Speaks to Believers in Exile*.
3. The worst hymns that I have ever had to sing are "Before Thy Throne, O God, We Kneel," which winds up as a masochistic request for divine punishment, and "Have Thine Own Way, Lord," which is an ultimate expression of wimpishly passive dependency that sounds like an invitation to abuse.
4. A quotation from the New Zealand *Anglican Prayer Book*. These are the words the person uses at the end of a scripture lesson in that church, instead of the Western "This is the word of the Lord." The New Zealand phrase is open-ended; the Western phrase encourages bibliolatry.

5. David Zuniga, one of my Harvard students, who is committed to incorporating the insights of Buddhism into the religious systems of the future, was the first to propose a liturgy to accompany the decision to abort. It has found a place in my mind from that day to this.

6. I find myself, at this point, strangely allied with the ultra-evangelical Anglican Archdiocese of Sydney (Australia), a circumstance that will surprise us both. They, however, arrive at their conclusion from a radically different perspective: out of their negativity toward anything that hints of a "Catholic" (Roman or Anglican) frame of reference. I arrive at my conclusion through the death of theism.

## CHAPTER THIRTEEN

1. Rudolf Bultmann, *Jesus and the Word*, p. 51.

2. Strauss has always fascinated me, and he is a person with whom I feel a great kinship. I was delighted when the Jesus Seminar set up the Order of David Friedrich Strauss as a way to honor groundbreaking, contemporary Christian leaders. I was pleased when I was chosen by the Seminar as one of their honorees and had the medallion depicting Strauss's image hung around my neck in the year 2000.

3. John Dominic Crossan, "A Future for the Christian Faith," in *The Once and Future Jesus*, Gregory Jenks, ed.

4. *The Once and Future Jesus*, p. 126.

5. Please note that I used the word *transgender* and not *transgendered*, the latter implying something that has been done to a person. We never say that one has been *maled* or *femaled*; we should likewise call no one *transgendered*. One of my students at Harvard raised my consciousness to this use of language.

6. Robert Funk, from his lead essay "The Once and Future Jesus," in *The Once and Future Jesus*, p. 21, Gregory Jenks, ed.

7. All of the "I am" sayings are found only in the Fourth Gospel.

## CHAPTER FOURTEEN

1. Katie Ford used *groundwater* not as a metaphor for God, as I noted earlier that Matthew Fox had used it. She meant nothing except literally "groundwater."

# BIBLIOGRAPHY

Altizer, Thomas J. J. *The Contemporary Jesus*. London: SCM Press, 1998.

———— (with William Hamilton). *Radical Theology and the Death of God*. Indianapolis: Bobbs-Merrill, 1966.

————. *Toward a New Christianity: Readings in the Death of God Theology*. New York: Harcourt, Brace, & World, 1967.

Aquinas, Thomas. *Summa Theologica*. London: Thomas Baker, 1906. (Written in the thirteenth century; available in numerous translations and editions since.)

Armstrong, Karen. *A History of God*. New York: Ballantine Books, 1993.

Augustine, Bishop of Hippo. *The Confessions*. Translated by Rex Warner. New York: New American Library, 1963.

Barbour, Ian. *Religion in the Age of Science*. San Francisco: HarperSanFrancisco, 1990.

Berger, Peter L. *The Social Reality of Religion*. London: Faber, 1969.

————. *The Voice of Solemn Assemblies*. Garden City, NY: Doubleday, 1981.

Bonhoeffer, Dietrich. *Letters and Papers from Prison*. Edited by Eberhard Bethge. London: SCM Press, 1953, 1971; New York: Macmillan, 1997.

Borg, Marcus. *Meeting Jesus Again for the First Time*. San Francisco: HarperSanFrancisco, 1994.

Bowie, Walter Russell. *The Story of the Bible*. New York: Abingdon Press, 1934.

Bowker, John. *Problems of Suffering in the Religions of the World*. Cambridge: Cambridge Univ. Press, 1975.

————. *The Sense of God: Sociological, Anthropological, and Psychological Approaches to the Origins of the Sense of God.* Oxford: Clarendon Press, 1973.

Breasted, James Henry. *The Dawn of Conscience.* New York: Scribner, 1933.

Bultmann, Rudolf. *Jesus and the Word.* Translated by Louise Pettibone Smith. New York: Scribner, 1958.

Catchpole, D. R. *The Quest for Q.* Edinburgh, UK: Clark, 1993.

Chilton, Bruce. *Judaic Approaches to the Gospels.* Atlanta: Scholars' Press, 1994.

————. *Rabbi Jesus.* Garden City, NY: Doubleday, 2000.

Cobb, John Boswell. *Christ in a Pluralistic Age.* Louisville: Westminster Press, 1975.

————. *The Structure of Christian Existence.* Philadelphia: Westminster Press, 1967.

Collins, John J. *The Apocalyptic Imagination: An Introduction to the Jewish Matrix of Christianity.* New York: Crossroad, 1984.

————. *Apocalypticism in the Dead Sea Scrolls.* London and New York: Routledge, 1997.

Cornford, Francis MacDonald. *From Religion to Philosophy: A Study in the Origins of Western Speculation.* Atlantic Highlands, NJ: Humanities Press, 1980.

Crockett, William R. *Eucharist: Symbol of Transformation.* New York: Pueblo, 1989.

Crossan, John Dominic. "A Future for the Christian Faith." Gregory Jenks, ed. *The Once and Future Jesus.* Santa Rosa, CA: Polebridge Press, 2000.

————. *Jesus: A Revolutionary Biography.* San Francisco: HarperSanFrancisco, 1990.

————. *Who Killed Jesus?* San Francisco: HarperSanFrancisco, 1995.

Cupitt, Don. *After God: The Future of Religion.* London: Weidenfeld & Nicholson, 1997; New York: Basic Books, 1997.

————. *Christ and the Hiddenness of God.* London: SCM Press, 1985.

————. *Crisis in Moral Authority: The Dethronement of Christianity.* Guildford, UK: Lutterworth Press, 1972.

————. *Mysticism After Modernity.* Oxford: Blackwell, 1998.

————. *Radicals and the Future of the Church.* London: SCM Press, 1989.

————. *The Religion of Being.* London: SCM Press, 1998.

————. *The Sea of Faith: Christianity in Change.* London: BBC Books, 1984.

————. *Solar Ethics.* London: London Xpress, 1993.

————. *Taking Leave of God.* London: SCM Press, 1980.

Darwin, Charles Robert. *The Origin of Species by Means of Natural Selection*. London: Hammondsworth and Penguin, 1988. (Originally published in 1859.)

Davies, Paul. *God and the New Physics*. London: Dent, 1984; New York: Simon & Schuster, 1984.

———. *The Mind of God*. New York: Simon & Schuster, 1992.

Dawkins, Richard. *The Blind Watchmaker*. London: Hammondsworth, 1991; New York: Norton, 1996.

———. *The Selfish Gene*. London: Granada, 1978; New York: Oxford Univ. Press, 1990.

Dixon, A. C., and R. H. Torrey, eds. *The Fundamentals*. Chicago: Testimony Publishing, 1910–1915.

Durant, Will, and Ariel Durant. *The Age of Louis XIV*. Vol. 7 of *The Story of Civilization*. New York: Simon & Schuster, 1935.

Durkheim, Emile. *The Elementary Forms of Religious Life*. Translated by Joseph W. Swain. New York: Macmillan, 1915.

Eckhart, Meister. *The Essential Sermons, Commentaries, and Treatises of Meister Eckhart*. London: SPCK, 1981.

Edinger, Edward. *Archetype of the Apocalypse: A Jungian Study of the Book of Revelation*. Edited by George Elder. Chicago: Open Court, 1999.

———. *The New God Image: A Study of Jung's Key Letters Concerning the Evolution of the Western God Image*.

———. *Transformation of the God Image: An Elucidation of Jung's Answer to Job*. Ontario: Inner City Books, 1992.

Edwards, Richard P. *A Theology of Q*. Philadelphia: Fortress Press, 1976.

Fosdick, Harry Emerson. *The Meaning of Prayer*. London: SCM Press, 1915; Nashville: Abingdon Press, 1980.

Fox, Matthew. *The Coming of the Cosmic Christ*. San Francisco: HarperSanFrancisco, 1988.

———. *One River, Many Wells: How Deepening Ecumenism Awakens Our Imaginations with Spiritual Visions*. New York: Jeremy Tarcher/ Putnam, 2000.

———. *Original Blessing: A Primer in Creation Spirituality*. Santa Fe: Bear, 1983.

Frankfort, Henri. *The Intellectual Adventure of Ancient Man: An Essay on Speculative Thought in the Ancient Near East*. Chicago: Univ. of Chicago Press, 1946.

Freeman, Anthony. *God in Us*. London: SCM Press, 1995.

Freud, Sigmund. *The Future of an Illusion*. Translated by W. D. Robson-Scott. London: Hogarth Press, 1943; New York: Norton, 1989. (Originally published in 1927.)

———. *Moses and Monotheism.* New York: Knopf, 1939.

———. *An Outline of Psychoanalysis.* New York: Norton, 1949.

———. *Totem and Taboo.* New York: W. W. Norton, 1950.

Fromm, Eric. *The Art of Loving.* New York: Harper & Row, 1956.

———. *The Heart of Man: Its Genius for Good and Evil.* New York: Harper & Row, 1964.

———. *On Being Human.* New York: Continuum, 1994.

———. *The Sane Society.* New York: Rinehart, 1955.

———. *To Have or to Be.* New York: Harper & Row, 1976.

———. *Ye Shall Be as Gods: A Radical Interpretation of the Old Testament and Its Traditions.* New York: Holt, Rinehart, & Winston, 1960.

Funk, Robert W. *Honest to Jesus: Jesus for a New Millennium.* San Francisco: HarperSanFrancisco, 1996.

———. "The Once and Future Jesus." Lead essay in *The Once and Future Jesus,* Gregory Jenks, ed. Santa Rosa, CA: Polebridge Press, 2000.

Funk, Robert W., Roy Hoover, and the Jesus Seminar, eds. *The Five Gospels.* New York: Macmillan, 1993.

Geering, Lloyd G. *Tomorrow's God: How We Create Our Worlds.* Wellington, NZ: Bridget Williams Books, 1994.

———. *The World to Come: From Christian Past to Global Future.* Santa Rosa, CA: Polebridge Press, 1999.

Glenn, Paul J. *A Tour of the Summa* [by Aquinas]. New York: Herder & Herder, 1960.

Gomes, Peter. *The Good Book: Reading the Bible with Mind and Heart.* New York: Morrow, 1996.

Goodall, Jane (with Phillip Berman). *Reason for Hope.* New York: Warner Books, 1999.

Goode, William Josiah. *Religion Among the Primitives.* Glencoe, IL: Free Press, 1951.

Goulder, Michael Donald. *The Evangelists' Calendar: A Lectionary Explanation of the Development of Scripture.* London: SPCK, 1978.

———. *Luke: A New Paradigm.* Sheffield, UK: JSOT Press, 1989.

———. *Midrash and Lection in Matthew.* London: SPCK, 1974.

———. *Type and History in Acts.* London: SPCK, 1964.

——— (with John Hick). *Why Believe in God?* London: SCM Press, 1983.

Greene, John C. *Debating Darwin.* Claremont, CA: Regina Books, 1999.

Haenchen, Ernst. *The Acts of the Apostles.* Oxford: Blackwell, 1971.

Hahn, Thich Nhat. *Living Buddha, Living Christ.* New York: Riverhead Books, 1995.

Hall, Douglas John. *The End of Christendom and the Future of Christianity*. Harrisburg, PA: Trinity Press, 1995.

Hamilton, William. *The New Essence of Christianity*. London: Darton, Longman, & Todd, 1966.

———— (with Thomas J. J. Altizer). *Radical Theology and the Death of God*. Indianapolis: Bobbs-Merrill, 1966.

Hampson, Daphne. *After Christianity*. London: SCM Press, 1996; Harrisburg, PA: Trinity Press, 1997.

Hanson, Paul D. *The Dawn of Apocalyptic*. Philadelphia: Fortress Press, 1975.

Hardy, Thomas. *The Collected Poems of Thomas Hardy*. London: Macmillan, 1974.

Hare, David. *Racing Demons*. 1991.

Harnack, Adolf. *What Is Christianity?* New York: Putnam, 1901.

Harris, Thomas A. *I'm OK, You're OK*. New York: Harper & Row, 1969.

Hart, David. *Faith in Doubt*. London: SPCK, 1993.

Hauener, Ivan. *Q: The Sayings of Jesus. With a Reconstruction of Q by Athanasius Polag*. Wilmington, DE: Glazier Press, 1987.

Hawking, Stephen. *A Brief History of Time*. London: Bantam, 1989; New York: Bantam, 1988.

Hick, John. *Death and Eternal Life*. Basingstoke, UK: Macmillan, 1985; Louisville: Westminster/John Knox Press, 1994.

————. *The Myth of Christian Uniqueness*. London: SCM Press, 1987; New York: Orbis Books, 1988.

————, ed. *The Myth of God Incarnate*. London: SCM Press, 1997.

———— (with Michael D. Goulder). *Why Believe in God?* London: SCM Press, 1983.

Higgins, A.J.B. *The Original Order of Q: Essays in Memory of T. W. Manson*. Manchester, UK: University Press, 1959.

Hodgson, Marshall G. S. *The Venture of Islam: Conscience and History in a World Civilization*. Chicago: Univ. of Chicago Press, 1974.

Holloway, Richard. *Godless Morality*. Edinburgh, UK: Canongate Press, 1999.

Jacobson, A. O. *The First Gospel: An Introduction to Q*. Sonoma, CA: Polebridge Press, 1992.

James, William. *The Varieties of Religious Experience*. London: Longman, Green, 1941; New York: Random House, 1999.

Jastrow, Robert. *The Enchanted Loom: Mind in the Universe*. New York: Simon & Schuster, 1981.

Jenks, Gregory, ed. *The Once and Future Jesus*. Santa Rosa, CA: Polebridge Press, 2000.

Jeremias, Joachim. *The Central Message of the New Testament*. London: SCM Press, 1967.

Julian of Norwich. *Enfolded in Love: Daily Readings with Julian of Norwich*. London: Darton, Longman, & Todd, 1980.

———. *A Showing of God's Love: The Shorter Version of the Sixteen Revelations*. Edited by Anna Maria. London: Longman, Green, 1958.

Jung, Carl G. *Answer to Job*. London: Routledge Kegan Paul, 1954; Princeton, NJ: Princeton Univ. Press, 1973.

———. *On Evil*. Princeton, NJ: Princeton Univ. Press, 1995.

———. *Psychology and Western Religion*. New Haven, CT: Yale Univ. Press, 1960.

Kierkegaard, Søren. *Sickness unto Death*. Translated by Walter Lowrie. New York: Doubleday Anchor Books, 1954.

Kloppenberg, John. *The Formation of Q: Trajectories in Ancient Wisdom Literature*. Philadelphia: Fortress Press, 1987.

Küng, Hans. *Does God Exist?* London: Collins, 1980; New York: Crossroad, 1994.

——— (with Edward Quinn). *On Being a Christian*. London: Collins, 1977; New York: Doubleday, 1976.

Latourette, Kenneth Scott. *Christianity in a Revolutionary Age*. New York: Harper, 1958–1962.

———. *The Nineteenth Century: The Great Century in the Americas, Australia, and Africa, 1800–1914*. New York: Harper Brothers, 1943.

Lowen, Alexander. *Narcissism: Denial of the True Self*. New York: Macmillan, 1983.

———. *Pathologies of the Modern Self: Narcissism, Schizophrenia, and Depression*. New York: University Press, 1987.

Lynch, David. *Yeats: The Poetics of the Self—The Narcissistic Condition*. Chicago: Univ. of Chicago Press, 1979.

Mack, Burton. *The Lost Gospel: The Book of Q and Christian Origins*. San Francisco: HarperSanFrancisco, 1993.

———. *Who Wrote the New Testament? The Making of the Myth of Christianity*. San Francisco: HarperSanFrancisco, 1995.

Marty, Martin E., and R. Scott Applesby. *Accounting for Fundamentalism*. Vol. 4 of *Fundamentalism*. Chicago: Univ. of Chicago Press, 1994.

———. *Fundamentalism Observed*. Vol. 1 of *Fundamentalism*. Chicago: Univ. of Chicago Press, 1991.

Meredith, Lawrence. *Life Before Death: A Spiritual Journey of Mind and Body*. Atlanta: Atlanta Humanics Publishing Group, 2000.

Minear, Paul. *I Saw a New Earth*. Washington, DC: Corpus Books, 1968.

———. *New Testament Apocalyptic*. Nashville: Abingdon Press, 1981.

Nietzsche, Friedrich W. *Thus Spake Zarathustra*. Translated by Thomas Common. New York: Modern Library, 1954.

Ogden, Schubert M. *Christ Without Myth*. New York: Harper & Brothers, 1961.

Otto, Rudolf. *The Idea of the Holy*. Oxford: Oxford Univ. Press, 1923, 1929, 1943.

Patterson, Colin. *Evolution*. Ithaca, NY: Cornell Univ. Press, 1999.

Patterson, Stephen J. *The Gospel of Thomas and Jesus*. Sonoma, CA: Polebridge Press, 1993.

Peacock, Arthur. *A Theology for a Scientific Life*. London: SCM Press, 1993.

Perkins, Pheme. *Resurrection: New Testament Witness and Contemporary Reflection*. London: Geoffrey Chapman, 1985.

Phillips, Dewi Z. *The Concept of Prayer*. Oxford: Blackwell, 1987. Originally published London: Routledge, 1965; New York: Schocken Books, 1966.

Pike, James A. *A Time for Christian Candor*. New York: Harper & Row, 1964.

Polanyi, Michael. *Personal Knowledge Toward a Post-Critical Philosophy*. New York: Harper Torch Books, 1958.

Robinson, James M., Paul Hoffman, and John S. Kloppenberg. *Reconstruction of Q Through Three Centuries of Gospel Research, Excerpted, Sorted, and Evaluated*. Leuven, Belgium: Peeters, 2000.

Robinson, John A. T. *But That I Can't Believe*. London: Collins, 1967.

———. *Honest to God*. London: SCM Press, 1963; Louisville: Westminster/John Knox Press, 1963.

———. *The Human Face of God*. London: SCM Press, 1973.

———. *The New Reformation*. London: SCM Press, 1965.

Rochlin, Gregor. *Man's Aggression in Defense of Self*. Boston: Gambit Press, 1973.

Russell, David S. *The Method and the Message of Jewish Apocalypse*. Philadelphia: Westminster Press, 1964.

Sagan, Carl. *The Demon-Haunted World: Science as a Candle in the Dark*. New York: Random House, 1995.

Sandmel, Samuel. *Judaism and Christian Beginnings*. Oxford: Oxford Univ. Press, 1979.

Schillebeeckx, Edward. *Christ: The Christian Experience in the Modern World*. London: SCM Press, 1980; New York: Seabury Press, 1980.

———. *Jesus: An Experiment in Christology*. London: Collins, 1979; New York: Crossroad, 1981.

————. *On Christian Faith: The Spiritual, Ethical, and Political Dimensions.* New York: Crossroad, 1987.

Schleiermacher, Friedrich. *The Christian Faith.* Edited by H. R. Mackintosh and J. S. Stewart. Edinburgh, UK: Clark, 1948.

Schopf, J. William. *Evolution: Facts and Fallacies.* London, San Diego, Boston, and New York: Academic Press, 1978.

Schweitzer, Albert. *The Quest for the Historical Jesus.* Translated by W. Montgomery. London: Black, 1936; Baltimore: Johns Hopkins Univ. Press, 1998. (Originally published in 1906.)

Segal, Robert, ed. *The Allure of Gnosticism: The Gnostic Experience in Jungian Psychology and Contemporary Culture.* Chicago: Open Court, 1995.

Sheehan, Thomas. *The First Coming: How the Kingdom of God Became Christianity.* New York: Random House, 1986.

Shepherd, Thomas W. *Glimpses of Truth: Systematic Theology from a Metaphysical Christian Perspective.* Chicago: Universal Foundation for Better Living, 2000.

Smart, Ninian. *The Concept of Worship.* London: Macmillan/St. Martin's Press, 1972.

————. *The Philosophy of Religion.* London: Sheldon Press, 1979.

————. *The Religious Experience of Mankind.* New York: Scribner, 1969.

Smith, John MacDonald. *On Doing Without God.* Oxford: Emissary, 1993.

Smith, Wilfred Cantwell. *The Meaning and the End of Religions.* London: New English Library, 1966.

————. *Toward a World Theology: A Faith in the Comparative History of Religion.* London: Macmillan, 1981, 1989.

Spong, John Shelby. *The Bishop's Voice: Selected Essays.* Edited by Christine M. Spong. New York: Crossroad, 1999.

————. *Born of a Woman: A Bishop Rethinks the Virgin Birth and the Treatment of Women in a Male-Dominated Church.* San Francisco: HarperSanFrancisco, 1992.

————. *Here I Stand: My Struggle for a Christianity of Integrity, Love, and Equality.* San Francisco: HarperSanFrancisco, 2000.

————. *Liberating the Gospels: Reading the Bible with Jewish Eyes.* San Francisco: HarperSanFrancisco, 1996.

————. *Living in Sin? A Bishop Rethinks Human Sexuality.* San Francisco: HarperSanFrancisco, 1988.

————. *Rescuing the Bible from Fundamentalism: A Bishop Rethinks the Meaning of Scripture.* San Francisco: HarperSanFrancisco, 1991.

————. *Resurrection: Myth or Reality? A Bishop Rethinks the Meaning of Easter.* San Francisco: HarperSanFrancisco, 1994.

———. *This Hebrew Lord: A Bishop Rethinks the Meaning of Jesus.* New York: Seabury Press, 1974; San Francisco: HarperSanFrancisco, 1988, 1993.

———. *Why Christianity Must Change or Die: A Bishop Speaks to Believers in Exile.* San Francisco: HarperSanFrancisco, 1998.

Stein, Murray. *Jung's Treatment of Christianity: The Psychology of a Religious Tradition.* Willamette, IL: Chiron, 1985.

Strauss, David Friedrich. *The Life of Jesus Critically Reviewed.* London: William & Norgate, 1865.

Streeter, B. H. *The Four Gospels: A Study in Origins.* London: Macmillan, 1930.

Sugarman, Shirley. *Sin and Madness: Studies in Narcissism.* Philadelphia: Westminster Press, 1976.

Swinburne, Richard. *The Cohesion of Theism.* Oxford: Oxford Univ. Press, 1977.

Tattersall, Ian. *Becoming Human: Evolution and Human Uniqueness.* New York: Harcourt Brace, 1998.

Teilhard de Chardin, Pierre. *The Appearance of Man.* London: Collins, 1965.

———. *The Future of Man.* London: Collins, 1964.

———. *Hymn to the Universe.* New York: Harper & Row, 1961.

———. *The Phenomenon of Man.* New York: Harper & Row, 1959.

Thomas, Keith Vivian. *Religion and the Decline of Magic.* New York: Scribner, 1971.

Thomas, R. S. *Collected Poems, 1945–1990.* London: Dent, 1993; Boston: Tuttle, 1997.

Tillich, Paul. *Biblical Religion and the Search for Ultimate Reality.* Chicago: Univ. of Chicago Press, 1955.

———. *The Courage to Be.* London: Nisbit, 1952; New Haven, CT: Yale Univ. Press, 2000.

———. *The Eternal Now.* London: SCM Press, 1963.

———. *The Future of Religion.* New York: Harper & Row, 1960.

———. *Morality and Beyond.* New York: Harper & Row, 1963.

———. *The New Being.* London: SCM Press, 1963.

———. *On the Boundary: An Autobiographical Sketch.* London: Collins, 1967.

———. *The Religious Situation.* Translated by H. Richard Niebuhr. New York: Meridian Books, 1956.

———. *The Shaking of the Foundations.* New York: Scribner, 1948.

———. *Systematic Theology.* Vols. 1–3. London: Nisbit, 1953–1963; Chicago: Univ. of Chicago Press, 1951–1963.

Valhanian, Gabriel. *The Death of God.* New York: George Braziller, 1957.

Van Buren, Paul. *The Secular Meaning of the Gospel.* London: SCM Press, 1963.

Vermes, Geza. *Jesus, the Jew.* London: SCM Press, 1994; Minneapolis: Fortress, 1981.

Von Rad, Gerhard. *Genesis: A Commentary.* Translated by John H. Marks. Philadelphia: Westminster Press, 1961.

———. *Old Testament Theology.* Vols. 1, 2. New York: Harper, 1962–1965.

Ward, Keith. *God, Chance, and Necessity.* Oxford: One World, 1996.

———. *Religion and Creation.* Oxford: Clarendon, 1996.

———. *A Vision to Pursue.* London: SCM Press, 1991.

Weber, Max. *The Sociology of Religion.* Translated by E. Fischoff. Boston: Beacon Press, 1993.

Wells, Harry. *Sigmund Freud: A Pavlovian Critique.* New York: International Publishers, 1960.

Whitehead, Alfred North. *Process and Reality.* New York: Free Press, 1978. (Originally published in 1929.)

———. *Religion in the Making.* Cambridge: Cambridge Univ. Press, 1929; New York: Fordham Univ. Press, 1996.

Zachner, Robert Charles. *The Comparison of Religions.* Boston: Beacon Press, 1967.

———. *The Concise Encyclopedia of Living Faiths.* Boston: Hawthorne Books, 1959.

Zweig, Paul. *The Heresy of Self-Love.* New York: Basic Books, 1968.

# INDEX